American Tropics

Critical American Studies Series

George Lipsitz, University of California–Santa Barbara, Series Editor

American Tropics

Articulating Filipino America

Allan Punzalan Isaac

Critical American Studies Series

University of Minnesota Press   Minneapolis • London

Published by the University of Minnesota Press
111 Third Avenue South, Suite 290
Minneapolis, MN 55401-2520
http://www.upress.umn.edu

Library of Congress Cataloging-in-Publication Data

Isaac, Allan Punzalan.
    American tropics : articulating Filipino America / Allan Punzalan Isaac.
        p.   cm. — (Critical American Studies series)
    Includes bibliographical references and index.

    ISBN-13: 978-0-8166-4273-1 (hc/j : alk. paper)
    ISBN-13: 978-0-8166-4274-8 (pb : alk. paper)

    1. Filipino Americans—Race identity. 2. United States—Race relations.
3. Racism in popular culture—United States. 4. United States—Relations—
Philippines. 5. Philippines—Relations—United States. 6. Postcolonialism.
7. Imperialism—History. 8. Filipino Americans—Study and teaching.
9. Imperialism in literature. 10. American literature—Filipino American
authors—History and criticism. I. Title.
    E184.F4I73 2006
    305.89'921073—dc22
                                                                            2006019665

Printed in the United States of America on acid-free paper

The University of Minnesota is an equal-opportunity educator and employer.

17 16 15 14 13 12 11 10   10 9 8 7 6 5 4 3 2

For my parents,
Felicidad and Lorenzo

Contents

Acknowledgments

An award-winning novelist from the Philippines who immigrated to the United States some years ago once complained about his novels' reception in the U.S. publishing industry. His U.S. publishers were confused as to why his novels did not "sound very Asian American." His writerly voice, they claimed, resonated more with Latin American novels straining with overwrought Catholic imagery and, well, outright overwroughtness. The publishing houses could not reconcile the Filipino American voice with what they have expected of the Asian American literary market. Social scientists have before observed this phenomenon about the Hispano-Malay's archipelago and its cultural and political-historical anomaly even in Asia. A writer friend once speculated that long ago the Philippine archipelago broke off from the Latin American landmass, floated across the Caribbean, across the isthmus, and into the Pacific and the China Sea. *American Tropics: Articulating Filipino America* attempts to map how U.S. imperial discourse and Filipino American writing could imagine such a fortuitous geographic turn.

The Philippines is neither a Caribbean nor a Polynesian island. Yet, as Édouard Glissant suggests in his literary-historical work *Caribbean Discourse,* seemingly divergent and unrelated cultures and spaces may be found to have similar, though not identical, histories if examined under the logic of empire. Wresting the Philippines and Filipino Americans away from Asia in this examination of U.S. imperialism refocuses the gaze to the center, to the equatorial axis of the Americas, and perhaps imagines if and how 7,100 islands may have floated away from Latin American shores. Inspired in part by Glissant's *Caribbean Discourse,* Paul Gilroy's *The Black Atlantic,* and Epeli Hau'ofa's "Our Sea of Islands," scholarly works that have treated lands and oceans together as sites of movement and exchanges of bodies and the imagination, I situate the Philippines along America's tropics to make apparent its conjunction with other colonized spaces—Puerto Rico, the historical borderlands of Panama and Mexico, and Hawai'i—to examine the breadth of U.S. imperial discourse and the depth of the American post-colonial imagination. This book owes a debt to Pacific, Caribbean, and U.S. Latino studies but is certainly not meant to inform those fields. Rather, I situate this study at the nexus of American, Asian American, ethnic, cultural, and postcolonial studies to offer strategies that enable new ways of telling the story of American nationhood and Asian American difference. What do Filipino Americans bring to Asian America as a sign of difference? Making an isthmian connection across islands and multiple American identities insists on the linked production of the Philippines with these other national spaces in the U.S. polity and imagination, but also on the construction of a uniquely Filipino American postcolonial aesthetics and politics.

While tracing the path of the 7,100 islands, I gratefully acknowledge the generosity and patience shown by teachers, family, and friends who have led me through my travels, twists, and turns. To fellow travelers who have shaped the course of my imagination, I thank you for taking me "elsewhere." From Manila to New York to San Juan, my conversations and education spanning many years with Oscar Campomanes have been crucial in the growth of this book and my own intellectual formation. I know he has been an inspiration to a whole generation of Filipino/Filipino American scholars. I thank Henry Abelove for his gentle guidance and fierce support as my mentor at Wesleyan University and beyond. Martin Manalansan has been tireless in his productive prodding and pushing of the project. Jennifer Wicke has been a friend and advocate these many years, and I thank her for giving me the freedom and support to explore the project during my time at New York University.

To the critical Filipino/Filipino American studies and Asian American studies communities from whom I have drawn much inspiration, many lessons, and immense pleasure, I owe much *utang na loob*: Lucy Burns, Anjali Arondekar, Sunaina Maira, Rick Bonus, Emily Ignacio, Augusto Espritu, Neferti Tadiar, Jonathan Beller, Carlo Tadiar, Mia Zamora, Jeffrey Santa Ana, Robyn Rodriguez, Greg Mullins, Nerissa Balce-Cortes, Fidelito Cortes, Richard Chu, Jessica Hagedorn, Quang Bao, Eric Gamalinda, David Eng, Sarita See, and Evelyn Hu-DeHart.

I have had many generative and vigorous exchanges with John Vincent, colleague and friend, whose provocative insights I have always learned from and appreciated. I thank Anita Mannur for her patient, thorough readings and the many hours of eating and laughter. Many thanks to Tara Fickle for her attention to detail. Their generosity is evidenced throughout the book; all faults, however, are mine. Richard Morrison has been a patient and wonderful editor who believed in the project from the beginning. I thank the anonymous readers of the University of Minnesota Press, who have been invaluable in pressing and developing my arguments. I am grateful for the generosity of George Lipsitz and for his insights and dialogue with the project.

Outside the continent, I thank Belinda Aquino of the Center for Philippine Studies at the University of Hawai'i–Manoa, who has welcomed me in all my comings and goings to Hawai'i since 1993. I thank friends at Alu Like, the Native Hawaiian Library, for their welcome during my visits. Further across the Pacific, my *bienvenidas* and *despedidas* were filled with many good friends who made a home for me in the Philippines, and to whom I owe much *utang na loob*; in particular, many thanks to Shirley Lua of De La Salle University–Taft, who has extended her friendship and worked so hard on my behalf. Isagani Cruz, Ronald Baytan, Marjorie Evasco, Jerry Torres, and Tet Wright warmly welcomed me into the faculty of the department of literature.

At Wesleyan University, my colleagues in the English department and the American studies program, as well as the Freeman Asian/Asian American Studies Initiative, have helped me immensely. I have learned much from exchanges and questions with colleagues; I thank J. Kehaulani Kauanui, Bill Johnson González, Christina Crosby, Joel Pfister, Indira Karamcheti, Sean McCann, Ann duCille, and Richard Slotkin. I have received much support through all my endeavors at New York University; for this, I thank Jack Tchen and the Asian/Pacific/American Studies Program, Ana Dopico, George Yúdice,

Andrew Ross, and the NYU Graduate School of Arts and Sciences. A special thank you to Fawzia Mustafa and Manthia Diawara, who introduced me to the passion for African and Caribbean literatures. In the early phases of this manuscript, Donette Francis provided me with motivation, friendship, and insights from the field of Caribbean and American studies while being my interlocutor at NYU Bobst Library. My warmest gratitude to Wendy Brown, Christopher Pye, and Anita Sokolsky, who introduced me to critical theory and literary criticism, and whose teaching at Williams College I still strive to emulate. I am deeply indebted to my students, from whom I have learned so much; in particular, the graduate students at De La Salle University–Taft (Eden Estopace, Genevieve Asenjo, Nette dela Cruz-Dalupan, Odette Negado, Ofelia Legaspi, Jennifer Balboa, Neri Marasigan, and Eileen Ang) and the Wesleyan students in my American Tropics class for their wealth of insights. Thank you for reading and rereading with me.

I wish to thank the wonderful folks at the Philippine-American Education Forum (PAEF), especially Esmeralda "E. C." Cunanan, for giving me the opportunity to teach and learn in Manila through the Fulbright grant in 2003–4. To unforgettable friends in Manila who have made it so worthwhile on those Malate nights: the Artery Group (Jae Robillos, Delan Robillos, Gary Devilles, Lito Zulueta), the witty and brilliant minds at University of Santo Tomas (Ferdie Lopez, Jack Quigley, Ralph Galan), *Kritika Kultura* at Ateneo de Manila University, and Roland Tolentino and Patrick Flores at the University of the Philippines: *Maraming salamat, mga kaibigan.*

I am grateful to Mark Berkowitz for his unwavering friendship and encouragement (and for providing a home for me whenever I needed it). *Agradezco a* Dennis Ortiz for sharing his overwrought Nuyorican sensibility ever since our adolescence at Regis. I wish to remember Dr. Shilpa Raval, Ovidian scholar, whose friendship since third grade at P.S. 38 in Jersey City remained fast for more than twenty-five years as we marched into academia and New Haven together. I cherish her memory as a generous scholar and dear friend.

From Manila eastward, I cannot give enough thanks to the many folks who have traveled and guided me: my gratitude to Reynaldo Alejandro, my guardian in the islands and on the continent; Roberto Caballero, Rommel Gonzaga, Martin Lopez, Lloyd Samartino, Raul Pertierra, Mike Rapatan, Peter Mayshle, Mike Santos, Mona Katigbak, Valerie Santiago, Kevin Bell, Mia Mask,

Donna Murch, Muna El Fituri, Laylah Ali, Ethel Brooks, Farhan Haq, Susan Tomlinson, Jim Palmer, Mary Ann Newman, David Diamond, and Bernard Croes for their patience, friendship, and endless humor. Special thanks to Rinehardt Zamora Linmark and Jeff Rebudal for flying with me, as angels do, across two archipelagoes and a continent. Thank you for being generous with yourselves; I am the richer for it.

Most important, I thank my family, who initiated the journey and withstood my subsequent turns and returns with unconditional love and unquestioning support: my mother, Felicidad Punzalan Isaac; my father, Lorenzo Isaac; my *ates* and *kuyas*, Grace, Susan, Lloyd, Lorenzo Jr., Roland, and their partners, Jun, Benny, Vanessa, and Ann; and their children, Allyson, Jillian, Tina, Leigh Ann, and Justin.

Thank you for showing me the breadth and depth of the American Tropics.

Introduction

So many faces. But, were the faces simply masks hiding a man no
one ever really knew? Could a smile so warm conceal evil so cold?
—Voice-over, *Dateline*, July 21, 1997

PHILIPPINES: WHERE ASIA WEARS A SMILE!
—Philippine tourism campaign

One of U.S. imperialism's great architects, Theodore Roosevelt,
once dreamed of a U.S. island empire consisting of an insular chain
connecting the Atlantic, the Caribbean, and the Pacific. Since the
mid-nineteenth century, the continual reinvention of the frontier
and manifest destiny propelled Americans across the continent and
into the Caribbean and the Pacific.[1] The United States claimed the
Philippine archipelago as property in the aftermath of the Spanish-
American War (1898) and the more bloody Philippine-American
War (1899–1902), in which one out of seven Filipinos was killed.
Against the national aspirations of the short-lived Philippine
Republic (1896–98), the United States incorporated the peoples of
the archipelago as U.S. territory.

Rather than begin in 1898 with the sale of the Philippines by
Spain to the United States for twenty million dollars under the
Treaty of Paris, I begin the larger American story a century later in
the summer of 1997, in sunny South Beach, Florida, where models,
actors, spring-breakers, retirees, and bon vivants frolic in the sand,

surf, and sun. This American chronicle takes a circuitous route through San Diego, Miami, and the Caribbean across the Gulf of Mexico, to the Philippines, then back again. The disjointed history of American empire makes for tortuous routes to recover its uncannily familiar trail.

Andrew Cunanan; or, The Manhunt for Filipino America

On July 27, 1997, a *New York Times* headline announced: "Suicide Brings Relief and Normality." The suicide in question was that of Andrew Cunanan, San Diego gay party boy responsible for the violent deaths of five people in Minnesota, Illinois, New Jersey, and Florida. His killing spree began on April 29 when he beat and murdered Naval Academy graduate Jeff Trail with a claw hammer. A few days later, he killed a friend, David Madson, and then tortured and killed Chicago businessman Lee Miglin. On May 9, he struck again in New Jersey, killing a caretaker, William Reese. He would steal the victim's red pickup truck. Police alerted gay communities from San Francisco to New York to South Beach. The shooting of Gianni Versace on July 15 brought the "spree killer" to international attention. A week later, South Beach police found Andrew Cunanan dead. The nation let out a sigh of relief; the summer's cross-country manhunt was over. The face horribly disfigured from a self-inflicted gunshot, Cunanan's body lay in the bedroom of a gleaming white houseboat. Thus did most Americans leave him—in glaring, if not blinding, whiteness, unaware that he was Filipino—a fact obsessed over by the Filipino American community media. Cunanan's fugitive status and his radically different treatment in the Filipino American press and in the national media are my starting points to illustrate the unrecognizability of the Filipino and the Philippines in larger U.S. narratives.

The "shape-shifting," "over-the-hill" Filipino rent boy with a reportedly "genius IQ" was an appalling and titillating late-twentieth-century media production. Andrew's image appeared on televisual and print media: *America's Most Wanted, Dateline, Newsweek,* and *Time,* with parallel coverage in local Filipino American newspapers across the continent. During those few weeks in 1997, I was struck by the different portrayals of Andrew Cunanan in the Filipino American papers and the national media.[2] Both savored the "true crime" story elements of the tragic events: gory murders, sadomasochism, hustlers, an Italian fashion designer, and anonymous gay men. However, the national American media, busy reveling in the mysteries of the gay demimonde, barely mentioned his Filipino heritage. Meanwhile, the mainstream Filipino American press could talk about nothing else, but kept his sexuality at bay. Of interest is not so much the ethnic consciousness of one or the homophobia of both, but rather the disconnect between two sets of media viewing points and reading practices.

The summer's spectacle is worth some speculation. Is this simply a case of a mixed-race Filipino American gone bad? Does he simply die in a blaze of whiteness in a white houseboat? What is the condition of this relieved "normality" brought about by Cunanan's demise? Three popular books have been published about Andrew Cunanan.[3] A musical titled *Disposable* is in development in La Jolla Playhouse in San Diego. With money, glamour, sex, and celebrities involved, he also becomes the stuff of which B movies are made. In the Philippines, Modesto Cunanan, his father, sold the film rights to Amable Aguiluz, the filmmaker who made *Rizal sa Dapitan* (Rizal in Dapitan), a story about the Philippine national hero José Rizal. In the United States, Mary Ann Schillaci Cunanan, his mother, sold movie rights of her son's life, and *The Versace Murder* was released a year after the tragedy. How did two historically and psychically linked nations on either side of the Pacific tell Andrew Cunanan's story to themselves? Is it an American story? Is it a Filipino story? Is it a Filipino American story? Is it a tragic, "gay" story? Or is it all of these with traces of America's empire?

Upon closer examination, Andrew's narrative and representation shatter a stable construct of the Filipino American, an Asian American subject distinguished by a history of U.S. colonialism and American racialization. As the offspring of a Filipino and an Italian American, he also embodies the cross-linkage of current and past American immigrations. Not only time but a history of colonization distinguishes these two moments of immigration. Furthermore, Andrew's story takes the immigration trajectory from a simple vertical transmission of "culture" from mythical origins and discharges it through a network of class and sexual stratifications, of immigrant and racialized subjectivities, and of transcontinental and transpacific global media. One of the many trajectories of the Asian American body, Andrew's refuses closure and raises questions about the stability of "ethnic" categories in light of an American colonial legacy and the movement and enfolding of fantasies and borders.

The Filipino American newspapers seemed compelled to mark and remark upon his Filipinoness and connection with the Filipino community. This countered the national media's initial insistence on his possibly Irish roots, his name presumably a version of Callaghan or Cullilane, but then decided to settle on his debauched and aberrant gayness instead. Of course, to a Filipino, the name Cunanan would already indicate his family's island regional origins. The nonmutual recognition—the disjuncture between the Filipino American press and the national coverage—characterizes the relationship between Filipino Americans and the American public at large. The national media's obsession and inability to recognize Andrew's supposed masks and alleged "shape-shifting," as *Newsweek* and *Prime Time* liked to report, not only laid bare American dis-ease with homosexuality, commodified or otherwise, but signaled the blind limits of the U.S. racial imaginary and its misreading and incomprehension of its imperial history.

Yet this does not explain the Filipino American press's insistence on Andrew's ethnic remarking. Was it not in their interest to ignore the fact of Filipinoness and let Andrew be a gay Irishman? The Filipino American papers reproduced a CNN video capture of the Filipino father donning a tank top in his Philippine home during the FBI and media manhunt. Might this reproduction be an anxiety about U.S. media tracing deviance back to its tropical roots? Or was it simply a voyeuristic desire to look for Andrew's *Filipino* father in the national media? In all cases, for the Filipino American press, the disclosure of his ethnic identity was a vital part of the pleasure *and* horror. Perhaps this compulsion stemmed from a longing to be reflected in the small screen in this American media sensation. Filipinos would in some manner be *part* of an American drama. *Any* American drama, even for the wrong reasons.[4]

The narrative disconnect between the Filipino American and U.S. national papers, I would suggest, signals two forms of cultural aphasia emerging from a racialization particular to U.S. imperial history. The Filipino American papers focused upon contiguity with Andrew, while the national press sought to establish his aberrant status. National papers saw a gay prostitute, Filipino American ones an act of assimilation gone wrong. U.S. Filipino papers continually marked Andrew's Filipinoness, an insistence that

certainly bespoke a fondness for the sensational, but, more important, the desire and pleasure to be a visible part of the national
story *as* a sensation. The papers at once claimed *and* disclaimed
him. A headline in the *Filipino Reporter,* "Cunanan Mourned and
Reviled by Fil-Ams," underscored this schizophrenic relationship
Filipino Americans had to their nonnative son.[5] The Filipino community papers' identification with and simultaneous disavowal
of Andrew indicates the conflicted position of Filipinos as postcolonial *and* ethnic Americans concerned with proper public presentation to an imagined (white) American audience. The Filipino
American press depicted the mestizo Andrew as having embodied
the promise of assimilation, by passing socially, economically, and
even phenotypically into the white American world, but something
went awry.

In the few short weeks that Andrew captured national attention,
the mainstream Filipino American press ran weekly reports on this
Filipino American run amok.[6] "Killer on the Loose," announced the
Filipino Express headline, followed immediately by another piece
titled "Cunanan's Father Found."[7] Modesto Cunanan had fled the
United States after charges of embezzlement. The excitement rested
not in the father's having been missing, but that he was "found" in
the Philippines. By extension, actual "proof" of Andrew's Filipino
ancestry had been uncovered. The FBI and the media reached
across the Pacific to the Philippines, which appeared, for a flash, on
national American television. The FBI had alerted Philippine authorities, who in turn colluded and put Andrew on an immigration
blacklist. Furthermore, the FBI asked Philippine police to monitor
relatives in case he attempted to hide out in the country. Andrew
had visited the Philippines only once before, as a child. Not since
Imelda's shoes after the 1986 People Power revolution and the
eruption of Mount Pinatubo in 1991 had the Philippines come to
mark excess in U.S. popular culture. Andrew was yet another case
of excess, but one that could not remain simply a spectacle but, as
a "spree" killer (note: not a serial killer, as that connotes careful
method), posed a real and unpredictable danger to American bodies inside U.S. national borders.

In the Filipino American press, the visual and narrative search
for the Filipino father forged the connection between Andrew and
Filipino American communities. The disclaimer was not far behind.
"Publicity on Cunanan Tarnishes FilAm Image," lamented the

Philippine News.[8] The lament was curious. What did the "FilAm Image" look like before the tarnish? Was there ever one? Was it possible that this man of many faces caused Filipino Americans to lose theirs? Furthermore, Filipino gay men might have appeared on the community pages before, but never in such a lurid and sensational way as to "tarnish" a whole group's image in the eyes of an imagined American public. More important, the Filipino American press marked Cunanan racially, whereas the national media did not: it barely mentioned his ethnic background. Was this national nonfact not the desired end and fantasy of assimilation?

When Andrew committed suicide, the first sentence of the *Filipino Express* report read: "Andrew Cunanan is remembered by his relatives as an altar boy."[9] Andrew's altar-boy past invoked a mainstay in Catholic Filipino (and Italian) iconography and tugged at parental heartstrings. Combined with his estranged father, he fit the facile image of the lost Filipino son. If only he had had a good home . . . and so forth. A week later, the same paper curiously informed its readers that there would be "no Philippine burial for Cunanan," as if anyone in his family had ever considered this possibility.[10] Would this not-quite native burial have brought closure to his broken body and promise?

In the meantime, most of the national American media fixated on a more delectable milieu by producing a flurry of articles about the gay underworld. Television news magazines predictably showed shots of frenzied gay men dancing in clubs engulfed by darkness and drowning in heavy hypnotic bass. Weekly magazines included short pieces on gay "glamour after dark," supplemented by blurry photos of more dance clubs.[11] The national press would have relegated Andrew to the middle pages as another tragic gay story were it not for Gianni Versace's murder. Concern then burst from the confines of gay communities onto the international scene. A *New Yorker* commentator described the tense atmosphere around Miami while Cunanan was at large: "every white male between eighteen and fifty walking the sandy streets drew stares."[12] Did Andrew make white males visible, or did the writer here simply misunderstand the practice of cruising in South Beach? Andrew, described as a "white male between eighteen and fifty," seemed elusive despite the sloppy trail of clues he left behind—a passport, a signature, a stolen red pickup, and video images. Yet none of these registered his actual whereabouts.

Some national press marveled at his ingenious shape-shifting abilities. A *New York Times* article reported: "For one thing, Mr. Cunanan, a 27-year-old native of San Diego, has a face so nondescript that it appears vaguely familiar to just about everyone."[13] Indeed, it was his ordinariness that made possible his blending that led Stone Phillips on *Dateline* to speculate that "he could look like any one of us." Being "5 feet 10 inches tall, slim build, olive skin" made him generic, but lurking behind this facade was a killer, engaged in "dark" sexual practices, purportedly evidenced by porn tapes found in his room. He was a societal aberrant who looked like one of "us," presumably olive-skinned Americans. Andrew did "pass" in American society in many ways. As an object of desire, he passed across racial, social, class, and sexual lines.

To Filipinos who held a different racial schema that recognizes a long history of cultural and national mixing, he looked like one of "us," Filipinos. He had the mestizo Filipino good looks often depicted, even celebrated, in Filipino and Filipino American magazines, newspapers, and movies that Filipino Americans consume in Flushing, Jersey City, Virginia Beach, or Daly City, places with large concentrations of Filipinos. He could have easily been featured in the center pages of the *Filipino Reporter* and *Filipino Express,* both based in New York, or the *Philippine News,* based in California. An interviewee in the *Filipino Express* bemoaned his death: "Andrew Cunanan is such a waste. He's an altar boy, a straight-A student, handsome, intelligent, articulate." His picture could have been in those social pages along with beauty queen Miss This-or-that from Chicago, Jersey City, Los Angeles, or San Francisco.

In the Filipino American press, his looks and profile appeared to embody all the mythic desires of the Filipino immigrant, yearning for that fantastic, one hundred-year-old promise of American assimilation. The Filipino American coverage of Andrew's story attempted to integrate him into the assimilationist promise, but something had gone awry. Perhaps the "mourning" and "reviling"—the sense of loss and denial—revealed the inability of the Filipino immigrant narrative to reconcile his many masks, especially the wasteful gay one. The traditional narrative for a smart altar boy could not piece together fully Andrew's masks and story. His became a cautionary tale. At what point did that Filipino American face evincing visible whiteness as a sign of assimilation into a national body stray from that promise? Unfortunately, that smiling face, horribly disfigured in the end, refused, or perhaps could not sustain, that promise. "Waste," unlike Imelda's material excess, seems to be defined by what assimilation cannot contain—racial, class, sexual, and violent excesses that do not add up.

Andrew's face bore the trace of the ambivalent century-long relationship between the Philippines and the United States. To reread the FBI manhunt with this relationship in mind would reveal clues to Philippine America and the seeming disconnect between the Filipino American and the U.S. national presses. How could a Filipino enter the United States without ever leaving the Philippines, without actually immigrating? To get on the fast track to U.S. citizenship, many Filipinos join the U.S. Navy, filling the menial jobs reserved for them at the military bases in the Philippines. The American Dream may be realized by way of the U.S. military and its neocolonial presence in the Philippines. Modesto Cunanan was a retired navy man. Like other Filipinos, he joined the U.S. Navy in the Philippines and wound up in San Diego, a military port city with a considerable number of Filipino residents.[14] There, he married Mary Ann Schillaci, an Italian American, descended from an earlier wave of American immigration. They had four children, Chris, Elena, Gina, and the youngest, Andrew.

The father's favorite, Andrew, the one with the most promise, the chosen one, was sent to an elite prep school, Bishop Academy, in a wealthier section of San Diego. There are two ways to realize the American Dream—hard work and education or social climbing—though the two may not be so different in the end. Choosing the latter, Andrew spent much time and money attaining and improving upon his social skills and symbolic capital—charm, manners, conversation skills, connections, money, and looks. A San Diego columnist commented: "He knew about the arts, the right kinds of fork to use, the right cognac to drink." In addition, he offered his sexual services. His social and sexual maneuvers obtained for him economic patronage from rich, older gay gentlemen, and, no less important, an essential part of the American Dream, astronomical credit limits on his platinum cards, which he unfailingly put to use. He enjoyed class mobility, as long as his looks and credit cards held out—both short-lived currencies that could buy and be bought.

With his biracial heritage and "olive skin," he passed himself off as a scion of a wealthy Jewish family or the son of a Mexican or Filipino plantation owner. Mexican. Filipino. Jew. Andrew occupied the hazy but all too familiar territory of brownness that the American racial schema cannot successfully apprehend in brown citizenry. The U.S. nation-state polices borders, as Filipinos and other migrants know only too well, and one of those borders is the color line. In many parts of the country, this line insists upon a peculiar binaristic black-and-white race paradigm. Sometimes, the binary is simply reduced to white and not-white. Historically, the United States has had to contain legally this blurry brownness.[15] Latinos and Asian Americans (and, in the past, Jews and Italians) fall into this yellow-brown category, a category reserved for what historian Gary Okihiro termed "custodial citizens." When strict categories, racial or sexual, fail to regulate identities and behavior such as Andrew's, stories remain incomplete. However, Andrew's "passing" narratives revealed another story.

Like the passport, the pickup, and the signature that he carelessly left behind, Andrew's masks also leave a trail of clues to America's past, its borders, its movement, and its unique trace. Two of these "masks"—the Mexican and Filipino—hark back to the United States' imperial past: 1848, the Mexican-American War by which northern Mexico was ceded to become California and the U.S. Southwest; and 1898, the Spanish-Philippine-American War, which resulted in the ceding of the Philippines and Puerto Rico as U.S. territories. Yet, they also hark back to a Philippine Hispanic past when the archipelago was administered by Spain *through* Mexico's viceroyalty, sharing culture and moneys for more than three centuries. Aside from mobile borders, mobile bodies are thrust into this circuit.

When a *New York Times* article puzzled over Andrew's enigmatic unrecognizability—"Mr. Cunanan appears to be everywhere and nowhere"—this national media blindness could have also described Filipino presence in the United States and in the Americas.[16] Like Andrew, Filipino Americans have left many clues to their existence and live as a testament to America's imperial past. They moved as labor to and from the continent as U.S. "nationals" then and as Philippine citizens now. Traces of this imperial past are indeed "everywhere," as the many pockets of Filipino communities show, and "nowhere," as American public memory and vision effectively overlook the Filipino and absentmindedly ask, "What American empire?" The Filipino wavers in and out of American vision and memory. For this reason, perhaps, the Philippines and its diaspora have, to echo Vicente Rafael, "a sense of elusiveness along with the unexpected familiarity."[17] In other words, the archipelago and its inhabitants' global dispersal have an uncanny effect on the American psyche to which Filipinos have an intimate and uncomfortable linkage.

Is the Filipino American but a set of traces, masks, and misrecognitions in American law, borders, and drama? This unrecognizability of the Filipino in the American imagination has roots in U.S. legal history in the construction of a colonial space rendered invisible to the American polity: the unincorporated territory. In a dissenting opinion in the creation of this geopolitical status for the newly acquired territories, the Insular Cases, a set of Supreme Court cases from 1901 dealing with the regulation of trade between the territories (Hawai'i, Puerto Rico, and the Philippines) and the continent, Justice Fuller rejected this American political entity that "Congress has the power to keep . . . like a disembodied shade, in an intermediate state of ambiguous existence for an indefinite period."[18] Thus, disembodied shadows have a legal and imperial history in the United States.

Perhaps this history of juridical disembodiment explains part of Andrew's enigma. Andrew generated speculations and ambivalence. In a position of unrepresentability and unrecognizability, Andrew mobilized strangely familiar images and narratives of exotic lands and plantations in Mexico and the Philippines to propel his body through the circuits of desire and money from San Diego to South Beach. He mimicked the social conventions of class and race to cross these boundaries. He manipulated sexual relations to reinvent himself at every turn. He played many parts shuttling between his clients' desires and his own. It is precisely his unremarkability that made possible his protean existence. How does one produce unremarkability and signature, a singular mark, at the same time? Through obfuscated boundaries and misrecognitions, Andrew's Filipino American stories mark the tragic possibilities and limits of the U.S. nation-state and its designated categories. In those summer months, Filipino American and other American subjects were on a manhunt for themselves: "Publicity on Cunanan Tarnishes FilAm Image"; "What does a serial killer look like? The answer is: he could look like any one of us." What were these stories if not the signature trace of American imperial narratives in the throes of paranoia and narcissism, to echo Homi Bhabha, for *both* nation and subnation? Colonies, like repressed memories, have a return effect on the metropole; they leave a ghostly, and sometimes bloody, trail that haunts the center.

These narrative paroxysms for both empire and postcolonial ethnic constitute what I term American Tropics as a set of regulatory tropes and narratives that reveal a particularly U.S. American imperial grammar that create ethnic, racial, and colonial subjects. American Tropics supplements the project of comparative ethnic studies. Ethnic studies is committed to creating a language connecting different communities of color suffering similar oppression under the U.S. nation-state. By formulating a language by which these spaces speak to each other, alliances are made possible. The postcolonial perspective would add that these ethnic spaces are also wrought with linkages outside the frame of the nation-state and its official identity designations; that is, there are narratives about identities, mainly but not limited to immigrant identities that precede a group's arrival on American shores. Identifications with other peripheral and racialized spaces within and without the U.S. national borders form and inform Filipino/Filipino American identity. These accounts fall outside apparent borders of the United States, and place the United States in a global context. Racialization in the American Tropics has a history steeped in imperialism, specifically U.S. imperialism.

The social pages in which Andrew would have appeared are usually found between articles about how horrible the situation is "back home" ridden with peso devaluation and typhoons, or about the plight of domestic workers in the Middle East and Southeast Asia. Because of global economic shifts, pockets of Filipino communities exist all over capital-rich cities in North America, Southeast Asia, Australia, Oceania, the Middle East, and Europe. Filipinos as subjects and Filipinoness are formed not only via the American racial classification system but also via identifications (good, bad, or ambivalent) with other Filipino translocal communities. According to Arjun Appadurai, the translocal differentiates itself from the country of origin, the culture of the host country, as well as other translocal communities.[19] Unable to fit into a unitary national narrative, the translocal is thus a troublesome category in that it complicates an easy understanding of ethnic formation in the United States.

The early-twentieth-century European-American immigration and assimilation model of ethnicity does not obtain so easily in the twenty-first century. There is no longer one way, if there ever was simply one, people become "ethnic" Americans. More simply, because of changing historical and geographic contexts, categories of race, identity, sexuality, and ethnicity cannot be taken for granted. Rather, the channels of power and the multiple *identificatory* historical and geographic sites produced by imperialism complicate the linear and singular trajectory of ethnic and national identity. Part and parcel of the Filipino American postcolonial imagination, these multiple identificatory sites suggest a terrain of social formations, still unrecognized by the U.S. nation-state, making the manhunt for Filipino America and Asian America that much more elusive.

Chapter 1, "American Tropics," examines the theoretical and historical underpinnings of the term in literary studies, postcolonial, American, and Asian American studies. The American Tropics forged out of U.S. imperial desire and fantasy presents another facet of the Asian American cultural imagination to decenter immigration and exclusion as the primary loci of Asian American racial formation. If American cultural and economic imperialism is an integral part of Asian American identities as a "social formation," to borrow Michael Omi and Howard Winant's phrase about race and racialization, how does this imperial desire inform Asian American social imagination? Forcible (un)incorporation of the Philippines into the U.S. domestic sphere created an anomalous form of "immigration" within national space as well as of "inclusion" of a subordinated legal subject. Accounting of U.S. history and state activities along enfolded—that is, simultaneously inside and outside—borders recognizes alternate American subjectivities emerging from such enfolding and suspension.

Part I, "An Imperial Grammar," explores misrecognitions and misreadings in the U.S. national imaginary that connect the Philippines to other geopolitical sites, understanding the archipelago through encounters with racial difference along U.S. geopolitical and moral borders. The Philippines has been variously articulated through Puerto Rico in turn-of-the-twentieth-century legal debates, as part of the Latin American borderlands in early-twentieth-century popular literature, and with Hawai'i and the Pacific Islands in mid-century cinema. The chapters foreground how American imperial and colonial subjectivities are codified by the legal clause, enclosed by moral borders, and projected into Hollywood romance. "America" on the move and in the movies negotiates its identity with the tropics to re-create the American domestic space and national family romance for its captive audience. Law, policy, education, and culture all mediate the way a subject comprehends, appropriates, and identifies with others. Law, literature, and film as producers of spectacles secure imperial fantasies that also manifest momentary crises of self-presentation for the imperial subject while managing racial difference. These tropical metaphors offer insight into the operations and processes of disavowal to make illegible the American colonial subject and to make legible the fantastic outlines of the U.S. nation-state.

Chapter 2, "Disappearing Clauses: Reconstituting America in the Unincorporated Territories," maps out the project's theoretical foundations in legal discourse through the historical emergence of the unincorporated territory and the noncitizen U.S. "national" designation. The early-twentieth-century constitution of the American Tropics is a legally unrepresentable geographic space constructed by U.S. juridico-economic discourse. This space became the object of the U.S. civilizing mission that produced colonial subjects out of the inhabitants of the American Tropics. The law calls into being the limbo state in which the Philippines and Puerto Rico find themselves property of the United States but not part of it.

Chapter 3, "Moral Sentences: Boy Scouts and Novel Encounters with Empire," examines the inaugural Boy Scout novels, which are a popular early-twentieth-century American adolescent series that imagined the moral and proprietary battles along U.S. borderlands. Published in 1911, the three inaugural novels, *Boy Scouts in Mexico, Boy Scouts in the Panama Canal Zone,* and *Boy Scouts in the Philippines,* all set in imperial milieus, venture into the nation's newfound empire along the Mexican border, in the Panama Canal Zone, and in the Philippine Islands to provide cultural lessons in the duties of U.S. imperial citizenship. As part of the American civilizing mission at home and abroad, the Boy Scouts symbolized self-reliance, citizenship, self-government, and civilization. In this popular literature, Progressive Era rhetoric imbued with a world mission propels this domestic masculinity to disseminate a universalist "Americanness" to its brown borders.

While the novels wrestle with transformation of impossible difference to its management through the specter of genocide, they also trace the hazy outlines and borders of whiteness and masculinity that travel with imperial paramilitary authority. Between genocide and ethnocide is the unstable project of whiteness and masculinity that cannot contain their paranoid borders.

Chapter 4, "Imperial Romance: Framing Manifest Destiny in the Pacific," moves to a mid-century point on the U.S. continent, where mainstream mass culture in the form of cinema re-created an Asian and Pacific image in the aftermath of Philippine liberation and the Japanese American internment camps, and during the civil rights movement. The chapter visits the fantasy spaces of "reconstituted" tropical America of the pre– and post–World War II era through popular American films and musicals that seek to incorporate colonized Asian and Pacific bodies in the American visual and geopolitical field. The romantic musicals are vehicles that serve not only to establish an American Pacific but also to drive away the specter of military violence visited upon Pacific spaces to constitute a new racially harmonious fantasy. The chapter interrogates imperial American tropes found in these cultural productions, from the United States as liberator of dependent Filipinos in *The Real Glory* (1939) to Elvis Presley as an island local in *Blue Hawaii* (1961). The films locate Pacific identity as an exotic but assimilable otherness, extending this to Hawaiʻi, then a dependency on the verge of becoming a state. The Pacific becomes the fantastical theater where, in place of the military violence visited upon the space, white American characters sing, dance, and fall in love with their own appropriated tropical identity.

Part II, "Toward an American Postcolonial Syntax," revisits the American subjects and predicates of the American Tropics by interrogating the works of two Filipino American writers, Carlos Bulosan from the 1940s and Jessica Hagedorn from the 1990s, read alongside the works of Hawaiian writer John Dominis Holt and continental Puerto Rican writer Piri Thomas. Proper syntax in English suggests a proper word order to make a chain of utterances have meaning. By virtue of U.S. colonization, military intervention, and occupation, the signs of "America" flow and disperse throughout Asia, the Caribbean, and the Pacific. Oftentimes the colonized subject never has to leave her island space to access the signs of America. When colonized subjects enter or are forced to enter the terrestrial space of the U.S. nation-state, how do the same tropes and fantasies inform their negotiation with Americanness? What happens when they come "home" to this fantasy? Like their continental counterpart, they too are reconstituted Americans, imbued by the developmental logic that insists that the completion of their modernity, even identity, can be realized in accessing the sign, if not the place, of "America." Writing against the ideological and narrative grain stemming from the imperial encounter, American writers whose identities are inextricably linked to this imperial history begin to reorder, literally and literarily, the American landscape. These American novels provide not only a critique of America as place *(topos)* and promise *(tropos),* but also imagine how place and promise order new identities and reorder national belonging.

Bulosan in 1943, before Philippine flag independence, and Hagedorn in 1990 articulate this syntax as they operate along two time lines: Philippine–U.S. colonial history and Asian American history. *America Is in the Heart* and *Dogeaters* mark pre- and post-Philippine flag independence as well as pre- and post-1965 Asian American immigration. Furthermore, I juxtapose these two works alongside those of Hawaiian writer John Dominis Holt and continental Puerto Rican writer Piri Thomas to suggest the contiguity of the American empire and to trace the narrative strategies of the American postcolonial imagination. By connecting these American island spaces, what can Asian American literary studies learn from Pacific and Hawaiian studies and Latino and Puerto Rican studies? How can one rearticulate the colonial/postcolonial convergence and contestation to bear upon the battles on the Asian American cultural and literary front? The readings demonstrate how the language of subjectivity challenges the language of imperial law and how the law shapes but, as these writers contend, fails to contain American postcolonial difference.

Chapter 5, "Reconstituting American Subjects: Proximate Masculinities," reads Carlos Bulosan's *America Is in the Heart* (1946) alongside Piri Thomas's *Down These Mean Streets* (1967) to explore the male abject body as the beginning of a new discourse. I argue that the obliteration of the colonized male's body is a narrative strategy that hedges and circulates alongside three modalities: imperial narrator, absented colonized, and the reconstitutive reteller. Bulosan making "visible the sores of history" complicates

the unincorporated subjects of the American landscape living within its enfolded borders, always on the verge of disintegration at the
moment of the subject's utterance. The moment of articulation
actually undoes the speaking subject, hence the circulating voice
strategically set to gain authority. This unstable relationship to language and authority suggests a precarious masculinity enmeshed in
nonnormative sexualities.

Chapter 6, "Reconstituting American Predicates: Troping the
American *Tour d'Horizon*," reads Jessica Hagedorn's *Dogeaters*
(1990) and John Dominis Holt's *Waimea Summer* (1976) as de-
ploying narrative strategies to expand the colonial spatial *tour
d'horizon* suggested by Benedict Anderson to extend to a more
sedimented postcolonial semiotic and temporal *tour d'horizon*.
Whereas *America Is in the Heart* and *Down These Mean Streets*
look back and reread life events to give meaning to them as new
subjects, *Dogeaters* and *Waimea Summer* reconfigure the landscape to reveal the sedimentation of meanings so that the abject
subject can make meaning and make itself signify to its surrounding objects. The novels expand not only national borders but also
national meaning making, as the protagonists grapple not only
with the familiar but also with the alienated meanings of this familiar to reread national subjectivity.

The Coda concludes the book with a consideration of ongoing
misreadings of Filipino bodies and history as they relate to U.S.
activity in the Middle East. The narrative disjunctures and spatial
occlusions produced by the legal and imaginative constructions of
the American Tropics also constitute the Filipino American postcolonial imagination as a critical and conjunctive practice. By connecting the works from dislocated American island spaces, the
vanishing point of unrecognizability and unrepresentability creates
a critical practice within American postcolonial history to reimag-
ine and relocate American cultural narratives.

1. American Tropics

"Tropic," Hayden White writes, "is the shadow from which all re-alistic discourse tries to flee. This flight, however, is futile; for trop-ics is the process by which discourse constitutes the objects which it pretends only to describe realistically and analyze objectively."[1] American Tropics interrogates the constitution of this fearsome shadow from which imperial discourse flees, making the U.S. nation-state legible and legitimate. Focusing on the Philippines and Filipino America as crucial parts of that shadow, the American Tropics turns upon "America" to demonstrate how America not only is itself a trope but continually gyrates and generates tropes about itself to underscore its identity or difference against its per-ceived others.

Etymologically, the word *tropics* is derived from the Greek word *tropikos* ("turn"). Geographically, the tropics bound the tor-rid zone marking the turning points of the sun. Literarily, tropics are the figurative turns in language wielded in narrative. Across the insular chain of what I call the American Tropics, marking U.S. territories in and adjacent to the torrid zone, the imperial encoun-ter has forced peoples, both within and without the U.S. nation-state, to negotiate legal, cultural, and imaginative borders to de-fine what is proper to "America." Each territorial enfolding under U.S. jurisdiction has inspired a flurry of narratives from histories and legal treatises to literature and cinema. These narratives about America's imperial mobility would seem to interrogate the carto-graphic place and placeness of this "America" appearing outside

the continental landmass and marking the globe with its paren-
thetical U.S. claims.

The American Tropics, then, is both discursive practice and
place. As place, the tropics geographically describe the region between the Tropic of Cancer and the Tropic of Capricorn. The quali-
fier "American" refers to the proprietary claims of the United States
over island nations around these latitudinal markers. Currently, the
American territorial landscape includes, in the Pacific, American
Samoa, the Federated States of Micronesia, Guam, the Northern
Mariana Islands, the Marshall Islands, and Palau, and, in the
Caribbean, Puerto Rico and the U.S. Virgin Islands.[2] In the early
twentieth century, Cuba, the Dominican Republic, and Haiti were
protectorates subject to U.S. military and economic intervention.
The Philippines and Hawai'i were also "organized" U.S. territories, that is, had organic acts. Both were annexed in 1898 as territories along with Puerto Rico and Guam; the former went the way
of independence, the latter qualified for statehood. Most of these
island nations suffered and continue to suffer military occupation,
cultural imperialism, and neocolonial underdevelopment.

The regeneration of the American frontier in the 1890s and the
formal institutionalization of American studies in the U.S. academy in the 1930s frame a critical span inaugurating, to paraphrase
Edward Said's observation of comparative literature and European
culture, the imperial interpellation of American culture.[3] In the
1930s, American studies, with its emphatic assertion of a distinctly
American, as opposed to European, civilization emerged as a formal discipline in higher education. Coterminous with this institutionalization of "American" culture, the 1934 Tydings-McDuffie
Act promised independence to the American colonial outpost of the
Philippines, effectively severing the archipelago from U.S. borders.
Thus, the United States demarcated its geopolitical boundaries at
the same time that it delimited its disciplinary and epistemological
terrain; it sought to circumscribe what was proper to, as opposed
to what was simply the property of, "America." Therefore, as a
disciplinary practice, the American Tropics constitute a set of controlling metaphors or tropes of imperial tutelage and containment
that separate the primitive from the civilized, chaos from order,
property from the proper.

Obversely, as a reading and cultural practice of those whose land
and imagination were shaped under these disciplinary tropes, the
American Tropics signal the presence of an invisible waterscape

and of the obfuscated narratives residing outside of, but produced as the by-product in the creation of, U.S. epistemological and geopolitical borders. The cultures of U.S. imperialism span half the world from Puerto Rico and the Virgin Islands across the Panama Canal to Hawai'i and the Philippines.[4] These territories were at one historical juncture or another "unincorporated" parts of the United States of America. The "unincorporated" state is also a geopolitical construction of U.S. juridico-political will that has served to obscure the contradiction inherent in a democratic republic holding colonial possessions. I use "unincorporated" in another broader sense to connote the excess assigned by the U.S. nation-state to the culturally secondary and politically dependent status of a state, nation, or people. American Tropics from the Caribbean to the Pacific and to Asia has been *formally* organized by the American polity and imagination even while setting it apart as legally "unincorporated" national entities.[5] Thus, the legal and political terrains structure the fantasy and imagination to fill the temporal and spatial distance assigned to them. As Neferti Tadiar has asserted, elaborating upon Slavoj Žižek, "Fantasy is a field of symbolically structured meaning (the unconscious) that shapes and regulates our desires, our modes of acting 'in reality.'"[6]

The Philippines, constituting part of the American Tropics, is where "America" meets its aporia, its impasse—a contingent but not contiguous source of difficult passages in legal, cinematic, and literary narratives, giving texture to the American story. Despite one hundred years of colonial and neocolonial relationship and exchange between the Philippines and the United States, the Philippines is virtually obscured in American studies and in American educational institutions. Amy Kaplan suggests that this oversight is symptomatic of American historiography; she notes in Oscar Campomanes's essay in *Discrepant Histories* (1995) that the "invisibility of the Philippines in American history has everything to do with the invisibility of American imperialism to itself."[7] American exceptionalist ideologues have characterized American imperialism as an aberration or euphemized it into more neutral terms such as "world power" and "benevolent assimilation." As Kaplan states in her introductory essay to *Cultures of United States Imperialism*:

> If the importance of culture has gone unrecognized in historical studies of American imperialism, the role of empire has been virtually ignored in the study of American culture. The current paradigm

of American studies today, still under intense debate, emphasizes cultural diversity and scholarly "dissensus" and analyzes American society and culture in terms of internal difference and conflicts, structured around relations of race, gender, ethnicity and class.[8]

Although scholarly work on race, gender, ethnicity, and class within U.S. national borders has been generative, the terrain of the respective debates might be altered if inflected with the discourse of empire that is so much a part of U.S. history but disavowed in its discursive imaginings. The cartographic contours of these debates become more complex when what is taken to be the outside, the colony and the regulatory prescriptions imposed on it, is imagined to be constitutive of these very debates on the inside. The refocus on the margins might bring a different view of the center, and, in fact, render the division to be an unstable one.

Given this colonial order, the stakes involved in interrogating neo-imperial discourse are even higher if we take seriously the exhortation made by Ann Laura Stoler in her book *Race and the Education of Desire* (1995). She supplements and expands on Michel Foucault's work on the history of sexuality by investigating the discursive practices of empire and race markedly absent in his work on nineteenth-century France. She challenges the notion of colonialism as a secure bourgeois project that imported metropole values into the periphery. On the contrary, she argues, the peripheral site helped constitute these very values.[9] This assertion proceeds from an elaboration on a passage in Foucault's lectures regarding a return effect *(effet de retour)* in the European colonial project:

> [C]olonization with its techniques and juridical and political weapons transported European models to other continents, but . . . this same colonization had a return effect on the mechanisms of power in the Occident, on the institutional apparatuses and techniques of power.[10]

In the U.S.–Philippine context, the colonial project mapped avenues by which concepts of "citizenship," "masculinity," "whiteness," and "Americanness" were sustained, forged, and filtered through U.S. activity in its colonies, including the Philippines. This is not to suggest that these formulations had a simple return effect back to the metropole, but that policy surrounding the colonies, later client states, informs and is informed by internal debates about race, gender, class, and ethnicity. These internal relations and techniques of power cannot be separated from the U.S. global and imperial enterprise. This book explores how Filipino American formation and American national identity have been shaped by the American vision of and activity among U.S. custodial populations at home and abroad. By extending its borders to incorporate tropical lands and peoples through its neocolonial adventures, the U.S. nation-state created an "American Tropics" as part of its national identity. While providing an imaginary space of fantasy, this tropical identity also required containment and discipline of potential excesses of both continent and territory.

Since the first covetous glance of American politicians and businessmen toward the fabled China market in the mid-nineteenth century, the Asia-Pacific region has played a crucial role in narrating the American story. The story has included Pago-Pago in American Samoa (1878), Hawai'i (1891), the Philippines (1898–1946), the Pacific theater during World War II (1941–45), Korea (1950–53), Vietnam (1955–75), and, most recently, the war in Iraq and the paranoiac war on terror. Lisa Lowe, in her influential book *Immigrant Acts: On Asian American Cultural Politics* (1996), and David Palumbo-Liu, in his work *Asian/American: Historical Crossings of a Racial Frontier* (1999), have argued that the Asia-Pacific region has been historically the site of American exoticization and exclusion, the repository of American fears and fantasy. Consequently, the region's various peoples were similarly disciplined, having been rendered inassimilable and "ineligible for citizenship" by American law under the Asiatic Barred Zone (1917), an area encompassing South Asia to Japan to Polynesia. Thus, peoples of Asia and the Pacific have been the "enabling exclusion" that made possible the consolidation of American identity and citizenship.[11]

In *Asian/American,* Palumbo-Liu locates the racialization of Asians in America as coinciding with U.S. modernization and industrialization. While "Asia" served as the locus of U.S. fantasy projection, Asian-raced peoples in the United States were the racialized, alien labor force in the modern economy on which such fantasies of threat and futurity were introjected. The racialization of the Asian American as the "foreigner within" is rooted in a history of recruiting temporary, noncitizen Asian labor in the nineteenth century and its enduring legacy into the early twenty-first century. Then, as now, Asians were expected to "go home" elsewhere. Born out of international politics and global industrial developments, Asian American racialization as a modern phenomenon was bound with paranoia surrounding Asiatic transnationals and their dubious allegiance to the U.S. nation-state. The Asian face as a sign of this transnationalism carries the threat of the porousness of national borders.

Lowe argues in *Immigrant Acts* that the subordination and racialization of the category "alien" from the category "citizen" gives epistemic force to Asian American cultural politics and criticism. Her exploration of Asian American subjectivities relies on Asian American culture as a condition of "alienated citizenship" or "disavowed citizenship." Asian American history, therefore, is fraught with negation of unequal race relations that has long defined national labor and political history. Therefore, Asian American culture becomes a repository for historical memory of race and class antagonism actively repressed by national memory.

Lowe couples the disavowal of a racialized imperial history with a negation of such a history. In looking at U.S. identity formation through enabling exclusions, I would distinguish between negation and disavowal of the racialized U.S. subject and her history. Negation and disavowal are two psychic operations that have very different consequences for the subjects of such a psychic and sociohistorical act. Following Gilles Deleuze's exploration of the masochistic imagination, negation is quantitative violence, a zero-sum game that institutionalizes negative valuation of a subordinate group.[12] Disavowal, on the other hand, is a qualitative violence, an act of the imagination effected by institutionalized invisibility.[13] It effects an active blindness to a fact, creating a suspended reality in its place.

Here, perhaps, we might distinguish black from Asian racialization. Frantz Fanon described blackness as negation within a colonial racial hierarchy in his psychoanalytic treatise *Black Skin, White Masks* (1952). In literary studies, Toni Morrison elaborates on the "Africanist presence" as an enabling trope that circumscribes the negative outline and projected limits of whiteness in the literary imagination in her essays *Playing in the Dark* (1993). On the other hand, the Asian-raced person bears on her body, as Palumbo-Liu suggests, the signs of transnational borders—the very transnationalism disavowed by U.S. national narrative. Asian-raced peoples living in the United States have posed a quandary for the nation-state that sought to exclude them from the national borders from 1882 to 1965 with immigration exclusion acts, and from the national body as citizens from 1790 to 1952 with the racial bar to naturalization.

A further complication of this enabling exclusion can be seen in the use of Filipinos as a colonized people from the U.S. "unincorporated" territories to further distinguish Asian racialization in the United States from U.S. colonial racialization. Colonials such as Puerto Ricans, Filipinos, Chamorros, and Samoans were given the status of U.S. nationals. This designation did not make them citizens, but neither were they construed as exactly alien. Critical legal scholar Natsu Taylor Saito has shown how congressional plenary powers as an extraconstitutional power derived from the notion of sovereignty wields two types of boundary making: the right to *exclude,* in cases of immigration, and the right to *dispose* of property, used in cases of territories.[14] While the former alludes to people, the latter applies to land and inanimate objects. The American dependent is poised precisely between these juridical powers, as both subject and object of a government external to herself. This strange doubleness results in the creation of parallel "Americans," one within and the other outside of the geocultural (not geographic) compass of the North American continent. This double identity compels me to route a comparative American studies across an East–West axis from the Philippines to Hawai'i, across the continent, and to Puerto Rico to mine the reading possibilities of the American Tropics.

This approach nuances Kaplan's claim of the invisibility of U.S. empire to itself and, by extension, the invisibility of Filipinos and their history as per Campomanes, in that the operation and production of empire is predicated on the legislative and cultural institutionalization of disavowal of these other American subjects. As a corollary to what Lowe terms alienated citizenship, these subjects bearing the official designation of "American" had the privilege of free travel and lived as *noncitizen nonaliens.* Thus, for Filipinos in the first half of the twentieth century, no borders that would obtain in what we often conceive of as immigration were crossed. Moreover, while Filipinos faced legal and violent extralegal disciplinary measures to regulate their sexual, racial, and class mobility in the United States, they were not officially excluded until flag independence after World War II. This anomalous position *within* the U.S. domestic sphere as a nodal point would signify for Asian

American studies a decentering of immigration and exclusion as primary sites in this investigation.

Reconstituting Americans Abroad

The unincorporated territory and the American national, both disembodied from the American body politic, became America's double in the Pacific. "Belonging to but not a part" of the United States, the Philippines and Filipinos occupied what Homi Bhabha calls "in that other scene of colonial power, where history turns to farce and presence to 'a part' can be seen the twin figures of narcissism and paranoia that repeat furiously, uncontrollably."[15] Within the laws of American polity, these spaces and their inhabitants were unrepresentable in Congress, the representative body of "We, the people," except through a nonvoting representative in the House—a presence without a voice. Constitutionally, territories being not proper to but property of the nation-state, their inhabitants were not part of that founding "We," and were subsequently severed from this representation, making possible the tenuous cultural and political integrity of the United States. Yet, these disembodied subjects were to be disciplined to become an (after)image of America overseas.

On July 4, 1902, Theodore Roosevelt by presidential fiat declared the end of the Philippine "insurrection," now recognized as the Philippine-American War (1899–1902). Roosevelt did not pursue the creation of a distinct colonial department. The ongoing conflict in the southern provinces of the Philippines, and the contemporary tension between military and civil authorities in different parts of the islands, made such an undertaking difficult. In international relations, the archipelago remained important to the U.S. military in order to keep the Japanese threat and European spheres of influence in Asia in abeyance.[16] The absence of an official colonial department (appearing later as the diminutive Bureau of Insular Affairs under the War Department) not only produced ad hoc colonial policies but also effectively erased the word *colony* from bureaucratic vocabulary.

The economic objectives of U.S. foreign policy mandated a structuring of a colonial society that would be dependent on the U.S. economy. A fast-industrializing United States sought the urbanization and integration of the Americas and the Philippine archipelago into the American sphere of influence in hopes of expanding its

markets. However, the dream of a vast Asia market never material-
ized with the Philippine colony.[17] Domestic sugar interests prevented development of a plantation economy in the Philippines for fear
of competition from the new territories.[18] The colony instead provided raw materials and imported finished American goods much
like the traditional European colonial pattern.

However, the banner of moral righteousness and civilization
became the cloaking mantle in the enforcement of imperial policies throughout the twentieth century. Empire building was dictated not solely by the masculinist rantings of Theodore Roosevelt,
but also by the sentimental desires of bourgeois reformist America.
The American imperial project was a meeting point of contending
ideologies and interests, conditioned not only by U.S. political and
economic needs, but also by domestic reformism. Progressive Era
rhetoric blurred the boundaries of foreign and domestic interests
to provide the subterfuge for "benevolent assimilation" and "sentimental imperialism" in the Philippines and other American territories. The domestic as a site of morality wove its way into foreign
and national policy. In President McKinley's oft-quoted words,
"there was nothing left for us to do but to take them all and to edu-
cate the Filipinos, and uplift and civilize and Christianize them."[19]

The reform movements and the concurrent disciplining of immigrants in settlement houses and civic organizations spreading
on the continent offered possibilities for American cultural education overseas. To administer the overseas territories and fulfill its
"civilizing mission," the United States undertook the tutelary project of Americanizing its insular "appurtenances" in preparation
for their self-government. In 1901, the USS *Thomas* brought to
Philippine shores the first group of more than a hundred American
public schoolteachers, later known as the "Thomasites," the new
evangelical missionaries of Americanism. U.S. educational policy for insular nationals was generally patterned after Booker T.
Washington's vocational program in Tuskegee and Hampton for
African Americans and Native Americans.[20]

As part of U.S. pacification measures, President Taft's "policy of
attraction" appropriated military funds to establish public schools
throughout the archipelago with soldiers already on the field re-
assigned as teachers.[21] Public primary schools were established
to teach agriculture and industry to make good, useful citizens
of the Filipinos.[22] The Philippine Normal School was opened to

train natives to become teachers. And in 1908 the University of the Philippines in Manila, the colonial administrative center, was established (five years after the founding of the University of Puerto Rico) by the U.S. administration and patterned after U.S. universities to prepare Filipinos for the expanding colonial bureaucracy.

> Its graduates and the graduates of other schools faithfully observing the mandates of American and US trained *pensionado* educators were to constitute the new intelligentsia that read, spoke and wrote English. Unlike the *ilustrados* of the late nineteenth century who belonged to the socio-economic elite, the new intelligentsia came from a broader sector of the populace.[23]

The predominance of English at all levels of education and in the bureaucracy facilitated the cultural Americanization and pacification of the Filipino populace. The imposition of American cultural norms severed Filipinos from the production of their own national texts and transformed Filipinos into consumers of American cultural products.[24] After pacification, the colonial situation, managed by Congress and the Philippine Commission, dictated the terms and conditions of eventual independence for the Philippines.

While remaining unrepresentable in the American polity and frozen in a political holding pattern, Filipino subjects were to incorporate American culture and values to "prove" their fitness for self-government. Metropolitan education and other disciplinary measures sought to make the little brown brothers "in our image," to echo the title of Stanley Karnow's book.[25] The imperious logic demanded that the colonized assimilate U.S. culture as part of their tutelage in self-government. Diana Fuss observes:

> It therefore becomes necessary for the colonizer to subject the colonial other to a double command: be like me, don't be like me; be mimetically identical, be totally other. The colonial other is situated somewhere between difference and similitude, at the vanishing point of subjectivity.[26]

Fuss underscores the split in both the colonizer and the colonized as a result of the imperial relationship. The colonized is enjoined to "assimilate but not incorporate, to approximate but not to displace."[27] Thus, while inhabiting "unincorporated" territory, the colonized subject must himself incorporate values and culture of the power that disowned him in the first place. In a state of political and cultural deferral, "at the vanishing point of subjectivity," the American Tropics produced an afterimage of the American.

Such incorporation by Filipinos of an institutionally teachable culture would assume a coherent U.S. culture in the first place. In order to create "Americans" abroad, colonial educational and civic institutions were established in which principles of Americanness were translated, systematized, and taught. "America" was defined by a systematic organization of U.S. culture, politics, history, language, and literature. However, "America" in the Philippines could be gleaned only in the exercise of U.S. dominance over the population. According to Stuart Hall, in colonialism, "the dominant regimes of representation were the critical exercise of cultural power and normalization."[28] In other words, in the Philippine case, "America" was what the U.S. colonial apparatus performed to discipline its subjects. "America" was a social relation as well as a set of knowledges. The enforced mapping of Filipino bodies along a developmental time line projected as its imperial goal a fantastical "American" telos.

The mimetic mandate creates symbolic infractions on two fronts. First, Filipinos as colonial subjects were being forced to mimic a fantastical projection of the American subject. They must accede to the *signs* of America—in speech, clothes, mannerisms, and cultural consumption. Second, mimesis, as with all desire, falters. Despite the mimetic discipline imposed on colonized subjects, assimilation could not but fail. If Americanization structured "reality" through cultural normalization, then "reality" is a product of the imperial regimes of representation. Reality, Slavoj Žižek warns, in a psychoanalytic context,

> is not "the thing" itself, it is always-already symbolized, constituted, structured by symbolic mechanisms—and the problem resides in the fact that symbolization ultimately always fails, that it never succeeds in fully "covering" the real, that it always involves some unsettled, unredeemed symbolic debt. This real (the part of reality that remains non-symbolized) returns in the guise of spectral apparitions.[29]

Applied to the colonial setting, assimilation fails because symbolic systems fail; that is, words, images, and discourses always already produce their own excess in the symbolic order, creating ghosts. In imperialism, the symbolic debt, or the inassimilable properties, of colonial reality return to haunt the center's narratives. Such is the case with the unincorporated territories of the United States and their inhabitants. Their narratives return to destabilize a facile American story of nationalism.

Bhabha suggests that "mimicry rearticulates presence in terms of its otherness, that which it disavows."[30] The emergence of "We, the people" was made possible in part through the disavowal of the colonial subject. Now this subject is forced to replicate "the people" while remaining unrepresentable to the original. In the course of the tutelary project, the excised portion of imperial narrative is the violence that originated and made possible the "critical exercise of cultural power and normalization" of one people over another. These imperial remainders or ghosts are the persistent but constitutive elements that are incorporated, however uncomfortably, into Filipino *and* American and then Filipino American narratives. This uneasy incorporation shapes the lives and imagination of American postcolonial subjects.

As Edward Said reminds us, colonialism is cultural. I use the term "postcoloniality" in Gayatri Spivak's sense to mean the condition of incomplete decolonization as lived in these spaces.[31] U.S. imperialism continues to produce what one recognizes as the everyday familiar of lived experience. Multiple waves of imperialism have washed on the shores of the Asia and the Pacific, carrying with them values, arts, aesthetics, politics, languages, and identities that become part and parcel of the local culture. Like waves, some practices converge and reinforce each other while others serve to continue silences and subordination. American postcoloniality marks how modes of power relations are dispersed and reconfigured in a world where the fact of colonialism still resides. At any given moment, there are multiple currents that texture the American postcolonial imagination. Instead of resulting in assimilation or identity crises, the postcolonial condition is a negotiation and performance of multiple identities, any one of which may surface according to the needs of the historical or political moment.

Colonialism creates a spatial and temporal differentiation and demarcation between ruler and ruled. As Fanon explains:

> The area of culture is then marked off by fences and signposts. . . .
> Every effort is made to bring the colonized person to admit the inferiority of his culture which has been transformed into instinc-

tive patterns of behavior, to recognize the unreality of his "nation," and, in the last extreme, the confused and imperfect character of his own biological structure.[32]

Native culture is thus relegated to nature, reduced to "instinctive behavior," the primordia on which the colonizer's culture is transplanted or tethered. If we take the spatial metaphor of culture's marginalization with "fences and signposts," natives are not only segregated, but their culture is relegated as the past to the colonizer's present and presence. Colonial and postcolonial conditions establish the coexistence of these nonsynchronal temporalities. If we take the image literally, we also see that these "fences and signposts" are but one of the many borders enfolded in the quotidian of the colonized. As Fanon suggests in his work, these spatial and temporal dislocations create a psychic circuitry in a raced and/or colonized subject that wavers between identification and resentment of the dominant culture. "Identification," Diana Fuss claims, "has a history—a colonial history."[33] These psychic productions have their own particular temporalities governing them, not necessarily synchronized with imperial political temporalities.

At the end of "On National Culture," Fanon locates the crystallization of decolonized national consciousness in an esoteric "zone of occult instability where people dwell."[34] This leads us to interrogate the lines and possibilities of multiple *temporalities* and *spaces* inherent in the colonial psychic order. If the nation is to "play its part on the stage of history," Fanon claims, "the first necessity is the reestablishment of the nation in order to give life to national culture in the strictly biological sense of the phrase."[35] If the nation is to be *reestablished* in the aftermath of colonialism, then this "national consciousness" must have borne its own temporality, having existed in some unrecognized form alongside official colonial chronicity.

Benedict Anderson has suggested the "inner compatibility of empire and nation," which denaturalizes the nation as a construct.[36] In his seminal work *Imagined Communities,* Anderson locates the construction of nationalism in a shift in the apprehension of time from the "medieval conception of simultaneity-along-time" to one of "homogenous, empty time," borrowing from Walter Benjamin.[37] Replacing messianic verticality in which past and present interact, the horizontal configuration of temporal coincidence opens up a spatialized notion for an "imagined community." This reorganization of consciousness emerged from capitalist conversion of production relations and the modular character of print capitalism in the hands of the national bourgeoisie. In the pages of the novel or newspaper, this fusion bounds the imagination of bourgeois nationalism to the plural spaces of the emergent nation, at least among the literate classes in colonial centers. Nationalism enforced homogenization and repression of inassimilable elements.

Multiple colonizations and varying modes of dependency make the horizons of the American Tropics not so clearly bounded. Postcolonial identity formation hinges upon the colonized space as the product of imperial sedimentation and the continual interplay of histories. Supplementing Anderson's analysis, at issue in narrating the postcolonial nation is the accommodation not only of the plurality of spaces within "homogenous, empty time," but also the tensile plurality of temporalities vying for hegemony in the island space and imagination.

I suggest that the U.S. symbolic debt in the American Tropics has produced spatial and temporal multiplicities that constitute postcolonial identities and imagination. The colonial space, the "unincorporated" "appurtenances," as an accessory and additive to the center, is transformative and betrays the fixity of American identity. Bhabha reminds critics to examine the ambivalent and productive effects of

> that "otherness" which is at once an object of desire and derision, an articulation of difference contained within the fantasy of origin and identity. What such a reading reveals are the boundaries of colonial discourse, and it enables a transgression of these limits from the space of that otherness.[38]

The colony's supplementary function in the Derridean sense of addition and replacement contradicts the notion that subjectivity is easily recognizable, quantified, isolated, then scientifically converted. The contradictions and boundaries produced by imperialism are elemental to racial and identity formation in these overwrought hybrid spaces. Samira Kawash suggests the productivity of scrutinizing identities along these boundaries:

> By considering the boundary itself, not simply as that which must be crossed over or crossed out, but as simultaneously limit and pos-

sibility. If the color line is such a boundary, then perhaps its beyond does arrive in the form of hybridity—but this will not be a hybridity that takes the place of, surpasses, or negates the identities legislated by the color line.[39]

If considered seriously, entry into these spaces does not offer facile liberatory narratives or alternatives. These boundaries mediate structures of knowledge and relationships between communities and individuals.[40] Similarly, American imperialism and its contradictions have defined the "limit and possibility" of American subjects inside and outside U.S. geopolitical borders. Imperial legislation has produced disembodied "shades," ghosts, and unrepresentable remainders that populate the "unincorporated" American territory and create other American narratives.

The task of reading the American Tropics, then, is first, to analyze the continual reinscription of U.S. imperial power in the subordinated American spaces, and second, to read cultural texts for the organizing binaries that gave and continue to give form to the colonial encounter and its furtherance. The second is reread "in light of" or in anticipation of the first; thus the task is always doubled. This rereading approach interrogates not simply the fact of colonialism but, more important, *how* colonialism continually reproduces this "fact." When U.S. colonial power forecloses the language that could make even description of colonial reality possible, what are the linguistic conditions that might mark postcolonial difference in Asian America? For the Filipino (American), produced out of such institutionalized disavowal of (non)belonging, neither alien nor citizen, a new type of national subject (and new predicates) would be necessary to tell her story. Is there space for her in Asian America?

Constituting Asian America

Lisa Lowe, in her oft-cited essay "Heterogeneity, Hybridity and Multiplicity: Marking Asian American Differences" first published in *Diaspora*'s premier issue in 1991 and later in *Immigrant Acts* (1996), called for an understanding of the nonequivalent matrix of differentials that compose Asian America as a field and as an object of study. If the two terms "Asian" and "America" are posited as conjunctive fantastic projections, "Asian America" then becomes a heterotopic formation in which real and unreal spaces shape social relations. This material/discursive formation demands alternative strategies for Asian American cultural politics and criticism. As Palumbo-Liu suggests in reading the solidum between "Asian" and "American" as different historical moments' imagining of each term's cultural distance from the other, the "politics of heterogeneity and difference is neither celebrated nor subjugated, but is instead historicized and particularized."[41] Meaning is derived from the particularity of the historical conditions in which the physical or imaginative separation is conceived. If we take politics, like narrative, as a practice in invention and (mis)recognition, I would suggest that it is precisely *mis*recognition that allows the distance to demand historical specificity to complicate the coalitional self-naming. The locution of individual subjectivity—her racialization and politicization—within the historical web of this more complex vision of Asian America is the beginning rather than the end point of this critical inquiry.

Kandice Chuh's work in *Imagine Otherwise* (2003) foregrounds the racialization inherent in the terms of U.S. national belonging and advances the critique toward the "*a priori* meaninglessness of 'Asian American,' the absence of an identity anterior to naming" to uncover the undecidability of American political subjectivity itself.[42] Along those lines, I suggest that the "U.S. national" as status and historical condition created by U.S. imperialism marks yet another moment of national undecidability in Asian America, for Filipinos in particular. Brought into being "precisely at the juncture of subjectification and subjection, 'Filipinos' may be understood as a category of critique rather than identity," Chuh argues.[43] Because Filipinos were, in fact, part of the U.S. domestic sphere, the category suggests a shift of critical inquiry from exclusion of "Asian America" to a critical challenge to the terms of forced membership. The ambivalent "inclusion" of the Filipino American in the U.S. polity as an American "national" reveals the contradictions in a political belonging founded on social domination. Moreover, I would underscore how this study (re)connects both Asian America and Filipino America to the Caribbean, the Latin American borderlands, and the Pacific in order to enable consideration of intellectual coalitions along and outside U.S. geopolitical borders.

The U.S. nation-state has a life beyond its geopolitical delineation. National belonging not only is a political subjectivity dictated by law but also disciplines that subjectivity into specific racial, gender, and sexual formations. These excesses of the legal proscription are expressed in terms of race, gender, and sexuality as unequal relations and as interrogations of ways of belonging to the nation-state that citizenship as equivalence denies. While law is concerned with justice and literature with imagination, the two come together in the double sense of "representation"—to represent politically and to re-present discursively—to which Gayatri Spivak has alluded to reveal the production of identities, meanings, and human relationships. Law and literature both inhabit the realm of interpretation, rhetoric, form, ethics, and epistemology; both mediate our relationship to society and shape how we imagine the world and ourselves. Both are practices in meaning making. Chuh reminds us of Jacques Derrida's "Afterword" in *Limited Inc.* (1988), which proposes that alternative paradigms must take into account the production of simple binaries and, at the same time, offer other epistemes within this political-ethical inquiry. Thus meaning making always carries with it "the specter of alternative possibilities."

"America" as contractual promise imagines the nation as both a terrestrial space and an abstract project that may be mobilized beyond its physical boundaries. In his study *Manifest Destiny*, Anders Stephanson uses the term "sacred-secular project" to describe how Anglo-American Puritanism attributed sacrality to the North American territory for the chosen people.[44] The land became the signifier and the "contract" or covenant, the signified. The distinction between the United States as a nation-state, the juridico-political entity that delimits borders, and "America," the sacred-secular project, the metaphor that imbues the metonym with its mobile moral force, was already operative from the start. The relationship between the U.S. nation-state as metonymic apparatus, and America as metaphoric contract, is contested terrain, a space of articulation and imagination.

The American Tropics signals the disjuncture between "America" as fantastic metaphor and physical metonymy. Between metonym and metaphor, between material reality and fantasy lie the American Tropics as a set of the cultural and reading practices that reveal the tropes that make possible "America's" global mobility, in particular tropes of enfolded borders and disavowed subjectivities. Roman Jakobson provides us insight into the operations of discourse along the metaphoric and metonymic poles:

The development of a discourse may take place along two different semantic lines: one topic may lead to another either through their similarity or through their contiguity. The metaphoric way would be the most appropriate term for the first case and the metonymic way for the second, since they find their most condensed expression in metaphor and metonymy respectively. In aphasia one or the other of these two processes is restricted or totally blocked—an effect which makes the study of aphasia particularly illuminating for the linguist. In normal verbal behavior both processes are continually operative, but careful observation will reveal that under the influence of a cultural pattern, personality, and verbal style, preference is given one of the two processes over the other.[45]

The culture of empire, I suggest, produces these two aphasic patterns, which are not mutually exclusive, but certainly one predominates over the other. In the metaphoric pattern, similarity implies its obverse, difference, so that this discursive cultural pattern reproduces the binary. U.S. imperial grammar operates under this principle of sameness and difference in a process of substitution. The self-disavowal of empire as a part of this logic erases the conjunction among colonized spaces and that relationship which tethers them to the U.S. nation-state. By contrast, subsumed under this logic of sameness and difference, colonized subjectivities within and without the continent continually, perhaps even obsessively, reintroduce relational predications. This type of aphasic cannot operate under a monologue, responds well only to a situation or an interlocutor, and is obsessed with conjunctions. The preponderance of metonyms in this form of cultural aphasia, the similarity disorder, Jakobson admits, defies easy interpretation.[46] With a predilection for "combination and contexture," this disorder, I would suggest, produces gaps in discourse not necessarily logical but aesthetic.[47]

By suggesting an interpretative lens to conjoin the disconnected insular cultures and spaces, the American Tropics further elaborates upon this similarity disorder as a rhetorical and narrative practice, akin to Paul de Man's definition of irony and allegory: "The sign points to something that differs from its literal meaning and has for its function the thematization of this difference."[48] The American Tropics, first, signals how U.S. imperialism creates tropes about the time and place of the colonized; that is, it turns upon "America" demonstrating how America not only is a trope but also continually gyrates and generates tropes about itself to underplay or underscore its identity and difference against its perceived others. Second, it invokes the multiplicity of landscapes and temporalities that inhere in imperial relations because of colonial sedimentation. Third, with transpacific migration, these American tropes and multiplicities have a return effect when the formerly colonized arrive on U.S. shores bearing this complex imagination. Finally, though fashioned under the grammar or logic of U.S. empire, such critical reading and writing practices reorder the syntax or order of meanings to perform and propel these multiplicities, destabilizing origin and destination, colonizer and colonized, spectator and spectacle.

Steeped in this imperial history and colonial and neocolonial relations, the Filipino American postcolonial imagination provides mapping possibilities in and along the reconstituted space of the American Tropics to suggest a reading and writing practice that addresses enfolded borders and disavowed meanings. The American Tropics as critical reading practice interrogates the instability of this imperial grammar, allowing for Filipino American writing using at once an ethnic and a postcolonial syntax that reorders, rearticulates, and reimagines the locution and location of America. The American Tropics is where "America" meets its aporia, its impasse—a contingent but not contiguous source of difficult passages in legal, cinematic, and literary narratives, giving texture to the American story. The American Tropics, as tropes are wont to do, turns America upon itself. Not a mere passive receptor of American ideologies and acculturation, this simultaneously ethnic (once foreign, now domestic) *and* postcolonial (once domestic, now foreign) imagination also tropes and imagines "America." I begin by exploring the cultural and narratological ramifications of the American Tropics as "unincorporated territories" of the U.S. geocultural and geopolitical landscape.[49]

I
An Imperial Grammar

2. Disappearing Clauses

Reconstituting America in the Unincorporated Territories

A year after Cunanan's spree killing on the centennial of the Spanish-American War, the U.S. Court of Appeals for the Second Circuit heard the case of *Valmonte v. INS*. The case involved a Filipina plaintiff, Rosario Santillan Valmonte, born in 1934 during the Philippine Commonwealth era. She claimed U.S. citizenship based on the equal protection and citizenship clause of the Fourteenth Amendment, which she claimed extended to the Philippines, then a U.S. territory. The final ruling upheld an immigration judge's decision to deny the petitioner's stay of deportation and to proceed with said deportation. The court held that birth in a U.S. territory did *not* confer U.S. citizenship.

Yet, the Fourteenth Amendment's citizenship clause states: "All persons born or naturalized in the United States, and subject to the jurisdiction thereof, are citizens of the United States and of the State wherein they reside." However, the courts do not rely on the citizenship clause but on what is referred to as "the revenue clause": "but all Duties, Imposts and Excises shall be uniform throughout the United States" (article 1, section 8). In actuality, the Philippines and Filipinos exist in the erasure and displacement of this clause in decisions involving Filipinos born during the U.S. territorial period claiming their right to citizenship. Court decisions have relied on this clause and its erroneous application to cast the Filipino's citizenship status at bay.

This was not the first case where Filipinos who have overstayed their tourist or working visas have tried to claim historical American belonging and allegiance bearing upon their right to stay in the United States. Also at stake in these cases is the argument that this claim to U.S. history is also a claim to American identity, something the courts are not prepared to recognize. When the Filipino claiming such an identity comes to court, she is characterized as "inhabitant of a former territory" or a "citizen of an alien state," thus revealing that the nation-state maintains not only spatial borders but temporal ones as well. Such a claim demands not only a contestation of U.S. history but the recognition of other Americans produced by this disavowed history. This temporal claim by former U.S. nationals juxtaposed to the national-spatial reality reveals the nature of the U.S. insular appurtenances, to use the early-twentieth-century characterization of the possessions, as one of suspended undecidability: U.S. and not-U.S.; foreign and domestic; neither alien nor citizen.

Throughout the first decades of the twentieth century, debates around the "Philippine question" and the status of the U.S. colonies in relation to the Constitution were crucial to the definition of American citizenship and Americanness. The possibility of a "citizen" existing outside the U.S. terrestrial compass prompted the Supreme Court to define the political relationship between what was *proper* to the United States and what was simply U.S. *property*. The nature of these territories and their relationship to the U.S. polity came under debate in the Supreme Court and Congress from 1898 through the 1930s, particularly in a series of court cases collectively known as the Insular Cases.[1] The Insular Cases were seven cases about trade and revenue in 1901, seven involving Puerto Rico, one the Philippines, and one Hawai'i; and thirteen cases from 1904 to 1914 and 1922, five involving Puerto Rico, six the Philippines, one Hawai'i, and one Alaska. The ambiguous relationship of the appurtenance to the United States proper posed a threat to the body politic itself in crisis over its racial and cultural boundaries. The court arguments and congressional debates held that, in contemporary parlance, the "Constitution did not follow the flag" in the territories; that is, constitutional rights did not automatically extend to the territories upon their acquisition. The Insular Cases held that the islands belonged to but were not part of the United States. They do not, in this sense, constitute part of the United States that claimed sovereignty over them. This raises the question as to whether the Constitution is a matter of membership or a mutuality of obligation. Legal scholar Gerald Neuman explains that whereas the first approach limits protection to members having a privileged relationship to the constitutional project, the second treats "constitutional rights and limitations as necessary to justify the exercise of governing power, and therefore extend those rights and limitations to persons or places that become subject to the governing power of the United States."[2] In other words, the extension of constitutional protection is a precondition to a relationship with a territory over which the United States has jurisdiction. Mutuality would force the question of the limits of the Constitution, including the question of other types of political belonging apart from full citizenship.

In 1901, in *Downes v. Bidwell,* the first of the Insular Cases, the problem before the Supreme Court—the same Fuller Court that ruled on *Plessy v. Ferguson* (1896) justifying racial segregation five years earlier—was how to legalize and constitute "separate" (but certainly not equal) *national* entities in relation to the American polity. Debates about tariff and territory shored up American boundaries through the "doctrine of territorial incorporation" as a legal reality. Subsequently, the controversy over commerce, on the one hand, and citizenship, on the other, resulted in constituting two types of American subjects for the new century: the imperial citizen and its uncanny "unincorporated" double, the colonial national—whose ghost still haunts Filipinos and Filipino Americans today.

This *other* American subject ineligible for representation was, as Justice Fuller announced in his dissent in *Bidwell,* "like a disembodied shade, in an intermediate state of ambiguous existence for an indefinite period."[3] The island territory and its inhabitants, by law, were made to appear and disappear in the same moment. While the islands' ambiguous tethering to the U.S. polity was based on economic demand, their exclusion was based on perceived racial and cultural difference.

The grammatical logic of U.S. imperialism is one of deferral and disavowal and continues to haunt Filipinos on both sides of the Pacific. I want to explore the emergence and implications of this ghostly status, the noncitizen U.S. national: first, I look at two deportation cases involving U.S.-based Filipinos; second, I examine the status's return effect in the Philippines, half a world away, in another Supreme Court during the country's 2004 presidential election: the historical ambiguity of the Philippine nation and the controversy over the citizenship of Philippine presidential candidate and former action-hero star Fernando Poe Jr.—"FPJ" or "Da King," as he is popularly known—who ran against incumbent and current president Gloria Macapagal Arroyo.

Constituting Unincorporated Space and Subjects

In the wake of U.S. emergence as a world power, Americans sought to consolidate the geographic and disciplinary borders defining the inside and outside of "America." With territorial expansion came a contraction of the United States' imagined borders.[4] The contraction of the U.S. domestic borders was already under way on the continent at the moment of economic and military expansion in the late nineteenth century. In 1882, the Chinese Exclusion Act barred Chinese from the United States; in 1891, Wounded Knee quashed Indian resistance on the Great Plains; in 1896, *Plessy v. Ferguson* sanctioned the political and social separation between African Americans and European Americans; European immigrant labor was disciplined in settlement houses and factories in the East Coast. With so many troublesome native and nonnative aliens already on the continent, the fear of aliens outside the borders becoming citizens intensified with the Philippine question.

The turn-of-the-century shifts in the economic modes of production from agrarian to corporate capitalism necessitated a rethinking of U.S. political self-definition. The corporate economy found its immediate political analogue in empire after the European example.[5] However, economic and social battles taking place in the United States would transform the traditional European notion of empire.[6] The American overseas appurtenances became the battleground on which economic (corporate versus proprietary capitalism) and sociopolitical (socialist versus capitalist) experiments were negotiated to realize the definition of the American republic from 1898 onward. The emergence of the market as a dominant force in determining social relations elicited the reinvention of colonial practice away from the traditional disciplinary apparatuses once wielded by European nations.[7] The legal, political, and cultural terrain would have to accommodate competing ideologies and the coterminous development of republic *and* empire under one United States.

By 1900, the United States was undergoing an economic boom. Historian Emily Rosenberg asserts that liberal developmentalism became the modus vivendi of the United States in its relation to the rest of the world. This social consciousness "merged nineteenth century liberal tenets with the historical experience of America's own development, elevating the beliefs and experiences of America's unique historical time and circumstance into developmental laws thought to be applicable everywhere."[8] The free flow of goods and information controlled by the invisible hand was the underlying faith of this developmentalism. Militarism was thought to be a necessary evil to mitigate the protectionist trade practices of other less powerful nations in the Americas and in Asia.[9]

Neither the anti-imperialists nor the imperialists were against U.S. *economic* expansion. They disagreed on the process of *political* expansion as both sides wrestled with the nature of the "American character" and its tenuous unity. During the height of scientific racism, both sides based their arguments on racial difference. Anti-imperialists feared that the incorporation of alien peoples into U.S. borders and the U.S. Constitution would destroy the delicate nature of the American government. Furthermore, this anxiety also contained the fear of alien peoples unable *by nature* to assimilate, as was evident in the immigration case of *U.S. v. Bhagat Singh Thind* (1923), one of a long line of cases that upheld the racial bar to citizenship from 1870 to 1952.[10] In the unincorporated territories, tropical peoples, anti-imperialists claimed, lacked the cultural and historical conditioning in Anglo-Saxon principles of government as had their counterparts in the more temperate climes. On the other hand, the imperialist camp did not disagree on the basis of the alien character of tropical peoples, but believed that part of the American destiny was to lead "inferior races" around the globe toward civilization.

From the anti-imperialist camp in Congress came a more serious charge that scrutinized the self-image of the United States and its republican principles. How would it be possible for a nation founded on the political self-determination of a people to hold colonial possessions like its European counterparts? How was it possible to preserve economic interests while not violating its founding principles? While liberalism guided the principle of competitive individualism, democracy guaranteed the collective participation of all citizens, equal in all respects before the law. U.S. mainland economic interests in foreign expansion had to be reconciled with the domestic reform agenda. Thus the U.S. government experienced a dual mandate of containment and expansion.

The Treaty of Paris ceding Spanish colonies to the United States led to debate over whether territorial annexation meant incorporation into the United States, thereby conferring citizenship on the former Spanish subjects. The Northwest Ordinance of 1787 contained a territorial clause that dictated the model for the process of statehood and the intermediate political status of territory. Thus, the Constitution provided the means to defer any formal *political* commitment to the newly acquired islands while maintaining *economic* advantages for the United States.

Other legal precedents dealing with trade and commerce helped shape the political status of the territory and its inhabitants. The 1901 *De Lima v. Bidwell* case forced the definition of "foreign territory." The Supreme Court found that the sugar tariff imposed on Puerto Rican sugar went against the uniformity clause found in the Dingley Act of 1897 before annexation. Thus, for revenue purposes, the territories would be considered domestic. However, the implication that Puerto Rico might be admitted and integrated into the Union incited fear of setting a precedent for the Philippines. After all, the two nations, along with Cuba, came under U.S. sovereignty through the same treaty. Active resistance movements obtained in Cuba and in the Philippines, but Puerto Rico did not offer a violent resistance. With the Philippine-American War under way, Filipinos were perceived as "unruly and disobedient" while Puerto Ricans were thought to be "well-behaved and well-disposed."[11]

Violent opposition also fed into the differing racial perceptions of these island nations' inhabitants. As a predominantly mixed-race population, Puerto Ricans would have been classified as nonwhite on the U.S. mainland, especially after *Plessy v. Ferguson*. However, dubious War Department reports to Congress highlighted Puerto Rico's purported "whiteness." This perpetuated the notion that most Puerto Ricans were of Spanish descent, with a slight commingling of Indian blood (acceptable in Virginia statutes). This purported whiteness would later be crucial for the passage of the 1917 Jones Act giving Puerto Ricans citizenship. According to political scientist Hazel McFerson: "The naturalization legislation prohibited nonwhites from acquiring citizenship. In order to grant Puerto Ricans citizenship, it became necessary to define Puerto Rico as white."[12] Meanwhile, the Philippines, thousands of miles away and waging guerrilla warfare against the United States, was perceived to be inhabited by inassimilable "Malays, Tagals, Filipinos, Chinese,

Japanese, Negritos and various more or less barbarous tribes."[13] The distance and density of the archipelago's population was the dark and barbarous specter feared by anti-imperialists.[14] The establishment of free trade with Puerto Rico and the new possessions had to bar any implication that the Philippines might later become part of the Union.

During the Philippine-American War, before the Insular Cases were settled by the Supreme Court, military legal expert Charles Magoon articulated the relationship between the United States and its new acquisitions for Secretary of War Elihu Root. His report stated that lands ceded from Spain "became land appertaining to the United States, but not within the territorial boundaries of the United States."[15] The language of possession stressed that the American Tropics *belonged to* but was certainly not a *part of* the United States. Therefore, these insular appurtenances could not enjoy the constitutional rights and privileges extended to continentals. The language is fascinating in that the word *appertaining* is defined as belonging "as part of a whole" or "as a possession"; the sentence immediately invokes "territorial boundaries" to bar the first meaning but also reveals the fragility of *domestic* or *national* boundaries that have expanded to include this property. As far as the Philippine case was concerned, Magoon continues, "wherever sovereignty of the United States may be asserted, the Congress of the United States may prescribe ways and means, the manner and methods by which such sovereignty is to be asserted."[16] The next sentence uses the passive voice in the first clause as there is no active subject actually founding the original assertion of sovereignty. Congress appears as the subject of the second clause, with sovereignty already sanctioned by an invisible force, presumably the Treaty of Paris. Having assumed this power, Congress would dictate the relationship and conditions of this sovereignty, thereby making the political status of the American Tropics contingent upon, but not contiguous with, the United States.

A year later, in 1901, the Supreme Court held that the treaties of annexation for each territory determined the political relationship of the acquisitions to the U.S. polity. On the issue of incorporation, Supreme Court Justice White opined:

> When a treaty contains no conditions for incorporation, and above all, where it not only has no such condition but expressly provides

> to the contrary, incorporation does not arise until in the wisdom of Congress it is deemed that the acquired territory has reached a state where it is proper that it should enter into and form part of the American family.[17]

The Constitution applied to the territories only to the extent that Congress allowed, thereby subjecting the territories to the plenary powers of Congress. The process of incorporation was therefore a decision made by the "wisdom of Congress." Congress, as the representative body of the "people," reserved the right of entry into the "American family." At issue was not whether Americanness was genetic or attainable through cultural nurture, as the imperialists and anti-imperialists were in part arguing. American citizenship and civilization (as a "proper" state) were clearly also *property* to be protected, rather than the political product of "consent by the people."

The inhabitants of the U.S. appurtenances were to be placed in a political holding pattern. The opinion distinguished "We, the people," as guardians of American status, from the inhabitants of "the territory or other property belonging to the United States," as per the territorial clause of the Northwest Ordinance. The attorney general in the *De Lima* case echoed Magoon:

> The inhabitants of the islands are not joint partners with the States in their transaction. . . . The islands are "territory belonging to the United States," not a part of the United States. The islands were the things acquired by the treaty; the United States were the party who acquired them, and to whom they belong. The owner and the thing owned are not the same.[18]

This line of argument sharply draws the line between subject and object, the active possessor and the "things" possessed. The possessive "their" might refer to "Spain" and the "States" or the "States" alone, but clearly *not* to the "inhabitants of the islands" because the statement stresses that the islands are *not* "partners" in their own transaction. However, the distinction between the islands, as owned "things acquired" and "things owned," and their inhabitants is unclear. As passive objects exchanged between Spain and the United States, they would seem to be disqualified from enjoying the right to self-determination as a fundamental, founding American principle; that is, the inhabitants would have no say as to their identity or destiny.

William Howard Taft would reinterpret the principle of "self-determination" as the "condition of the locality." "Self-determination" was not a *political* consensus negotiated by a people, but rather the *cultural* (civilizational) state of the island inhabitants, who might not comprise a "people" after all.[19] He thus conflated the locality or place with its inhabitants. Congress, or "We, the people," would judge whether constitutional principles, and perhaps citizenship, would extend to the tropical peoples according to the perceived fitness for democracy of the "locality."

The "unincorporated territory" and the redefinition of self-determination in cultural terms paved the way for the creation of a category within the postslavery Constitution for an American subject who is *not* a citizen. In this way, the U.S. republic secured power over another people who are treated as "property." The anti-imperialists invoked the specter of the U.S. slavery past by citing Judge Taney's opinion in the *Dred Scott* (1857) decision: "There is certainly no power given by the constitution to the Federal Government to establish or maintain colonies bordering on the United States or at a distance, to be ruled or governed at its own pleasure."[20] This decision allowed the absolute negation of the political and civil rights of African-descent peoples in the United States. At the turn of the century, anti-imperialists invoked the decision to satisfy the political, economic, and cultural exigencies of the United States concerning the territories.

As Priscilla Wald has demonstrated in her analysis of *Cherokee Nation v. Georgia* (1831) and *Dred Scott v. Sanford* (1857), the law "names property into existence," as well as the relationship that governs the possessor and property. By naming the "terms of assimilation" in contract with the United States, the law legislates the subjectivities of inhabitants on and off the American continent. In her case studies, the emergent American nation attained a tenuous national unity by maintaining that Native and African-descent peoples were neither citizens nor aliens in relation to the United States, thus casting them out from legal representation in the U.S. polity.[21] Wald notes that this unrepresentability and racial bar to the "American family" returns again in the Insular Cases dealing with the outlying territories:

> The 1901 Supreme Court case of *Downes v. Bidwell* forcefully registers the return of the issues (and decisions) of *Cherokee Nation*

and *Dred Scott.* The case which explicitly sanctions the nation's right to own territory and legislate over subjects that it does not incorporate, declares inhabitants of the United States overseas territories neither citizens nor aliens, hence, again, legally unrepresentable. . . . In legislating the ambiguous status of (non-white) inhabitants of overseas territories, however, the Court creates disembodied subjects who bear witness to the fate most feared.[22]

"Neither citizens nor aliens," this other American subject ineligible for representation was, as Justice Fuller announced, "like a disembodied shade, in an intermediate state of ambiguous existence for an indefinite period."[23] The American Tropics and its inhabitants, by law, were made to appear and disappear in the same moment. This ambiguous space was created by the very laws that sought its exclusion from the "American family," highlighting the latter's cultural and political boundaries by creating property contingent on but not contiguous to the United States. The legal construction of this geopolitical boundary at once founded and conserved the cultural divide between what was and was not "American." To reformulate Samira Kawash's "geographies of the color line" in African American texts, the enabling legal fiction that constituted the islands as possessions came *after* the hierarchical laws established by scientific racism.[24] Whereas their ambiguous tethering to the U.S. polity was based on economic demand, the islands' exclusion was based on cultural difference. The juridically imposed geopolitical—and geocultural—scoring simply made apparent and reaffirmed the cultural difference that was always already assumed between continent and archipelago.

With Congress having plenary powers over the possessions, "We, the people" was named as subject with sovereignty over the destiny and identity of insular appurtenances and their inhabitants. Justice Marshall in the *Cherokee Nation* case described the Native nation and its members as a "domestic dependent nation. . . . Their relation to the United States resembles that of ward to his guardian."[25] Seventy years later, this designation shaped the formation of the Philippine tutelary state as a domestic-foreign dependency inhabited by, in Taft's words, "little brown brothers."

The Philippine case differs from the *Cherokee Nation* case, where the Native nation was deemed ineligible to possess private property collectively, and also from the *Dred Scott* case, where African-descent persons were barred from self-ownership. The nature of the Filipino's legal unrepresentability lay in his disqualification for a nationality and control of national destiny. Like the nation-within-a-nation model instituted for Native peoples, the United States mediated foreign relations for the Philippines, but for domestic purposes the archipelago remained culturally foreign and alien.

During the congressional debates in 1901, Rep. Joseph Holt Gaines (D-Tennessee) challenged the Republican side of the house: "are you fitting these people for the citizenship of the United States or the citizenship of the Philippine islands?" The imperialist Sereno Payne (R-New York) responded dismissively:

> Mr. Payne: "Oh, my friend, we will cross that bridge when we come to it, and if you will cooperate with us, we will fit them for the citizenship of the Philippine Islands, or the citizenship of the United States, or of any other country." [Applause and laughter on the Republican side][26]

Training for citizenship in the Philippines was an abstract concept and exercise that did not pertain to any land base or people. Filipinos and their citizenship were in an indefinite state of deferral. Thus, unlike the legally incorporated territories of Hawai'i and Alaska, as Salvador P. Lopez, political critic and onetime Philippine ambassador to the United Nations, summarized, the Philippines

> was part of the United States and subject to its jurisdiction, [but] the Constitution did not follow the flag to the Philippines. The Filipino was not an American citizen but a citizen of the Philippines owing allegiance to, and under protection of the United States. Most aptly was it said that the Philippines was foreign to the United States for domestic purposes, but domestic for foreign purposes.[27]

The "unincorporated territory" as a legal, geopolitical term gave Congress flexibility—in time and political space—to maintain the ambiguous status of the American Tropics for the duration of the colonial project.[28]

At issue in the immigration case of *Valmonte v. INS* (1998) and others like it a century after *Downes v. Bidwell* is not only the racial history behind the creation of the "unincorporated territory." According to Judge Meskill, the judge writing the majority opinion in *Valmonte,* at issue is the scope and meaning of "the United States" in the Fourteenth Amendment—a virtual constitutional crisis that asks, What is the United States? He relies on the decision of another immigration case three years before *Valmonte, Rabang v. INS* (1995), heard by the U.S. Court of Appeals, Ninth Circuit. Applying the Fourteenth Amendment, the *Rabang* plaintiffs and their parents, born in U.S. territory, claimed U.S. citizenship on the *jus sanguinis* (blood) basis for the children and *jus soli* (territory) for the parents. In a *split* court decision, they were denied citizenship. Meskill, of the majority opinion, depends on three bases for denying Filipinos the right to claim U.S. citizenship—article 4, the Treaty of Paris, and *Downes v. Bidwell.*

Article 4 of the Constitution states that "Congress shall have power to dispose of and make all needful rules and regulations respecting the territory or other property belonging to the United States." Congressional plenary power is an extraconstitutional right issuing from the nature of national sovereignty and its power to exclude and its power to dispose of property. But "other property belonging to the United States" creates an ambiguity between territory as member and territory as mere appendage. The unincorporated status would imply that the status of "property" extends to inhabitants. But if the distinction between land as geopolitical property and citizenship as political right were maintained to resolve this problem, the question remains whether Congress has the power to withhold that right when a whole people is absorbed unilaterally into its jurisdiction. In the nineteenth century, birth in U.S. territory in the west guaranteed citizenship, but turn-of-century citizenship was divorced from territory with the foray beyond the continent.[29]

The terms of the Treaty of Paris ending the Spanish-American War (but not the ensuing unrecognized Philippine-American War) empowered Congress to determine the civil rights and political status of the native inhabitants of the Philippines. The inhabitants of the territories were guaranteed *ex proprio vigore* (by its own force) certain fundamental rights upon cession and entrance into U.S. protection. Yet the question that was answered without judicial review was whether citizenship was a fundamental right for Filipinos in the unincorporated territory.[30] The dissenting opinion of Judge Pregerson in *Rabang v. INS* (1995) argues that the court of appeals opinion relies erroneously on the revenue clause of article 1, section 8 of the Constitution and only on *Downes v. Bidwell* of the Insular Cases to adjudicate on a citizenship case. *Downes v. Bidwell,* the first of the Insular Cases, decided that Puerto Rico was a foreign territory, but only insofar as import duties were concerned. The case dealt with the Constitution's *revenue* clause and did not offer interpretation of the Fourteenth Amendment's *citizenship* clause. The Insular Cases were themselves not consistent in defining domestic and foreign territory. Whereas *Downes v. Bidwell* defined Puerto Rico as foreign, by contrast, *De Lima v. Bidwell* expanded the definition of "domestic" as being under the sphere of U.S. sovereignty. In *De Lima,* for revenue purposes, Puerto Rico under the Dingley Act of 1897 would be considered domestic. Thus, relying on only one case would erase the specificity of the precedents and would seem to form judgments that are arbitrary. The language in *Downes v. Bidwell* is clear in its exclusive reference to Puerto Rico: "Puerto Rico is a territory appurtenant and belonging to the United States, but not a part of the United States within the Revenue clause of the Constitution." The case therefore does not interpret citizenship at all, only the revenue clause as applied to Puerto Rico.

Neither *Downes v. Bidwell* as precedent nor the revenue clause on which the *Rabang v. INS* and *Valmonte v. INS* decisions rest interprets the citizenship clause. Yet courts rely on the imaginative erasure of the phrase "within the revenue clause," leaving only "Puerto Rico is a territory appurtenant and belonging to the United States, but not a part of the United States." This legal magic of the post-Bidwell courts expands the strictly worded decision to interpret political and civil rights of territorial inhabitants. The political status of insular inhabitants and the maintenance of colonial status depended on this erasure. Thus, the United States' economic relationship overrode, indeed underwrote, the political civil rights of insular inhabitants and the question of their relationship to their sovereignty and to the United States.

Legal scholar Avelino Halagao Jr. has questioned this interpretative authority that would derive meaning of citizenship from the history of revenue clause, rather than construction via the history of the citizenship clause itself. The legal-historical life of the citizenship clause brings us back to English common law. The Pregerson dissent in *Rabang v. INS* relies on *United States v. Wong Kim Ark* (1898), which involved a child born of Chinese parents who were, by being Asian, ineligible for naturalization. Here, Asian American history intersects U.S. imperial history. Ark sites the Anglo-American common law of *jus soli,* which states that those born in a territory and who owe complete allegiance to the U.S. government are not subject to the Chinese Exclusion Act. The citizenship clause in Ark "affirms the ancient and fundamental rule of citizenship by birth within the territory, in the allegiance and under the protection of the country." We can read this historical turn between 1898 and 1901 this way: because *Wong Kim Ark* removed the racial bar to citizenship through *jus soli,* it became even more important to reconstitute the *soli* (territories) and divorce its inhabitants from automatic citizenship in the doctrine of incorporation. Opinion in *Rabang v. INS* responds that *Wong Kim Ark* offers ambiguous dicta (commentary not part of the holding) regarding territory and is therefore not admissible as a legal holding.[31] Yet the doctrine of territorial incorporation was itself culled from dicta around the Insular Cases.

Although the Treaty of Paris might have dictated the terms of assimilation of a territory, were these terms in line with constitutional guarantees? In 1902, civilian rule was established in the Philippines providing that inhabitants, who did not preserve their allegiance to Spain (an option granted only to Peninsulars), were "citizens of the Philippine Islands and as such entitled to the protection of the United States." Do debt of allegiance and status of territory (December 10, 1898–July 4, 1946) suffice to introduce inhabitants of the Philippines into the U.S. body politic as per the Treaty of Paris, which ceded the Philippines to U.S. control? Subsequent court decisions seem to reject complete allegiance as belonging, by holding race over allegiance as the predominating qualifying term for U.S. citizenship.

From 1790 until 1952, naturalization to U.S. citizenship excluded Asians. The 1790 naturalization act made alien "free, white persons" eligible for citizenship. The act was revised in 1870 to extend citizenship to those of African descent or nativity and in 1906, at the height of U.S. empire, to include those "owing permanent allegiance" to the United States. Examining the citizenship petitions of *In re Alverto* (1912) and *In re Rallos* (1917), Kandice Chuh recounts that the plaintiffs in these cases filed for citizenship under an 1894 statute that accelerated citizenship for those who had served in the U.S. Navy. The Filipino plaintiffs had served in the navy as U.S. nationals. However, the courts denied them citizenship because of the racial prerequisites targeted against Asians. The courts dismissed the idea that dying for one's country of allegiance qualified one for citizenship. For Chuh, the denial of entry into citizenship via the military not only racializes national belonging but also "denies access to and/or possession of that masculinity," one based on legitimated state violence.[32] Thus, state power as manifested in violent masculinity in the early twentieth century is constitutive of Filipino racialization under U.S. empire. Subsequent chapters will continue to look at the representational implications of this racial bar to masculinity and belonging.

Instead of the full protection of citizenship, the U.S. nationals "who nevertheless owed permanent allegiance to the United States and who were entitled to the United States protection" received simply a deferral of their rights. In 1950, in *Cabebe v. Acheson* (Ninth Circuit), a Filipino born in the Philippines in 1910 and who then migrated to Hawai'i, another U.S. territory, in 1930 petitioned for a U.S. passport in 1949. The court denied him the passport because U.S. sovereignty over the Philippines ceased to exist as of 1946, and thus found the plaintiff to be an alien. Beyond the disappearance of borders, the court also said of this "hybrid status . . . the so-called non-citizen national": "While Congress, by declaring such persons became Philippine citizens, contributed to the national dignity of the Philippine people, the status had no international effect prior to the relinquishment of the United States sovereignty but rather served a useful internal American function." This implies that the "Philippine citizenship" the United States granted to Filipinos during the colonial period had no international standing or meaning until relinquishment of territory in 1946. Thus, the categories "Filipino" and "U.S. national" were, for a half century, legal placeholders of not-quite-belonging in the U.S. imperium.

By 1934, under the Tydings-McDuffie Act or the Philippine Independence Act, the Filipino was designated "alien," but only under U.S. immigration laws. This act was also effectively the last of the Asian exclusion acts starting with the 1882 Chinese Exclusion Act up to the 1924 Johnson Act, which barred entry for those "ineligible for citizenship," and which targeted Asians. Notably, the Commonwealth Act of 1934 did not relinquish the islands as foreign territory but merely classified Filipinos as aliens for immigration purposes. "Alienated" inhabitants were thus divorced from a "domestic" territory. During the Commonwealth era, the United States still had complete dominion over the archipelago; the act, following the anti-Asian legal pattern, thus created aliens within

U.S. domestic space and restricted migration within domestic space. Hence, the concept of immigration (a dominant concern in Asian American studies) is historically and conceptually problematic in reference to Filipinos, who did not necessarily move through borders, but rather, borders continually enfolded them.

On July 4, 1946, now called Philippine-American Friendship Day in the Philippines, the United States, in a fit of narcissism, declared the Philippines independent, terminating its territorial status and terminating the Filipino's "noncitizen national" status.[33] Given this domestic dominion over the Philippines, did Congress overstep the constitutional bounds of its plenary powers by designating Filipinos as U.S. noncitizen nationals in the first place—and later, by taking away free travel attending such a designation in 1934 and then revoking it completely in 1946?[34] The Insular Cases held that fundamental constitutional rights cannot be abridged in the unincorporated territories. The question thus remains: is citizenship one of these fundamental rights? The judicial branch of the United States, as Halagao argues, has to this day not performed its duty to review congressional action on citizenship for nationals, nor has it addressed the meaning of "the United States" to include "the United States of America, Philippine Islands" during the colonial period. The Fourteenth Amendment overturns *Dred Scott* (1857) by making "all persons born within the jurisdiction *citizens* of the United States." Is the right to citizenship one of the fundamental constitutional rights that apply by their own force and do not rely on the particularity of the land in question?

Many inhabitants of U.S. insular possessions, including the Philippines, Guam, Puerto Rico, the Virgin Islands, and American Samoa, currently or in the past inhabited this ghostly other legal fiction under the U.S. imperium: the U.S. national. Such designation embodies in law and in person the contradiction and ambiguity of the U.S. republic's relationship to these insular territories and their inhabitants. Indefinite governance of a subordinate location underwrote the logic of the U.S. noncitizen national designation. In the U.S. courts, Filipinos on the continent have been characterized as either aliens in a state of the Union (space) or natives of a former U.S. territory (time). The designation provided a legal logic by which Filipinos during the territorial period would always be out of sync with national time and space. Enfolded borders create a condition for territorial inhabitants in which articulation or disarticulation from national space and time remains dangerously imminent and unilateral according to the imperium's economic and political needs. The noncitizen national status signals the legal unrepresentability of the Filipino in the United States, however, this legal fiction would also pose a representational and legal conundrum for Filipinos themselves for half of the last century. What are the ramifications of this legal triangulation among the United States, Puerto Rico, and the Philippines a hundred years later?

Bastardy and Belonging in the Philippines

On December 10, 2003, the United Opposition (Koalisyon ng Nagkakaisang Pilipino) nominated Fernando Poe Jr., action-hero star of the 1950s through the 1980s, as its candidate for the president of the Republic of the Philippines. A month later, on January 9, petitioners Tecson, Velez, and Fornier, sought to "cancel the certificate of candidacy," claiming that Ronald Allan Kelley Poe, or FPJ, "is not even a citizen of the Philippines." The petitioners claimed that Poe's grandfather did not renounce his Spanish citizenship, and that even if he did, the candidate was born out of wedlock and therefore, under U.S. law operative at the time, took the citizenship of the mother, Bessie Kelley, whose father was an American. After the commission of elections, COMELEC, dismissed the case, it was brought to the Philippine Supreme Court.

How did the case against FPJ frame citizenship and legitimacy and how do these tie in with the historical deferral of Filipino political rights in relation to the United States? Like the *Valmonte* and *Rabang* cases, at issue on this side of the Pacific is the interpretative authority over sovereignty, citizenship, and the constitution during the Commonwealth era to reveal the hazy outlines of Philippine citizenship enfolded in U.S. nationality.

The court dramatically stages the question as follows:

> Our people are waiting for the judgment of the Court with bated breath. Is Fernando Poe, Jr., the hero of silver screen, and now one of the main contenders for the presidency, a natural born Filipino or is he not? The moment of introspection takes us face to face with Spanish and American colonial roots and reminds us of the rich heritage of civil law and common law traditions, the fusion resulting in a hybrid of laws and jurisprudence that could be no less than distinctly Filipino.[35]

The event provided an opportunity to see how Philippine courts and media would interpret Philippine citizenship. Unlike the all too silent erasure of the U.S. cases, law and spectacle in the Philippine courts came together to mutually enforce and produce each other. This dramatic paroxysm in Philippine history raised the question about the very nature of Philippine national belonging that had been enfolded under the sign "U.S. national" for the first half of the century.

Various opinion columns and coverage of FPJ a month before the decision rested their arguments on U.S. law. "FPJ, American citizen, by US Law," said one headline, and a few others depended on the seemingly ubiquitous handbook of U.S. naturalization and citizenship—as if U.S. law continued to be the final arbiter of Philippine citizenship and legal thought. Such an approach by Filipino intellectuals and opinion makers was symptomatic of the colonial legacy echoing through facile narratives. However, this gesture cannot be simply dismissed as it also expressed the conundrum of a legal history sedimented by various imperial histories. Law as a cultural production is not impervious to hybridization and incommensurability as it is a continuing legacy negotiated through imperial, anti-imperial, and nationalist histories. This line of argument claims that national subjectivity in 1939 when FPJ was born must recognize U.S. authority, the final colonial arbiter of the time.

The shift in emphasis by FPJ's opponents to the "natural-born" character of his citizenship made legitimacy an issue. The petitioners set the rhetorical terms of familial legitimacy with its moral undertones in the predominantly Catholic country. This shift imaginatively connected legitimate birth status with eligibility— legitimacy—for holding elected office. However, this proves troublesome. First, this rhetorical move elides civil (family) with political (nation-state) rights. Second, the natural-born qualification was philosophically about unquestioned (and presumed) allegiance, yet the colonial condition of the Philippines in that era and, indeed, the current condition of the labor diaspora raise doubts not about the legitimacy of this allegiance but about its legibility. Rather than raise questions about the terms of allegiance and other ways of belonging, discussion relied on tropes of bloodlines to serve as *evidence* of allegiance.

Only the principles of *jus soli,* birth in territory, and *jus sanguinis,* birth to citizen parents, as legal fictions for citizenship qualify one to be classified as a natural-born citizen. *Jus soli* was briefly a basis for citizenship from 1912 *(Roa v. Collector of Customs)* to the adoption of the 1935 constitution.[36] There was no argument that FPJ was not born in the territory defined as the Philippines in 1939. Since the 1935 and 1987 constitutions make no mention of legitimacy in qualification for citizenship—simply that the offspring of a citizen father *or* citizen mother is a citizen—the courts sought to establish *jus sanguinis* through paternal filiation and recognition. FPJ's grandfather, Lorenzo Pou, was deemed by the courts to have been a Philippine citizen, in the absence of any proof that he declared continued allegiance to Spain in 1898. FPJ's father, therefore, was Filipino, by lack of evidence to the contrary.

However, legitimacy remained an issue. Some Filipino intellectuals questioned why the political status of the child, her relation to the nation-state, is necessarily connected to the parents' social contract before the child is born. The 1935 constitution explicitly states that either mother or father bestowed Philippine citizenship to the offspring. The separate entry of mother and father originated from the past complication of cases involving citizen mothers who lost their citizenship upon marrying an alien, usually Chinese. As an expression of nationalist sentiment, citizen fathers outside of the islands were secure in bestowing citizenship to offspring born outside the territory—a right not extended to citizen mothers. FPJ's mother, Bessie Kelly, was a U.S. citizen and therefore an alien. Furthermore, he was born outside the marriage contract. Therefore, recognition by the father became the issue. Two judges looked for paternal recognition to prove FPJ's citizenship. What does paternal recognition actually mean?

Constitutional scholar and adviser Joaquin G. Bernas, S.J., in his amicus brief found the classification and distinction of illegitimate children as source of unconstitutionality. Also, legitimation here is based on a different treatment depending on gender. Having a different relationship to reproduction and reproductive labor, the male in the formal act of recognition would be given de facto plenary power over political borders, whether or not to confer citizenship on the child, as was argued by two other judges. The law would create a figure of the male citizen who embodies congressional plenary power and the interest of the state through bestowal of citizenship through the recognition of the child. The father would thus embody national sovereign power.[37] This recognition and subsequent legitimation (retroactive or not) is based on a sexual hierarchy that does not withstand the constitutional guarantee of equal protection. Bernas astutely distinguishes between legitimacy and proof of paternity: "What flow from legitimacy are civil rights; citizenship is a political right which flows not from legitimacy but from paternity."[38] Civil rights are concerned with the protection of private interests while political rights deal with one's relationship to the state. Yet, this notion of paternity as guarantee of citizenship also offers a troublesome, if not messy, visual narrative.

I do not suggest that the Philippine Supreme Court was wrong in relying on the *jus sanguinis* basis; however, I hope to underscore the suspect history and logic of both *jus sanguinis* and *jus soli* as the basis of citizenship. The history of the abandonment of the *jus soli* basis emerged not only from the instability and international nonrecognition of Philippine sovereignty but also from the racial and anti-Chinese character of Philippine citizenship as mandated by the U.S. administration in the early twentieth century. Under the U.S. colonial state, as historian Richard Chu has noted, Chinese Filipinos were racialized differently from *indios* or native Filipinos.[39] The tripartite system of *mestizo, indio,* and *sangleyes* under the Spanish was converted under the U.S. administration, according to Chu, to the binary citizen Filipino and alien Chinese, one docile, the other unassimilable. The abandonment of the *jus soli* basis for citizenship was thus buttressed by the controlling principle of naturalization to Philippine citizenship under the Jones Act for the Philippines in 1916 wherein those "ineligible for citizenship" under U.S. law could not be naturalized in the Philippines. Thus the fear and subsequent exclusion of Chinese as unassimilable on the continent was extended to the archipelago as a U.S. territory. "Filipinos" as U.S. nationals and as cheap labor were allowed free travel to the continent, but the Chinese were not.

The United States thus dictated the terms of Filipino national belonging along racial lines. Abandonment of *jus soli* pressed upon *jus sanguinis* in the myth of blood, so closely tied with race. In 1939, the *Chua v. Secretary of Labor* case in the Philippines declared that "Chua Uang cannot invoke Filipino nationality merely because of the fact that she was born in this country." Explicit abandonment of the *jus soli* basis in favor of *jus sanguinis* came with *Tan Chong v. Secretary of Labor* in 1947, a year after flag independence, a moment in Philippine history when the outlines of the archipelago's new national borders had to be made legible. Anti-Chinese sentiment from both sides of the Pacific in part underwrote this legibility. The ruling in the *Tan Chong* case stated: "Dual allegiance must be discouraged and prevented. But the application of the principle of *jus soli* to persons born in this country of alien parentage would encourage dual allegiance which in the long run would be detrimental to both countries of which such persons might claim to be citizens." This decision is the uncanny opposite of the U.S. landmark case of *United States v. Wong Kim Ark* (1898) half a century earlier, which removed the racial bar in *jus soli* claims on the continent. As if in a fit of fantasy fulfillment, the U.S. imperium *reintroduced,* beginning with the 1916 Jones Act, the racial bar to citizenship by nativity in the Philippine territory as an extension of the domestic space. This series of Philippine cases accomplished what could not be overturned in the continental United States precisely because of the dual nature of plenary power derived from national sovereignty: the right to dispose and the right to exclude. The U.S. administration had the absolute power over its territory and its citizenry; thus it had the power to exclude in the territories on the basis of race, translated into nationality. In comparative perspective, these cases bring to light the doubled versions of "America"—one continental, the other insular.

These cases do not address U.S. alien citizenship, which FPJ's mother, Bessie Kelley, acquired through her father, but hers was a citizenship in which Philippine citizenship was enfolded. In 1939, Philippine citizenship was based precisely on a dual allegiance embedded in national subordination, producing two knowledge systems in which one clearly can veto the other. How does one determine foreign from domestic on either continent or territory given this enfolding? In twenty-eight single-spaced pages in its FPJ decision, the Philippine Supreme Court did not decide whether FPJ was a natural-born citizen; it did not decide whether FPJ was eligible for candidacy on the basis of citizenship. The court dismissed the first two petitions on the basis of jurisdiction; that is, the court had jurisdiction only after elections, not before. On the third petition regarding misrepresentation of citizenship, the court decided that FPJ was eligible because "he cannot be held guilty of having made a material misrepresentation in his certificate of candidacy." Material misrepresentation, the court held, required willful misrepresentation. As far as FPJ was concerned, he always considered himself a Filipino citizen regardless of the national affiliation of his parents. The court refocused the case on intent and knowledge of misrepresentation, but by implication it turned the natural-born citizenship question into one of affect in the absence of definitive proof of noncitizenship.

The question posed at the beginning of the Philippine Supreme Court decision was not answered: "Our people are waiting for the judgment of the Court with bated breath. Is Fernando Poe, Jr., the hero of silver screen, and now one of the main contenders for the presidency, a natural-born Filipino or is he not?" The question itself contains two articulations of belonging appealing to affect, one dependent on fantasies of popular culture (FPJ, the public hero of the silver screen) and the other on the fantasies of law (FPJ the private citizen). His was a powerful image on the screen spanning four decades of playing vigilantes, appealing to the disenfranchised poor, and playing Muslim Filipino law-enforcement agents, appealing to Muslim Filipinos of the disenfranchised southern islands. Furthermore, the question acknowledges the power of the masses, 80 percent of whom live well below the poverty line who are also voters, much to the dismay of the middle classes. The June 30 count tallied 9.7 million votes for FPJ and 10.4 million for Gloria Macapagal-Arroyo in a country of 60 million. One reading might suggest that the courts deferred the decision of his belonging and raises the question of which belonging had more influence with the mass of voters.[40]

For the middle-class newspaper reader, the front page of the *Philippine Daily Inquirer* (PDI) on the day the court issued the decision cast a happy ending on this national trial. It printed what FPJ submitted in support of his father's recognition: the Poe nuclear family picture with the elder Poe looking adoringly at his children Elizabeth and young FPJ. The figure of Bessie Kelly the American citizen is at the center, her face cast in the shadows above the children. The caption reads: "A Filipino Family." Out of the political maelstrom of paranoia and narcissism, a hermetic mestizo national family picture emerges on the front page. Perhaps this visual evidence stands for the vexed triumph of the greater illegitimacy that continues to condition the lives of Filipinos in the Philippines and abroad. Notably, the addenda to these articles continually pointed out that Philippine stocks had risen since FPJ's legitimacy for candidacy was announced, quelling middle-class and elite fears of mass revolt. Such an ending revealed the financial and political interest of the writers and readers and a state dependent on foreign investments. Pushed further, this economic addendum may be read as a historical continuation of the time when U.S. international revenue concerns underwrote the anomalous enfolding of Philippine citizenship into U.S. nationality. Political and economic interests converged to exclude and include the territories at once. A century later, the neocolonial Philippine state's and elite's international revenue concerns would underwrite FPJ's claim of "vindication" of his Philippine citizenship to avoid depriving a mass of voters of a popular "public hero" and candidate that had represented its interests on the silver screen.[41]

In addition to these class-inflected readings of this event, one could also interpret this deferral of a decision as illustrating how both *jus sanguinis* and *jus soli* have defined Philippine and other citizenship in two necessarily limited ways of defining and articulating national belonging on which a painful history of deferral, erasure, contradictions, suspension, and illegitimacy cannot rest so peacefully. Filipinoness rather than Filipino citizenship is perhaps an aporetic sense of belonging. Historically "belonging to but not a part of" the United States, and in turn belonging to but not part of a Philippines under colonial rule, the Philippines and Filipinos as categories might suggest different types of belonging outside the imperial nation-state. Perhaps FPJ's popularity is one such expression of a different sense of belonging—one neither about blood nor about land, but about a desire for justice that a client state run by elites and beholden to U.S. policies cannot fulfill.

U.S. citizenship in relation to Filipinos has had an unstable, perhaps unconstitutional, and certainly unexhausted legal, ethical, and political history. Until more than fifty years ago, Philippine citizenship was enfolded within U.S. nationality under the designation of U.S. noncitizen, national. Philippine citizenship inhabited the contradictions of an imperial democracy, because the archipelago's sovereignty itself was held in a state of suspension, and had no international recognition. By bringing into the world the sign of the "U.S. national," U.S. law troubled its own Constitution and produced this state of undecidability for Filipinos. In one sense, the Philippine courts could only remain inarticulate under this contradictory sign, which left the Philippines in international limbo and whose legal history the U.S. courts have refused to examine. The

Philippine courts decided the case using paternal bloodlines going back to the colonial transfer of citizenship by treaty—in line with the Philippine constitution of 1935 in order to avoid the founding colonial undecidability.

Laws on immigration and citizenship contain the rhetorical gymnastics nation-states must perform to imagine and make real what is outside of themselves and what they incorporate. By naming the "terms of assimilation" in contract with the United States, the law historically legislates the subjectivities of inhabitants on and off the American continent. Reading legal fictions—such as the U.S. national designation, a legislated and institutionalized disavowal—reveals the porousness of the body politic but also the assumptions and ethical thinking that ground the presumed integrity of such a body.

I would suggest that the Philippine U.S. "noncitizen national" status—while characterized by suspension or intermediateness—is not one of static or suspended animation, but one of active *deferral* of nationality, identity, and meaning. It is this deferred identity that informs such a problematic designation as "Filipino *American*," along with those for Puerto Rico, the U.S. Virgin Islands, American Samoa, and Guam. Under the operation of legal grammar, these American subjects were embedded "within the revenue clause," which was subsequently erased and displaced, and in its place emerged the illusion of U.S. national legibility and legal objectivity. As such, these legally "unincorporated" subjects are remainders and reminders to the U.S. national imaginary of those ghostly, unincorporated appurtenances, which must intermittently haunt the American sentence. Making legible the erasure makes possible the seeming contradictory desires of belonging in multiple and unequal spaces that I will examine further in novels written by these other American subjects.

The U.S. imperium legislated disavowal and erasure for these territorial spaces. But such a spectacular reality for many across the imperium has also enabled a rhetorical strategy to articulate demands and lay claims from within a nation-state that historically and legally misrecognizes them. On one side, Filipinos in the United States have used this strategic belonging to gain economic and political rights, though not always successfully, and, on the other side, to express a desire that a postcolonial nation-state cannot represent. Yet both claims reveal how the temporal realm also commands a national boundary. I would suggest another mode of understanding borders distinct from the immigration or post-colonial models. Rather than the movement of bodies across borders in the former or the movement of borders across bodies in the latter, U.S. legal discourse around the unincorporated territories and its inhabitants has created the condition of *enfolded* borders that produce and erase dangerous and endangered extranational subjectivities with which nation-states must grapple.

Cast out of political and legal discourse, these reminders find expression in cultural productions and social movements emerging from the spaces I call American Tropics, in tropes in the law's articulations and in the shape of cultural narratives. First, they bear imaginative critiques of U.S. empire and its hegemonic power to make meanings and relationships beyond *jus sanguinis* and *jus soli*. Second, these critiques offer alternative imaginings of belonging beyond the imperial nation-state. Third, they trouble the privileged paradigm of a type of understanding of immigration and exclusion in Asian American studies—an understanding based on a domestic/foreign binary. Both alien and citizen cover a complex range of overlapping possibilities if we view borders as undetectably enfolded. Finally, these subjectivities of the American Tropics born out of legal unrepresentability and deferral made legible may offer much-needed conversations across their respective geopolitical spaces, from the Pacific to the Panama Canal to the Caribbean, together and comparatively, that articulate this vexed geocultural heritage.

3. Moral Sentences

Boy Scouts and Novel Encounters with Empire

On the border between civilization and barbarism war is generally normal because it must be under the conditions of barbarism. . . . It is only the warlike power of a civilized people that can give peace to the world.

—Theodore Roosevelt in *The Strenuous Life* (1911)

"[Mexicans] are selfish and cruel," Jimmie said, "and no nation of that stripe ever prospered. What they need here is less strong drink and more school houses—more real freedom and less mere show of republican government."

—Jimmie McGraw in *Boy Scouts in Mexico* (1911)

While touring the Philippine Islands in 1914, an American society woman, Mrs. Spencer of Newport, approached one Lieutenant Sherman Kiser, an officer in the occupying forces stationed in the southern Philippines, and told him of her son's involvement in the Boy Scout movement in New York City. Her son was Lorillard Spencer Jr., who organized the first American Boy Scout organization in New York City in December 1910. She suggested that Lieutenant Kiser might do the same for the native boys to make useful citizens of the lads. A year later, Lieutenant Kiser formed a Boy Scout troop among "Moro" boys of a village in Zamboanga City in the predominantly Muslim southern Philippines. The *New York Tribune* introduced "Kiser's Sturdy Brown Boy Scouts of Moroland," marveling how a "Group of Bare, Dusky Lads Developed into a Band of Martial Youths."[1] Whereas American boy scouting grew out of nostalgia for a lost frontier, in the new imperial frontier boy scouting was born in a fit of nostalgia for home, for the United States. Nations (the United States and the Philippines) and histories (America, once a frontier, and America, having just acquired a frontier) become entangled in these fantasies of national and boyhood development.

Within the continental United States the Progressive movement had been consolidating "uplift" discourse toward the impoverished populace of the burgeoning city. The movement characterized "the other half" made up of the poor and immigrant masses of society as ignorant, unsanitary, foreign—therefore uncivilized—urban dwellers to be uplifted for the good of the sanitized whole.[2] Domestic racial, scientific, and civic discourses were to spill into the subtended borders of the United States, into the colonized islands, as part of the American civilizing mission. U.S. soldiers traded their guns for schoolbooks throughout the archipelago by order of the War Department as part of Taft's "campaign of attraction." As the U.S. administration continued to prepare the denizens of the Philippine archipelago for an American form of citizenship through "more schoolhouses," civic organizations on the U.S. continent, such as the Rotary Club, the 4-H movement, and the Boy Scouts of America, emerged to prepare Americans for their new role as productive leaders and world citizens. As part of the American civilizing mission at home and abroad, the international Boy Scouts movement provided lessons in self-reliance, citizenship, self-government, and civilization.

Having acquired a new frontier a little more than a decade earlier, if Theodore Roosevelt is correct, U.S. activity in this borderland would normalize war as a general condition to "give peace to the world." Therefore, for him, civilized war meant peace on the borders. The military (Kiser) and the civic-minded (society matron Spencer) banded together to make possible this contradictory sentence of the Progressive Era. Each fueled by the fantasy of national development, the two worldviews of the early twentieth century sought to turn the colonized brown youth into youthful versions of masculine violence that the occupying power symbolized. The early Boy Scouts organization inside and outside of the continental United States had a double identity as a paramilitary organization and as a boyhood development project. Thus it was poised between national violence, on the one hand, and domestic assimilation, on the other. The cultivation of good citizenship depended on the protection of national and moral borders.

Fictional Boy Scouts made their appearance in the Philippine archipelago three years earlier than the real Muslim Filipino Boy Scouts, just a year after the establishment of the Boy Scout organization in New York City by the younger Spencer. Fantasy production eliding national and moral borders was already in the works in mass culture and in para-educational institutions. While political and legal discourse created a persona for those who had been conquered in the American Tropics, these popular narratives codified notions of "Americanness" through empire. In 1911, M. A. Donohue and Company of Chicago began publishing a boys' novel series featuring a small group of U.S. Boy Scouts. Over a period of three decades, "that Great Nature Authority and Eminent Scout Master, G. Harvey Ralphson of the Black Bear Patrol," as the book jackets introduce the author, wrote more than thirty "Boy Scout" novels, which featured scouts in the most unlikely scenarios as champions of American democratic civilization.[3] The American empire was only a little more than a decade old when the Boy Scout novels were published. Inheriting the tradition of the U.S. dime novel of late nineteenth century, these novels portray the youthful vim and vigor of American boys in search of adventure while making the world safe for democracy.[4] Like their forefathers, American youth could reclaim their lost frontier heritage and conquer the frontier as configured by the novelistic imagination.

The three inaugural "Boy Scouts" novels, all published in 1911, recount the adventures of these boys working covertly with the U.S. Secret Service outside the United States and in the imperial borderlands. Contemporary anxieties about the safety of the American nation prone to domestic and foreign corruption and infiltration provide the paranoid backdrop of the first of these novels. They displaced domestic, continental anxieties about immigration, racial purity, and masculine degeneration along the border, creating an uneasy suture between the United States and its tropical other. In *Boy Scouts in Mexico; or, On Guard with Uncle Sam,* the boys jaunt across the Texas–Mexico border to prevent a Mexican raid across the Rio Grande. *Boy Scouts in the Canal Zone; or, The Plot against Uncle Sam* finds the boys farther south outwitting a group of treacherous Japanese to prevent them from destroying the Gatun Dam. From there, the boys sail across the Pacific in their imperial journey to the Philippine Islands in *Boy Scouts in the Philippines; or, The Key to the Treaty Box* to bring order to Uncle Sam's new, but unruly, possessions. The novels' itinerary roughly maps the United States' borders and preoccupation during the first decade of the twentieth century: Mexico, militarized at the border in 1910 at the revolution's outbreak; the Panama Canal Zone, made U.S. territory after an orchestrated revolution against Colombia and a treaty with the new nation in 1903; and the Philippines, where war with Filipino revolutionaries ended by presidential fiat in 1902 despite continued guerrilla activity through 1913.

In normalizing war as a condition of these borders, the fictional Boy Scouts carried the U.S. border along nation-state claims to the territories. However, the domestic frontiers of the past mapped onto the imperial outposts created a temporal loop in imagining these spaces. Domestic discourse about these spaces structures the disavowal of imperial violence. In turn, this violence may be further divided into genocide and ethnocide. David Lloyd terms the destruction of ways of life and ways of being in the world "ethnocide."[5] Genocide is the material destruction of bodies usually accomplished by military force; ethnocide is the destruction of structures that give meaning to these bodies accomplished through war by other means. As the fictional boys traipse through the newfound empire, the novels walk this fine line between desire for genocide and desire for ethnocide.

Carrying the fetters of a mobile American civilization in their backpacks, the Boy Scouts find adventure along the Mexican border, in the Panama Canal Zone, and in the Philippine Islands to provide phantasmic cultural lessons in the duties and difficulties of U.S. imperial citizenship. The boys embody U.S. sovereignty as they define the moral compass of American culture. While defining what is proper to the United States, the novels confuse national histories and spaces to make claims for U.S. property. Only through the reclamation of their frontier past are they able to claim real property so that the moral boys become propertied men. Thus, as the boys outline the U.S. borders, they outline the limits of American violent masculinity and imperial citizenship.

The Case of the Missing Class Conflict

In the novelistic space, the amalgamation of social Darwinism with manifest destiny leads the offspring and charges of the middle classes to the imperial outposts of the United States. The Boy Scouts series does not use rural America as its trajectory but rather New York's Fifth Avenue. Upper-middle-class New York City, from which the real Boy Scouts of America gained prominence, and home of the intellectual and political leaders of the Progressive movement, is the point of dissemination for civilization. From the comfort of an uptown clubhouse, the fictional boys bypass the countryside and venture directly into the jungles of Mexico, Panama, and the Philippines.

The opening scene of the first novel, *Boy Scouts in Mexico,* introduces the group "gathered before an open grate fire in a luxuriously furnished clubroom of the Black Bear Patrol, in the upper portion of a handsome uptown residence, in the city of New York."[6] The author describes the luxurious surroundings, taking pains to list sporting equipment proper to a vigorous boy:

> The walls of the apartment were hung with guns, paddles, bows, arrows, foils, boxing gloves, and such trophies as the members of the patrol had been able to bring from the field and forest.

An assortment of manly tools from the frontiersman and the Indian—guns, paddles, bow and arrows—decorates the room. Trophies from field and forest attest to the persistence of the frontier even on Fifth Avenue. The boys' uptown bourgeois residence clings to the trappings of the frontiers. A corner of the privileged American domestic space is transformed into a museum for the preservation of American manhood, already a thing of the past. In New York City, America's center of finance, media, and culture in the early twentieth century, a middle-class home maintains an image of the strenuous life to ward off the enervating effects of wealth, gentility, and overcivilization.

That the Boy Scout protagonists are all New Yorkers is no accident. The organization came into national prominence in New York, the leading city in American modernization, commerce, and media. Elite families merged in Manhattan in the late nineteenth and early twentieth centuries. On the afternoon of December 16, 1910, Lorillard Spencer Jr., son of the woman who was to bring the

Boy Scout idea to the Philippines, was made temporary chairman of the New York City Council of the Boy Scouts of America.[7] The council was made up of "over a hundred prominent men" of New York. President Taft (later governor-general of the Philippines) and then Colonel Theodore Roosevelt were the honorary president and vice president, respectively, of the new national Boy Scout organization. Spencer's plan was to increase enrollment fifteenfold from six thousand boys to ninety thousand in ten months. The problem was finding enough scoutmasters to lead the boys. These he soon found among "young society men" of the city. By 1912, Boy Scouts in the United States numbered three hundred thousand from New York City to San Francisco to its colonial outposts in Honolulu, Puerto Rico, and the Philippines.[8]

Like real Boy Scouts, pedigree in addition to property completes the fictional Boy Scouts' domestic scene. The Black Bear Patrol is composed entirely of sons of very wealthy parents, furnished with time and wherewithal to go off to the woods and water whenever opportunity offered:

> There were Harry Stevens, son of a manufacturer of automobiles; Glen Howard, son of a well-known board of trade man; Jack Bosworth, son of a leading attorney; George Fremont, adopted son of James Cameron; Frank Shaw, son of a newspaper owner. (15–16)

The boys are unmistakably native-born, white, and privileged in a city where 40 percent of its denizens were foreign-born in 1910. They are the male offspring of a new breed of privileged Americans—manufacturers, bankers, businessmen, lawyers, and newspapermen—and leaders of American modernization. At the turn of the century, these had risen to challenge the power and privilege of the traditional American plutocracy.

The new professional class, overwhelmingly urban, middle-class, white, native-born, and Protestant, and with claim to knowledge and skill, provided the moral and intellectual content to the contemporary Progressive movement.[9] Historian Richard Hofstadter characterized Progressivism as

> a mild and judicious movement, whose goal was not a sharp change in the social structure, but rather the formation of a responsible elite, which was to take charge of the popular impulse toward change and direct it into moderate and, as they would have said,

"constructive" channels—a leadership occupying . . . "a position of independence between the wealthy and the people, prepared to curb the excesses of either."[10]

Drawing leaders from the privileged classes of the city, the Boy Scouts of America had no intention of changing the structure of society either. The organization aspired to build a better society by building character in the American boy.[11] Character building aimed to channel boys' energies into constructive activity, thereby instilling stronger moral character. These boys would then grow up to direct and "curb" the excesses of the wealthy and of the masses. The Boy Scouts organization was the breeding ground for the offspring of the new professional-managerial class. Later, it functioned as an entrée into middle-class respectability for the offspring of the skilled working class. Equating class attainment with racial vigor, this emergent class became the self-appointed guardian of American masculinity, of American society entering the twentieth century, and, subsequently, of the U.S. empire.

This effort at class consolidation took place amid troubled times. In the domestic arena, the relationship between capital and labor, between rich and poor, was tense. When the Boy Scout organization was introduced into the United States from England in 1910, its bourgeois origins and its paramilitary image were a source of anxiety for the laboring classes, whose ranks had swelled with the influx of new immigrants. Indeed, the novels' easy alliance with the Secret Service and the U.S. military went against the attempts of the Boy Scouts of America (BSA) to disaffiliate with either capital or labor. Labor groups were suspicious of the organization. In response to public objections to the BSA, James West, executive secretary of the BSA, wrote that the movement "is not interested in preaching capitalism or labor" and that "there is nothing military about the Boy Scout movement."[12] Organized unions, however, kept a suspicious eye on the organization. In 1910, the American Federation of Labor criticized the organization for having "too strong a military flavor, and giving the impression that the Boy Scouts might be called on to take a hand in labor disputes," as they had in Cuba. Later that year, however, the American Federation of Labor returned a resolution approving the BSA. The objections were initially based on the *Boy Scout Handbook,* which deviated very little from Robert Baden-Powell's handbook in England, which emphasized militarism and experiences from the imperial Boer War. This purported misinterpretation compelled the U.S. organization to revise its handbook, emphasizing civic and moral duties over military drills and weapons.[13] Americanized abstractions of civilization codified Roosevelt's "warlike power of a civilized people" in the handbook to displace the Scouts' origins in military genocide and violence in the British imperial wars in Africa.

Amid the clashes between rich and poor, the Boy Scouts as a fraternal organization was committed to the American democratic ideal of a society unmarred by class conflict. The first novel offers the Boy Scouts organization as a way to promote class cooperation and interaction, just falling short of class integration. Among the wealthy Black Bear Patrol is George Fremont, an orphaned newsboy, who works in the employ of James Cameron, a lawyer from a prestigious New York family. However, George's true bourgeois origin is later revealed in the course of the boys' adventure in Mexico. The wealthy Black Bear Patrol is joined and led by members of the working-class Wolf Patrol, a Scout unit from the Bowery made up mostly of newsboys and messengers. Working-class downtown travels uptown led by Ned Nestor, the novels' main protagonist as the boy detective, and his impetuous sidekick, Jimmie McGraw, both of the downtown Wolf Patrol. Ned Nestor remains unmarked by class, though the reader is made aware of his incredibly intimate connection with the Secret Service and the U.S. military command.

Young Jimmie McGraw, on the other hand, is a caricature of a feisty Irish street lad who stands in direct contrast to the privileged and pampered Anglo-Saxon boys of Fifth Avenue. The novel underscores his class and ethnic difference through his speech, peppered by colloquialisms, clipped words, and the occasional uncontrollable racial and ethnic slurs evincing his lower-class origins. Among the boys, he epitomizes the little urban savage, able to survive by pluck and resourcefulness. He is what the pampered, more reserved uptown boys are not in the urban jungle. He is the richer boys' other, less inhibited in speech and more likely to get into trouble. As such, he provides comic relief. Although never the hero, he does follow Ned Nestor in his adventures more closely than the others, whether he is invited to do so or not. Yet he is welcomed into the boys' middle-class fold as the troublesome younger brother.

This homosocial world is not without its romance and "crushes."

When little Jimmie introduces George Fremont to the main protagonist, Ned Nestor, his "patrol leader and the bulliest boy in
New York," George is immediately entranced by this older youth
described as

> a sturdy boy of little less than eighteen, a lad with a face that one
> would trust instinctively. His dark eyes met the blue ones of the pa-
> trol leader steadily. There was no suspicion of guilt in his manner.
> Ned Nestor extended his hand frankly, his strong clean-cut face
> sympathetic. Fremont grasped it eagerly, and the two stood for a
> moment looking into each other's eyes. (32–33)

This touching scene is also the first time that Ned Nestor the Boy
Scout leader is introduced to the reader of the novels. The distressed
boy is spellbound by the young man, holding his grasp eagerly and
his gaze steadily. Like lovers, they "stood for a moment looking
into each other's eyes." Like Fremont, the reader is implicitly made
to look into his blue eyes and take Ned and his trustworthiness at
face value. The moment is described in rapt detail and the passage
reads as if from a romance novel without the promise of heterosexual union.

  If a romance novel is about fantasy fulfillment and cathexis to
a heroic figure, the boy reader, like the younger characters, bonds
with the brave older boy hero. He follows him to the ends of the
world, or at least to the ends of U.S. borders, with the pretense
of safeguarding democracy. The books are peppered with these
poignant romantic moments wherein the nascent homoerotic desire for the "bulliest" patrol leader is displaced into hero wor-
ship and a desire to be *like* Ned rather than desiring him directly.
Emphasizing mimetic over erotic desire, the novel allows for same-
sex desire without admitting to homosexuality. The distance af-
forded by wanting "to be like" rather than simply "liking" Ned enables homoerotic desires to persist while being properly displaced
onto a fraternal love of nation. The homoerotic romance is turned
into a tight-knit family romance, albeit without females.

  Without apparent desire for female company, the adolescent
boys, upon crossing borders, check the specter of miscegenation as
they roam the wilderness. The anxiety of miscegenation was acute
in early-twentieth-century New York, the boys' home, where opportunities for social, cultural, and racial mixing increased because
of immigration and population concentration. This anxiety had to

be checked at the racially different borders that the white, native boys must cross to spread the boons of civilization. Their homosocial bond broke class barriers but not racial ones. It expanded the interpellative power of whiteness across class lines to create a hermetic and masculinist nationalism unhampered by heterosexual reproduction with racial others. The mentor–mentee relationship uses and momentarily diverts homosexual desire toward fraternal and the asexual reproduction of "manly" and nationalist values. In the wilderness, the boys compose a makeshift all-male and all-white civilization in the frontiers. True to the purpose of the fraternal organization, the fictional boys cultivate loyalty to abstract ideals rather than to class or social origins, and encourage a form of a racialized homosocial domesticity.

This mobile domesticity delimits boys' feral energies, thus offering a resolution to any class conflict that might arise with boys from different class backgrounds. The novel series opens with paternalism and fraternalism that manage the potential eruption of class antagonism and latent homosexuality. These necessary fictions follow the logic of middle-class guardianship of the less fortunate. The novel diffuses contemporary class anxieties, first, through paternalism within the organization and, second, by dispatching the boys to foreign lands in service of the U.S. government. Routed into the imperial circuit, the boys leave their class identities and potential violence behind to recover a shared American nationality imbued with the values of their culturally and racially Anglo-American, middle-class sponsors.

The emerging professional-managerial class claimed to inherit and guard the peculiar Anglo-Saxon racial vigor needed for political and cultural expansion. In his analysis of "red-blooded fiction" at the turn of the century Richard Slotkin observes:

> These novels are not chiefly concerned with the loss of democratic opportunity entailed by the closing of the frontier, but with the potential loss of opportunities for exercising the peculiar warrior virtues of the Anglo-Saxon race. Some question whether the racial vigor of the Anglo-Saxon can survive the passage from the age of conquest to the age of trade.[14]

For the United States, as with all modern imperial powers, the age of trade coincided with its age of conquest. Trade fueled and buttressed expansionist desires so as to make the age of trade and the age of conquest indistinguishable from each other. Although politicians and businessmen shared interests in expansionism, they did not necessarily agree on economic or territorial expansion or on the U.S. empire's political and institutional elaboration. The "peculiar warrior virtues" would be manifest in the civilizing mission in the borderlands to secure property.

Mexico; or, The Case of Misguided Nationalism

The Boy Scouts begin their lesson in world citizenship close to home in neighboring Mexico. Throughout the nineteenth century, U.S. manifest destiny pushed borders westward and southward to the detriment of native peoples and at the expense of Mexico and Spain. After the Mexican-American War of 1846–48, Mexico found it difficult to maintain its northern provinces owing to internal strife and out-migration.[15] On the U.S. side of the Rio Grande, Texas Rangers were dispossessing and terrorizing Mexican Texans. At the time of the novel's writing, the Mexican Revolution had destabilized the republic, forcing the United States to intensify militarization in order to quell uprisings along the border.[16] Here is where the Boy Scouts would stand "on guard with Uncle Sam," as the book's subtitle announces.

The Secret Service called upon Ned Nestor, the seventeen-year-old patrol leader, to avert "serious complications between the government of that rebellious republic and the government of the United States," by checking a threatened raid across the Rio Grande. Ned Nestor discovers that the culprit is one Don Miguel, a Mexican diplomat, who wanted war between Mexico and the United States as a way to generate unity among Mexican factions. He would then lead a united Mexico in a war against the United States to further his nationalist cause. Don Miguel's case is one of misguided, therefore false, nationalism based on war and hatred. Such a nationalism endangers the well-being of the mass of Mexicans and that of U.S. citizens.

At the base of this false nationalism, the Boy Scouts learn, is not political or social conflict, but rather a major flaw in the Mexican national character that makes the mass of Mexicans so easily fooled by deceitful leaders. The patriotic Boy Scouts are patronizingly sympathetic to the plight of the gullible Mexicans. Amazingly, Jimmie's Bowery accent disappears when he speaks on the subject of foreign peoples requiring U.S. guidance. Jimmie's class difference disappears when he begins to espouse theories about Mexicans, who

> have never been favored as the people of our country have, and that they've got years of national childhood to go through yet before they become a great people. (139)

Jimmie's sudden erudition provides the necessary contrast between the boys' American national maturity and the cowardly Mexicans' national childishness. According to Jimmie, Mexicans have not had the formative advantages, namely, Anglo-Saxon principles and discipline, necessary to become a "great" nation like the United States.

Human development becomes the metaphor for national development. Developmental theory in the early twentieth century proposed that (Western) civilization's evolution parallels individual development and vice versa. Boy Scouts of America secretary John L. Alexander suggested that "from babyhood to manhood, a boy passes through all the stages through which civilization has passed. The intensely individual boy of 7 or 8, grabbing everything in sight and storing it away in his pocket, was the savage. With the beginning of adolescence, at about 12 years, he developed social instincts, and in his romantic and chivalric outlook upon life was like the men of the Middle Ages."[17]

If young boys were akin to savages in their development, then what differentiated them from borderland savages? The phylogenetic model of boy development portrays males in puberty as vulnerable, therefore, malleable in terms of moral and civic education. The Boy Scout organization curbs and directs boys' natural savagery toward productive activity, such as camping, playing sports, and, in the novels, aiding the Secret Service in their spare time. With the organization's guidance, they can hone their survival skills in the tropical jungles, as their forefathers had in the western frontier, while rendering valuable service to their country.

By contrast, Mexican or other un-American, native savagery, it was believed, is savagery without purpose, unbridled by the disciplinary and character-building process as only the Boy Scout organization could provide. Because democratic institutions, like scouting, are absent in the borderlands, the preponderance of savagery leads to revolution and anarchy as found in undisciplined boys. A nation in its childhood has hardly reached the "Middle Ages" and remains selfish, savage, and unfit for self-government.

Such savagery cannot simply run its destructive course. Like boys, childish nations and their savage energies have to be mastered and channeled by, in Theodore Roosevelt's term, "manlier" nations.[18] A manly nation (i.e., the United States) would "arrange" the environment for these child-nations, much as Ernest Thompson Seton and Daniel Carter Beard suggested for proper boy development, through the establishment of democratic institutions and the inculcation of democratic principles. As the Boy Scout organization "arranges the environment" for the boys, so too would the Boy Scouts as representatives of American civilization rearrange the colonial environment to fit into America's image.

Inherent in this developmental model is a contradiction. As the telos of national development, the United States sets the example of true nationalism for the world. Some nations, like Mexico, must necessarily experience growing pains in their struggle to reach national maturity. Such growing pains might include continual revolutions occasioned by false and faulty nationalism. However, the tautological implication is that U.S. Americans are a "great" people because they are *by nature* predisposed to greatness, whereas other nations remain undeveloped because they are not "favored." Not wars of conquest, but some divine force has bestowed might to the United States. Unfortunately, national development for other nations will remain retarded because of flaws inherent in the people themselves. Thus the tautology cancels the possibility the teleological view entertains—that others might achieve a similar greatness in due time. In truth, greatness cannot emerge naturally from semi-barbaric peoples; greatness must be bestowed upon them and continue to be guided from the outside, by the United States. In this way, "America" as represented by the traipsing Boy Scouts is an independent force that transforms peoples and history—the transcendent unmoved mover of world history. America is a sign for the modern and the transmitter of modernity.

The difference "Aztec-Spanish" inhabitants in the Mexican borderland present is understood in the same terms as that of Native Americans in the mythical American western frontier. By invoking Aztecs and "tribal relations," the Boy Scouts collapse the mass of Mexicans with Native Americans—"primitive," "unsettled," and "selfish and cruel." This knowledge reproduction reads the Mexican case as a mere replication of the American frontier, wherein a childish race requires discipline and subjugation by a greater power. Like Native Americans, Mexicans cannot be considered a "people" because "tribal"—rather than truly national—relations predominate. Resisting the state's civilizing force, both groups remain outside a proper relationship with a democratic government. The facile substitution of Aztec Mexicans for American Indians thus creates the illusion that Americans could readily understand Mexico's political and cultural reality.

The boys would contend that the retardation of Mexican national development is the result not of political and historical circumstances suffered by the people under Spanish and American imperialism, but, more fundamentally, of the defective blood coursing through the Mexican. The boys discuss the matter to offer a pseudo-socio-anthropological analysis of the Mexican and his national character:

> The Aztec-Spanish blood is still in his vein. Of course, there are cultured and refined Mexicans, but the great mass of the people are still pretty primitive. Outside the cities, in many instances, old tribal relations continue, and the people are unsettled in habitation as well as in spirit, selfish and cruel, too. (141)

Aztec blood and Spanish blood are conveniently commingled with a hyphen to produce the "selfish" and "cruel" Mexican. This mixing of European and native blood precipitated the downfall of the Mexican and barred the way to national "greatness." The novel implies that in the U.S. American case, European blood did *not* intermix with native blood to cause racial and national degeneration. In other words, the preservation of "whiteness" in the United States guaranteed its national greatness. The retention of Anglo-Saxon purity, among the privileged classes at least, paved the way to the "greatness" the United States enjoys. Whether urban or rural, refined or illiterate, blood—not history—distinguishes the neighboring Latin republic from its Anglo counterpart. For Mexicans to develop democratic institutions like those of their Anglo neighbor is impossible. To do so is not in their "blood." "Bad blood" inherited from native savages and degenerate Europeans is a fundamental obstacle to natural maturation.

The boys pursue their query into the possible future of Mexico into more insidious terrain. In the short term, dictatorship is the discipline needed to check unruliness:

"It requires a strong hand to rule such a people," Jimmie mused. "I guess Diaz has troubles of his own."

"There is no doubt of it," the drummer continued. "In future years Mexico will become one of the garden spots of the world. It is clear why one people after another selected the Valley of Mexico for their abiding place. But blood will tell for evil as well as good, and the bad strain in her must be thinned down. The hills are rich in minerals, and the valleys are fertile, and all the land needs is a race of steady, patient workers—fewer bullfights and less *pulque* and more days' work. (Ibid.)

The "Valley of Mexico" is romanticized, but the present inhabitants disappear from the discussion altogether, replaced by waves of "one people after another." The tension between the desire for genocide and for ethnocide is clear. The current inhabitants are depicted as a transient "race" that would eventually vanish like the others. The boys figure that the land needs a new "race of steady, patient workers," perhaps similar to those who settled the American West in order to realize the promise of a land in chaos. How the "bad strain in her must be thinned down" disturbingly suggests, at best, displacement or land appropriation and, at worst, genocide as a policy toward Mexico. However, the history of military and paramilitary "bloodletting" along the U.S.–Mexican border reveals that the boys are not the first to suggest these options for the neighbors on the other side of the Rio Grande.

The boys conclude their stay in Mexico not only by asserting the need for Anglo-American presence and influence, but also by reclaiming U.S. property there. The boys' errand into imperial wilderness yielded not only the recovery of their masculine selves, but also the recuperation of one of the Boys Scouts' rightful bourgeois identities, as the owner of real estate in the borderlands. While searching for the rabble-rouser, Ned and the boys come upon an ancient underground complex, which is "coincidentally" the lost mine they are seeking: "It seems that they have unconsciously followed the directions given in the paper they copied." The papers reveal that the New York lawyer's adopted son, Boy Scout George Fremont, is the long-lost heir to an estate that includes the Mexican mine. The poor newsboy, having already been adopted into the "Cameron family, one of wealthiest and most exclusive in New York," was a rightful member of the bourgeoisie after all. As the boys intimated about the future of Mexico, "blood will tell," and this proves true for the American boy who finds his proper place not only in the national but also in the imperial bourgeois order.

Although most of the boys are already heirs to fortunes at home, by successfully promoting American virtues in foiling their degenerate adversaries, as King Arthur claims his Excalibur, the Boy Scouts prove themselves worthy to lay claim to the fortunes of the American empire. As the Boy Scouts continue their imperial journey, Secret Service men are left to guard the mine until peace comes to the rebellious republic. The Boy Scouts' claim to property guarantees the continued presence of Americans in the borderlands and affirms U.S. ascendancy in the region. More than this, the introductory novel set in Mexico addresses the initial class anxiety in the beginning. Given enough time, the boys can find their fortunes abroad. With the proper claim to property intact, the Boy Scout also cements his claim to class status, manhood, and belonging to America.

The Panama Canal; or, The Case of Yellow Fever

Reclamation of property resurfaces in the second novel, set in the Panama Canal Zone. Sailing across the Caribbean from Mexico, the boys track down a four-hundred-year-old emerald necklace originally owned by "some secret order of natives." Someone had stolen the necklace from a Boy Scout's home along with papers that might reveal the nature of a plot to blow up the Gatun Dam in the Zone. The thefts in the Shaw home illustrate the U.S. domestic space's permeability and the need for close monitoring of such spaces. Possible infiltration by foreign or un-American elements is a prevalent anxiety in all three novels.

As U.S. borders grew increasingly distended to encompass the globe in the early twentieth century, points of vulnerability along the border also multiplied. At the time of the novels' publication, the United States was stricken with the fear of Japanese encroachment, the so-called Yellow Peril. Japan had just annexed Korea as part of its eastern empire the year before, in 1910. A growing economic and industrial power, Japan proved its military might against a European nation in the Russo-Japanese War in 1904–5 and now posed a threat to U.S. sovereignty over the Philippines and Hawai'i. The perceived economic threat of Japanese within the continent and the real and imagined Japanese political and military threat outside the continent over what has become *domestic* territory led to the Gentleman's Agreement of 1907 restricting Japanese immigration into the United States.

In the novels' world, although the vestiges of the Spanish Empire might offer some resistance in the Panama Canal Zone and in Mexico, the Japanese Empire lurks menacingly along the borderlands in all three novels. The Japanese menace first appears as a possible border threat in the first novel, set in Mexico. When Ned Nestor suggests that other nations might benefit from a war between the United States and Mexico, Frank Shaw, son of the newspaper owner, exclaims:

> You mean Japan. . . . I've heard that Mexico is full of Japs, all trained and ready to fight. And I've heard about a secret treaty between Mexico and Japan, too. Let the Japs butt in, if they want to. We'll drive them into the Pacific. (124)

"Secret" treaties, especially with Japan, threaten the U.S. hegemony that the Monroe Doctrine (1823) and, later, the Roosevelt Corollary (1904) sought to secure in the Western Hemisphere. While the United States tightened its doors to Japanese immigration in 1907, neighboring Mexico kept its doors wide open. Many feared that imagined Japanese presence right at the border and the Mexican Revolution in 1910 jeopardized the security of the U.S.–Mexican border. However, the Yellow Peril proved false in the first novel. In the Canal Zone, the Japanese turn out to be the culprit, and the boys bring a quick end to the threat that sought to sabotage America's future. The boys catch "four Japs with lighted fuses in their hands" thwarting plans to make Japan "mistress of the Pacific."[19] One of the saboteurs confesses that spies "were working for the Glory of the Emperor, but he forbade it" (243). In a diplomatic move, while the novels seem to place blame on Japanese characters, they fall short of condemning the Japanese Empire.

In the course of wresting the canal away from the encroaching Japanese, the boys also do double duty by staving off the last vestiges of old Spanish rule on the isthmus. A former servant in the Shaw home named Pedro Pedrarias follows the boys to the Canal Zone. Pedrarias was the "pet servant" of Frank Shaw's father, in whose home the double theft of the emerald necklace and some important documents took place. He disappeared after the Secret Service came to investigate the theft. Nestor learns that the treacherous Japanese hired Pedrarias to steal papers revealing the sabotage plot before the U.S. government could find out about the scheme. Thus, in this fantasy, Spanish treachery collaborated with the Yellow Peril. From the outset, Nestor had been suspicious of this non-American presence in the Shaw home. Suspicions of this foreign domestic's perfidious international links proved to be correct. The Latin manservant is introduced to the reader as

in intellectual capacity and breeding far above the menial position he occupied in the house. . . . But even as he stood subserviently by the couch of his employer, his slender hands at his side, there seemed to be something of the alertness of a wild beast in his physical attitude of suppression. Somehow, he gave Ned the impression of one about to spring forth upon an enemy. . . . [T]here was something in the voice which told as plainly as words could have done that English was not the native tongue of the speaker. (48)

"His physical attitude of suppression," decidedly not Anglo-Saxon reserve, seemed to conceal some nefarious secret. Besides being the "pet servant," he possessed "slender hands" and seemed "about to spring forth upon an enemy," to continue the feral feline metaphor. As if these were not sufficient evidence of his un-American status, his speech proved once and for all that "English was not the native tongue of the speaker." The un-American intruder stands in stark contrast to manly, all-American Ned Nestor, whose honesty could be taken at face value and who cleverly deduces that Pedro might be an intruder in the American domestic space.

The Boy Scouts discover later that Pedrarias, descended from old rulers of the isthmus, is the former owner of the emerald necklace and came to work in the Shaw residence to reclaim his family treasure. The Boy Scout Frank Shaw is inexplicably the current owner of the stolen emerald necklace. Emeralds, apparently a Boy Scout's best friend, become a subplot in the fight for democracy. In the American allegory, the struggle for ownership of the necklace between the untrustworthy Pedrarias and the Boy Scout is the contest between old culture and new and the initially missing class conflict is transformed into an international one between a degenerate Spanish aristocracy and a righteous American bourgeoisie. Pedrarias represents the cunning deceit of the old Spanish aristocracy who has infiltrated the American bourgeois home for selfish gain. Eventually, the moral superiority of the American bourgeoisie represented by the Boy Scouts triumphs over the old aristocracy. In this light, the real jewel at stake was not the emerald necklace but the control of the isthmus and the future of the American hemisphere. As Boy Scout Peter Fenton explained to the boys in the club room before setting sail for the Canal Zone:

> The Spaniards who lived in the Province of New Granada, on the Isthmus of Darien, as it was then called, planned a ship canal across the neck in the year 1518, and there has been talk of the big ditch ever since. (14)

What the boys sought was the recovery not of a four hundred-year-old emerald necklace but of a four hundred-year-old dream of a canal connecting the two great oceans. Like the necklace, the isthmus is a four hundred-year-old treasure linking the Atlantic and Pacific oceans to be claimed by the United States. The passing of the necklace's ownership from the Spaniard Pedrarias to the American Shaw represents the arrogation of the right of imperial succession to the United States from Old World to New.

As the boys sail south on the Caribbean to the isthmus, one of the boys gives the others a quick history lesson:

> "Over there is the oldest country on this side of the world," said Peter Fenton, pointing over the rail of the vessel and across the smooth waters of the Caribbean Sea. . . . "Just ahead, rising out of the sea, is the Isthmus of Panama. Down there to the left is the continent of South America, where there were cathedrals and palaces when Manhattan Island was still populated by native Indians." (55)

As the boys travel from east to west, the isthmus "rising out of the sea" separates "to the left," South or Spanish America and to the right, North America designated by the tiny island of Manhattan, the boys' home. The boys' journey organizes the hemisphere such that only the Caribbean Sea seems to separate Manhattan Island from South America. In the middle of this reorganized hemisphere, the boys again straddle a border between Spanish and Anglo America, between barbarism and civilization, between the old and the new. This imaginative cartography elegantly naturalizes the intimate link, symbolized by the emerald necklace, between United States and the rest of the Americas as its manifest destiny and locates the boys at the gateway—the isthmian center—of this destiny.

Linking together space and history, the isthmus as the passage to the future is described in terms of modern New York wonders:

> The great trees lifting their heads out of the jungle reminded the boys of the electric towers of New York, the twists of vines resembling the mighty cables which convey light, heat and power to the inhabitants of Manhattan. (60)

Trees become electric towers; vines turn into cables; the jungle of the Canal Zone transforms into Manhattan. For Peter Fenton and the rest of the boys, the isthmus is not only a spatial and cultural gateway, but also a temporal passageway between the Spanish past and the U.S. future. While "Manhattan was still populated by native Indians," according to Fenton the expert, the Spanish had conquered and populated this *other* America. Because Spanish culture has reached its zenith in a bygone era, "cathedrals and palaces" must give way to the skyscrapers of Manhattan, the new center of hemispheric finance and culture. Manhattan, a burgeoning metropolis by 1911, stands in for the whole United States as the new center of modernity, civilization, and empire.

The superimposition of New York soon ceases to be imagined and becomes literal. The boys come out of the jungle into an American settlement:

> [T]he jungle disappeared as if *by magic,* and the train was winding up grassy hills. Beyond, higher up, the scattered houses of a city of fair size came into view.
>
> "That's the Gatun," cried Fenton. "I've read half a dozen descriptions of it lately. Great town, that."
>
> "The houses look like boxes from here," Jimmie observed.
>
> "Of course," Peter replied, "they are all two-story houses, square, with double balconies all screened in. Might be Philadelphia, eh?"
>
> There were smooth roads in front of the houses, and there were yards where flowers were growing, and where neatly dressed children were playing. Jimmie turned from the homelike scene to Frank.
>
> "I thought there would be something new down here," he complained. "This is just like a town up the Hudson." (61; emphasis added)

Jimmie is not as prepared in the Canal Zone as he was in Mexico faced with this "homelike" scene. Contrary to Jimmie's complaint, thanks to American "magic" there is something "new" but strangely familiar down there in the zone—just about everything. The jungle has disappeared and metamorphosed into "smooth roads" and "two-story houses." Natives have been displaced and transformed into "neatly dressed children" playing in the yard. The boys were hoping for a jungle adventure in Panama, only to find a reproduction of the eastern seaboard from "Philadelphia" to a "town up the Hudson." The "magic" of American technology and empire building has swept away Spanish and indigenous history and culture, leaving only a homogeneous replica to be experienced by the boys as strangely familiar and "homelike" in this other America.

This "homelike" experience was created by treaty and a bit of imperial imagination. The Panama Canal Zone became American in 1903. Theodore Roosevelt's romantic vision of an Atlantic and Pacific fleet was realized with the purchase of the Panama Canal in 1902 for fifty million dollars. From 1904 to 1914, construction on the canal continued. Both the Philippines and the Canal Zone were under the War Department, fusing economic and military concerns.[20] Through the clever machinations of the U.S. government, Panama was severed from Gran Colombia so that the United States could secure control of the isthmus and the future of world commerce. Years later, in 1911, Roosevelt spoke proudly of his outright appropriation of the Canal Zone: "I took the Canal Zone and let Congress debate; and while the debate goes on the Canal does also."[21]

The isthmus represents an imaginary space where the United States successfully transforms a savage land into its image. The introduction of American technology delivers the wild tropics to the twentieth century. Modernity is the gift of American civilization to the tropics and the rest of the world:

> From the distance came the clamor of the greatest work the world has ever undertaken. The thud and creaking of machinery mingled with the primitive noises of the forest. (73)

Amid the industrial clamor, the United States and Manhattan, in yet another metaphoric turn, magically disappear from view and reappear as "the world." The clamor "from the distance" that the boys hear is not simply that of industry and technology at work but that of the American empire re-creating the world in its image. Distracting and dazzling the rest of the world with technological noise and wonder, the United States of the early twentieth century emerges to hammer out the world's future: "Night and day under the great white lights the work went forward cutting a way for the commerce of the world" (137). Cutting across the continent to conjoin the Atlantic and Pacific oceans, "the greatest work" is not just the United States changing the world's physical and commercial landscape; it is the United States building its empire.

The Philippines; or, Confederates in the Tropics

Having ensured the safe passage of American manifest destiny through the treasured emerald jewel lacing the Western Hemisphere with the Pacific, Ned Nestor "accepted the invitation to enter the Secret Service, stipulating that his chums should be permitted to accompany him to Uncle Sam's new and somewhat unruly possessions in Asia."[22] *Boy Scouts in the Philippines; or, The Key to the Treaty Box* finds the boys "assisting in the uncovering of an alleged treasonable plot against the peace of the Islands and the continued supremacy of the United States government" (10). The novel pits the Boy Scouts against corporate villains who have infiltrated the Secret Service to bring chaos to the archipelago. This time, the hidden danger lurking in the borderlands no longer wears a visibly racialized face. Corruption from within white American ranks now disrupts Pax Americana in the Pacific. Although they are sons and heirs of businessmen themselves, the boys maintain a suspicion of "big business."

In the Canal Zone, "railroad interests" were under suspicion as they stood to lose profit to the canal by displacing the transcontinental lines as the main route for goods and trade. In the Philippines, Nestor suspected that corporate interests might be behind the uprisings in the islands: "I am not an anarchist, but it is my belief that there are many corporations in the world who would set the nations at each other's throats if profit could be made out of it" (35). Freed of national governance, the boys believe that corporations rage unchecked across the globe, wreaking international havoc. As Boy Scouts, they are products of reform-minded America. While supporting the structures of capitalism, Progressive rhetoric objected to the worst practices of big business, and sought to ameliorate the inequities of undisciplined capitalism. Unruly corporations and their corrupting influence must be reined in to prevent anarchy. But, why must the Boy Scouts travel halfway around the world to the Philippines to confront U.S. corporations?

The boys uncover a plot by people connected with the U.S. Navy
and working with some commercial interest on the continent to in-
cite a Philippine insurrection. In his Bowery slang, Jimmie points
to the son of a U.S. senator as the main culprit, who

> "is here representin' some big interest, an' that's the treaty box he's
> got. Say, if they ever get all these native kings an' queens an' prime
> ministers to goin', there'll be bloody war in the Philippines, an'
> Japan, or China, or Germany, or France will butt in, an' there'll be
> a fine time." (188)

Although the identity of the "big interest" is never divulged, the
outrage stems from betrayal of the American nation by men among
its trusted ranks. The paranoia of infiltration found in the previous
two novels reappears in the form of corporate interests. Roosevelt's
border between savagery and civilization is no longer so clearly
delineated between foreign and domestic spaces. Capitalist barbarism originating from within the American borders has infiltrated
military and government institutions to disturb the peace of the
colonial world.

The senator's son and other unidentified culprits were attempt-
ing to convince the native chiefs to build a "confederacy" to wage
war against the United States. The traitors kidnap the boys' Secret
Service contact to give the "confederates time in which to complete the work of organizing the tribes" (245). The case in the
Philippines is similar to that in Mexico in which a deceitful leader
tries to mislead gullible natives. Like Mexicans, Filipinos have no
true national ties because "tribes" and "natives" with "many odd
customs" inhabit the "twelve hundred islands . . . [that] constitute
the group" (11):[23]

> There is a notion at Washington that it may be some financial inter-
> est. The newspapers were saying, when we left civilization, that a
> certain monopoly was financing the Mexican revolution, and there
> is a suspicion that some disloyal men in the United States are doing
> the same with the ignorant natives of the Philippines—urging them
> on and supplying them with guns and ammunitions. (97)

Again, like their Mexican brethren, the tribal-like people are easily fooled and misled by sophisticated American urban financiers
and commercial interests into thinking that rebelling against Pax
Americana might be advantageous. In other words, the Filipino is

like the vulnerable adolescent, susceptible to bad influence. As upright men guide the moral development of boys, the Boy Scouts too must protect the impressionable savages, prone to revolt and treason, from civilization's corrosive influences. Without the discipline Americans provide to "arrange a proper environment" for the colonized borderlands, anarchy would ensue and impede the development of these colonial appurtenances.

However, in this case the perfidy hails from the American continent itself. Unlike the infiltrating foreign domestic Pedrarias of the last novel, locating the proper borders of America becomes even more complicated with this internal savagery.[24] Consequently, identifying the battlefront for the struggle between civilization and savagery becomes equally difficult because corporations have caused the borders of America to become unfixed and uncertain. However, the text itself experiences a difficulty in sustaining the border between the boy's crusade against the unidentified corporation and the colonial setting on which the battle is being fought. The Philippines is cast as a battleground on which the nefarious tendencies of American commercial interests and the unassailable virtues of the Boy Scouts fight for ascendancy. The novel displaces Roosevelt's contemporaneous New York trust-busting campaigns onto the colonial possession.

The invocation of "confederate" factions in the Philippine situation holds the real "key" to the text's own confusion. The language of the U.S. Civil War first imagines uncontrolled capital and its infiltrating agents as rebel forces fighting against the sovereignty of the Union. However, the reference to "confederates" and "confederacy" slips ambiguously between the U.S. plotters and the potential association of native chieftains being organized by the plotters. The novel unwittingly deploys the specter of the U.S. Civil War—half a century and half a world away—to embed the historical reality of the Philippine-American War and to deny the persistence of Filipino opposition to the American administration. Interestingly, the novel avoids any direct allusion to the protracted war being waged by Filipinos against the U.S. pacifying forces even up to the novels' publication. Even more than a decade after Roosevelt declared the Philippine-American War officially over in 1902, military pacification campaigns continued, especially in the southern provinces, through 1913.

During the Philippine-American War, the U.S. military administration revived a law passed in 1863 against Confederate forces, this time in 1902 against Filipinos. The 1863 War Act stated that Confederate combatants were to be treated as rebels or "bandits" within the territory rather than as prisoners of war. The law was revived and used against Filipinos, whose guerrilla tactics proved a nuisance to American forces. The tropical possessions became defined as domestic territory for pacification purposes. The U.S. forces thus treated Filipino guerrillas not as combatants of an independent nation but as rebels within American territory. Filipino resistance was treated as being outside the bounds of recognized warfare, thereby sanctioning barbarity in the treatment of the "rebels."[25] Governor-General Taft later declared all guerrilla activity *criminal* rather than *military* aggression against the United States. Under U.S. military and civil administration, the Filipino struggle for independence against the new colonizers was effectively erased and renamed "banditry" and "brigandage," thus rendering the enduring conflict unrecognizable in official discourse.

The Boy Scout novel set in the Philippines is more ambivalent about the U.S. role in the Philippines than are the novels set in Mexico and the Panama Canal Zone. One of the American officers in the novel expresses his confusion over who the enemy is in the archipelago:

> "[It is] hard to tell who is the enemy as people in the pueblo help bandits. . . . About a thousand of these brown leaders will have to be killed off before there will be any security of life and property here," said the captain. "The natives would behave themselves if let alone." (55)

The "bandits" seem to have popular support, to the bewilderment of the characters themselves. The very labels "banditry" and "brigandage" served to confuse issues and erase any chance of understanding the Philippine situation. What is repeated from the other novels is the desire for order at whatever cost, and, as in the Mexican case, genocide is invoked as an option: "about a thousand of these brown leaders will have to be killed off" so that peace can be secured.

The resurrection of the U.S. Civil War in the Philippines in the historical and fictional narratives underscores the tenuous position of the archipelago in relation to the American polity and imagination. Although the Philippines was unincorporated into the United States, as a "possession" or property, Congress held plenary powers over it, bestowing and withholding rights to a subject people according to the metropole's political or economic exigencies. Unlike the cases of Mexico or Panama, which sought to replicate the American space and order, this ambivalence about the Philippines located the archipelago both inside and outside the U.S. nation-state, configuring an enfolded border between them.

The novel redraws the boundaries of the United States to encompass and domesticate the colonial archipelago. By "domesticating" the Philippines in the American imagination, Filipino insurgency becomes a criminal act against the Union, of which the archipelago is not technically a part. Recalling the U.S. Civil War, any "confederacy" including the demand for Filipino independence would constitute an act of secession, and therefore an act of treason on the part of the colonized. By capturing and bringing to justice the corrupt elements in the islands, the boys make them safe for democracy and save the Filipino natives from themselves. Doing so brings order to the untidy flow of ideas along this border to assert U.S. sovereignty over its colonial possessions. The novel, like official discourse, denies the reality of Filipino resistance under American administration. As in the Canal Zone and in Mexico, the fictional Boy Scouts arrive in the Philippines to secure the American claim to overseas property, but in this case the novel refuses allegories of a mine or a necklace; instead, the Philippines itself is the property to be claimed.

Although the character flaw rests this time on immoral continental Americans, the exoneration of the natives of any misdeed eventuates the erasure of any native agency. By placing culpability on metropolitan agents, the narrative diminishes Filipinos, who are characterized as mere pawns of metropolitan desires, both moral and immoral. If the colonized subject is but a cipher susceptible to the evil influence of commercial interests and civilization, then the possibility that Filipinos might actually have a reason to revolt is forestalled. This transformation of the Philippine landscape (like Panama) and the Filipino mind (like Mexico) reflects the ideological needs of American colonizers to legitimize U.S. guardianship of these territories by naturalizing the power of white American bodies to appropriate and command the islands.

As the novel reconfigures American borders to domesticate the tropical archipelago, it also domesticates the inhabitants through two minor Filipino characters: Tag and Minda. The only independentist

sentiment voiced in the entire novel is from the fleeting appearance
of a Tagalog servant, unimaginatively named Tag, who was staying
at the boys' camp. When questioned of the whereabouts of a suspect, he cries:

> "You *Americanos* expect us to see everything and know every-
> thing! If we are so wise and capable, why don't you permit us to
> govern ourselves—send away your soldiers and let us handle the
> situation here?" (42)

However, his appeal for Filipino self-government is never engaged
in the course of the novel. The reader is simply made aware at the
end that Tag has been arrested along with other rebels. Like his
name, Tag's role in the Boy Scout novel is abbreviated. And, like
the Philippine archipelago, his character is reduced to an appurtenance or a literal "tag" to the grander narrative of U.S. exploits in
the tropics.

However, the Filipino is redeemed later. Tag disappears from
the story and another Filipino character, Minda, a local Boy Scout
from Manila whose name is a shortened form of the southern island
Mindanao, takes his place. The protagonists meet Minda, of all
places, atop a tree:

> "What does the badge say?" asked the voice, then.
> "Be prepared!"
> "Now, what do you think of that?" Pat demanded. "What do
> you think of meeting a Boy Scout out here?"
> "What patrol?"
> "Wild Cat, Manila!" came the reply. (173)

At first the boys think the figure up the tree is little Jimmie "made
up as a little brown man." In fact, the Filipino Boy Scout is made up
as a little American boy dressed in a simple Scout uniform. Minda
predates by three years the first recorded Filipino Boy Scout troop
formed in the southern provinces. Ironically, it was in the southern provinces that U.S. pacification campaigns met with fervent
Filipino Muslim resistance, which endured through 1913.

In the novel, Minda serves to redeem the Filipino native by sup-
planting the rebellious Tag and transforming him into a faithful
little boy. The Filipino body is remodeled into that of a Boy Scout.
The boys learn that Minda came as a servant on a steamer after running away from Manila, because, like the adventurous American

boys, he was tired of the city. Through a combination of the boys' ventriloquism and Minda's one- and two-word responses, the native Boy Scout proceeds to tell the boys of a conference of native chiefs about to take place, thus helping to foil the treasonous plot. As with little Jimmie from the Bowery, the middle-class boys adopt the brown scout. In the end, their little brown brother is sent to Washington to become a "real" American. The future of the Philippines resides in "little brown brothers" like Minda, the Filipino boy remade in America's image. He proves himself the perfect colonized native—childish, loyal, and ready for American tutelage—the tamed offspring of benevolent assimilation. Like the Panamanian landscape, the inhabitants of the Philippine tropics are recast in America's image, wiping way all memories of conflict between the colonizer and the colonized.

Born of the imperial encounter, the Boy Scouts movement reaches past the Philippines, past the American frontier, past England, and all the way to Africa. "The story begins in Africa, in Mafeking, in 1899–1900," began an account of the Boy Scouts movement in *Outlook* magazine.[26] The Boer War forced every Englishman into combat. As military reinforcement, boys were put in uniform and acted as messengers, lookouts, and orderlies. The boys provided valiant and much-needed service to the British Empire's efforts in its African frontier. Years after the war in 1908, General Robert Baden-Powell gathered some English boys to teach them scouting skills as wartime would require and "showed them how to play at Indian and Knights of King Arthur."[27] Decimated North American peoples and mythic English lore together laid the imaginary foundation for transforming the English boy into a modern-day noble savage in service of empire.

These mythic foundations crossed the Atlantic to inspire American middle-class men to save their sons from the deleterious effects of prosperity, modern comforts, and overcivilization. The Boy Scouts in the United States rose to national prominence in 1910 during the Progressive Era. The King Arthur myth of fifteenth-century English invention appealed to the rising middle class's aristocratic pretensions, but the treatment of North American Indians was a brutal reality from America's recent past. Only a generation before the Scout movement's formation, the Dawes Act of 1887 dismantled the reservation system and began the "Americanization" of American Indians in an attempt to erase Native culture from the continent. Yet, the myths of the noble savage and of the Indian's intimate relation to the wilderness provided necessary counter-point to the thundering call of American industrialization and over-civilization. The American Indian's domestication through violent erasure and containment in myth would make possible for the American boy a "strenuous life."

Prominent political figures shared fears about the state of Ameri-can masculinity. Daniel Beard formed a society in 1905 called the Sons of Daniel Boone, later known as the "Boy Pioneers of America," moving away from the American Indian as ideal and fo-cusing on European-American frontier settlers. Beard expressed his concern about American boys' general helplessness and inability to be self-reliant like their pioneering forebears. "This state of affairs seemed to me to bode ill for the future crop of men," he lament-ed, "and I have now spent some thirty years in a modest endeavor to bring our boys back to a state where they are more in accord with the all-around useful men from whom they sprang."[28] In his view, the American boy—or at least, his urban manifestation—had degenerated and become a weakling compared to his heartier fore-father. Bringing the ailing boy back to the woods under the guid-ance of sturdy men in a controlled environment, much as Seton rec-ommended, might cure him of his weakness in character, strength, and spirituality.

Progressive rhetoric rested on nostalgia of small-town democ-racy and belief in social amelioration with the bourgeoisie or elite as leaders of a better and more just society. The widening commer-cial and political stage after the Spanish-American War compelled some guardians to extend the geographic boundaries of their social responsibility. "Society" as sphere of responsibility came to encom-pass the whole Western Hemisphere *and* Asia.

The novels' necessarily expansive geography renders a world be-yond the protagonist's locale and encompassing the imperial cir-cuit. The novels translate the nineteenth-century myth of the fron-tier into a twentieth-century errand into the imperial wilderness. This errand into the imperial outposts is not simply an errand to recover American masculinity and cull lessons in self-government, but to claim property and management rights over the colonies. Under the pretext of upholding American virtue and battling sav-age vice along the borderlands, the fictional Boy Scouts natural-ize the right of the American colonizers to rule over other peoples.

Contemporary concerns and threats about American borders arising from this encounter are projected onto villains from semi-barbaric Spaniards and treacherous Japanese to native savages and rapacious capitalists. The novels simplify and bring to satisfactory and patriotic conclusion the conflicts and anxieties arising from the U.S. imperial enterprise.

The international Boy Scouts' itinerant nature is a fitting vehicle to demonstrate the global mobility of American values and citizens as transmitted by the Boy Scouts. During peacetime, these boys demonstrate not only America's geographic mobility, but also, with the presence of Boy Scouts everywhere trained by upright and virtuous men of the American bourgeoisie, American universality. The genre lends itself well to a display of American masculine prowess in logic, deduction, ingenuity, and courage, in contrast to the cowardly, insidious, and feminized depictions of the enemy, whether Japanese, Filipino, Spanish, or Mexican.

The novels make the world seamless, organized by American values. These values give meaning to the new frontier, the American world mission for the twentieth century, and imperial citizenship. While teaching about the evils of cigarette smoking, the novels allow readers to live vicariously through mythical boys who prove their patriotism in colonized spaces. Thus, the reader learns about the colonial world and its peoples as mediated by the imperial relationship and the compulsion to introduce Pax Americana into the otherwise disorderly realm of browner, less civilized, border states, always on the brink of anarchy. U.S. citizenship brings with it the burden of empire.

In *A Strenuous Life,* Theodore Roosevelt and the imperialists conceived of an American-controlled Philippines as a field in which an enervated white masculinity could restore itself to a primal vigor by subduing primitive men.[29] There, the American frontier and the frontier spirit could be reinvigorated. In 1911—the same year the Boy Scout novels were published—William Cameron Forbes, governor-general of the Philippine Islands, described central Mindanao in the southern Philippines as "white man's land." He saw in this "white man's land" an opportunity "to get to work and cultivate the virgin soil and undertake other enterprises," known only to hearty American forefathers of the western frontier.[30] A year later, Woodrow Wilson more ambivalently admitted: "The Philippines are at present our frontier but I hope we presently are to deprive ourselves of that frontier."[31] Twenty years after Frederick Jackson Turner's famous frontier thesis lamenting the loss of the western frontier that extinguished American vitality, the frontier found a new home outside U.S. borders. The colonial possessions provided this frontier. The "white man's burden" turned out to be the white man's—and boy's—savior after all.

4. Imperial Romance

Framing Manifest Destiny in the Pacific

> Next time you're going to play these games in the jungle, why don't
> you take me with you? I'm good at that sort of thing. I can start a fire
> by rubbing two Boy Scouts together.
>
> —Lieutenant McCool in *The Real Glory*

> I could have been an actress in one of those romantic musicals, back
> in the days when movies were movies and everyone loved romance!
> Ay—where is the romance, these days? . . . We Filipinos, we know
> how to endure, and we embrace the movies. With movies, everything
> is okay lang?
>
> —Madame in *Dogeaters*

Whereas early-twentieth-century popular literature imagined
the adventures of Boy Scouts in the borderlands, mid-century
Hollywood produced movies recounting the heroic exploits of
Americans in the Pacific. U.S. films and musicals would continue
to resonate with tropes of masculinity, heroism, nationalism, and
benevolence throughout the Pacific region. The spaces of tropical
America would incorporate Asian and Pacific bodies in their visual, and this time heteroerotic field. Saved by the white man's burden, the American boys must now grow up to weave more complex
stories about difference within the bounds of their moral compass. Much as the tropical mise-en-scène would seduce audiences,
American male characters would tame, if not seduce, their brown

love interests. From the moral sentence of adolescence emerges the romance in the American Tropics.

The romantic musical as a genre celebrates the coming together of a heteronormative dyad to guarantee a seemingly satisfying "happily ever after" fantasy for the characters. This narrative trajectory posits sexual difference as the primary sign of difference and desire, relegating race to a minor subplot in the grander resolution in heterosexuality. Empire and race when thrown into the mix of musical numbers, however, question the primacy of sexual difference and reveal gender and sexuality to be as susceptible to social negotiation as class and racial difference. The seemingly natural process of seduction based on sexual difference when complicated by race and empire destabilizes the facile development of the white male figures. These moments in which masculine authority is destabilized are the moments during which the U.S. imperial project seems to founder. The ways these crises in masculinity are managed reveal the operative tropes of imperialism.

The beginnings of American filmmaking were coterminous with U.S. empire building. Images of the Pacific were already being captured on film by May 10, 1898, when a Thomas Alva Edison camera crew filmed the Republic of Hawaii, three months before its annexation as U.S. territory and five years after the illegal overthrow of the Kingdom of Hawai'i. Part of a cinematic diary of their voyage from Asia back to the East Coast, these images are the first known "Paci-flicks," as film historian Luis Reyes terms South Seas cinema.[1] Entertaining audiences for generations, movies set in the Pacific used the exotic milieu either to stage wartime American heroism or as a fantastic retreat from the changing world of post–World War II United States. The war in the Pacific theater and its aftermath was an opportunity to stage the revisioning of the American project, bringing the islands of the Philippines and Pacific nations, including Hawai'i, then a dependency on the verge of becoming a state, into sharper focus. Images of the Philippines and the Pacific appeared in a range of movies, from the heroic retelling of military valor in *Bataan* (1943), *Back to Bataan* (1945), and *From Here to Eternity* (1953) to the tropical romps of star vehicles such as *Song of the Islands* (1942) and *Blue Hawaii* (1961). These transpacific flights of fancy reassured audiences of the United States' rightful place in the vast Pacific world and reinscribed notions of American manliness and citizenship that attended that right. On the shores of war-torn Pacific islands, white American characters would sing, dance, and fall in love with their assumed tropical identities.

Like many Hollywood films of the period, white American actors enchantingly played brown characters to stage American tropical dramas.[2] Dorothy Lamour played Balinese Princess Lalah for Bing Crosby and Bob Hope in *Road to Bali* (1952). Esther Williams played a beguiling half-American and half-Tahitian maiden in *Pagan Love Song* (1950). *Song of the Islands* distracted audiences from the war with the legs of flaxen-haired Betty Grable peeking through plastic grass skirts. Exotic ethnic white beauties of the era such as Maria Montez, Dolores del Rio, Yvonne De Carlo, and Rita Hayworth among many others donned their sarongs and grass skirts in feminized and erotic visualizations of the Pacific. Meanwhile, when not slugging it out in the American West, John Wayne could also be found in the Pacific isles in *Back to Bataan* (1945) teaching Filipinos to be better nationalists, and, nearly twenty years later, in *Donovan's Reef* (1963), taking care of Pacific Island children. Whether featuring white bodies playing natives or caring for them or both, the movies mark the various ways U.S. cinema laid claim to Asia and the Pacific as sites of American fantasy and identity formation.

I highlight the tensions inherent in producing visual cultural artifacts that construct an American Tropics as the repository of U.S. nationalist fantasies. I do not wish to rehearse here misrepresentations or to point out cases of bad representation, only to reinscribe the power of the defining terms and thus imply the inevitability of American manifest destiny. I take Viet Nguyen's insight seriously in refusing a type of Asian American cultural criticism that assigns aesthetic value to an object via the political binary of resistance or accommodation.[3] Tropes deployed for whatever (a)political purpose do not work in such a facile manner. Therefore, I do not focus my analysis on the misrepresentation of local peoples and whether or not brown characters are played by whites or locals. This practice of "misrecognition" is inherent in fantasy production as an expression of imperial desires. What interests me instead are the narrative operations through metaphor and allegory that carve out the unquestioned place of white American bodies in the Pacific, as liberators and eventually as rightful, if not righteous, settlers and "natives" to the islands. These national fantasies inform the United

States' quest to regulate these spaces and peoples and shape the terrain of Asian American and Pacific social realities.

Like the Boy Scout novels, each film makes use of the trope of the frontier to justify the place of American bodies in the islands, which are then made to depend on such intrusive bodies for their very existence. These filmic narratives about American bodies proliferating in and populating the Pacific emerge at a time in the mid-twentieth century when immigration laws excluding Asians and Pacific Islanders were in place and increasingly enforced. The Immigration Act of 1917 circumscribed the "Asiatic barred zone," extending exclusion from Arabia (or western Asia) to South Asia out to the Polynesian islands.[4] While American bodies peopled Asian and Pacific islands on film, Asian and Pacific bodies were still barred from immigrating in large numbers into the continental United States.[5] The mainstream mass culture in the form of cinema recreated a Pacific image locating the conflated Asian-Pacific identity as an exotic and foreign otherness against which U.S. masculinity and nation were defined. With each narrative, the encounter imposes U.S. culture on hapless natives, but, at the same time, it changes the American character and identity to create a new vision of themselves during the social challenges faced by the mid-century United States.

I examine three films, *The Real Glory* (1939) with Gary Cooper, *Donovan's Reef* (1963) with John Wayne, and *Blue Hawaii* (1961) with Elvis Presley, with references to other contemporary movies to illustrate how these popular American films and musicals revive the trope of the frontier and manifest destiny in the Pacific. These movies depict white Americans (1) as founders of nationalism in the Philippines; (2) as noble settlers in a mythical Pacific; and (3) as natives or "naturalized" elite in Hawai'i. These three fantastical visions of island Southeast Asia and the Pacific manage to clothe native bodies for civilization even as they enable white American bodies to disrobe and appropriate Asian and Pacific spaces *and* identities. Yet all three create moments of instability in which the management of masculinity becomes the operative trope to resolve internal anxieties of national integrity.

Coming-of-Age in the Philippines: The Real Glory (1939)

Philippine training for citizenship operative in the legal, political, and educational realms since the early twentieth century makes it to the big screen just before World War II. Movies like *Bataan* and *Back to Bataan* depicted the U.S. war effort in the Philippines and its moral investment in this Pacific ward. The struggles of Americans and, only secondarily, their Filipino allies underscore the pivotal role the United States played in bringing to fruition a proper Philippine nationalism, that is, a nationalism based on U.S. democratic principles and notions of manhood. In *Back to Bataan,* for example, John Wayne, playing Colonel Madden, resuscitates Philippine nationalism by creating a viable army out of Filipino guerrilla forces. However, the rebirth of the Philippine nation, against the encroaching Japanese, rested on John Wayne playing Colonel Madden as a romantic broker between Andrés Bonifacio III (played by the ethnic-looking Anthony Quinn) and the beautiful Dalisay Delgado (Fely Franquelli), a radio star and spy for the United States and the Philippines.

The movie openly recalls memories of the Philippine-American War as Madden recruits a descendant and namesake of the Filipino revolutionary leader Andrés Bonifacio, whose heroic leadership continued to be remembered and to serve as an inspiration even after his death in 1897 in the Filipino "insurrection" (recently acknowledged as the Philippine-American War) against the Americans (1899–1910s). Madden needs the revolutionary descendant to inspire the Filipino guerrilla forces against the Japanese. Unfortunately, the younger Bonifacio is a pale shadow of his great-grandfather. A disaffected officer of the Philippine Scouts, Bonifacio III has lost all faith in Filipinos and the Philippines. Madden gives the Filipino descendant a history lesson about the Philippine revolution against the invading Americans: "A handful of revolutionaries calling themselves the *Katipunan* took everything we could throw at them, fought us to a standstill with bolos and clubs."

Madden (Wayne) later encourages the scant Filipino troops to use the same guerrilla tactics Filipino rebels used against the Americans, but this time to defeat the Japanese. Ironically, although Madden's version of history depicts Filipinos as feisty savages "with bolos and clubs," he offers the very prehistory that the American education system sought to erase in Philippine history books. Perhaps this systematic erasure justifies the retelling of Philippine history to the Filipino Bonifacio (Quinn) by the American Madden. After all, as Bonifacio admits in his apology to Madden: "I don't mean that, Joe. I know you're a better Filipino than I am." This deference to the American about proper Philippine patriotism reflects the general view the movie takes on the Philippine–American conflict: the violent and genocidal episode in Philippine–American history is reduced to a simple misunderstanding between the two peoples, after which the contrite Filipinos were grateful to learn proper nationalism from the Americans. More interestingly, Bonifacio's substitution of "Filipino" in the set U.S. English phrase "you're a better man than I am" reveals that the lesson in patriotism is also a lesson in proper manhood.

Not realizing that perhaps he might have historically contributed to the affliction, Madden cures Bonifacio's nationalist impotence by reuniting him with his former girlfriend, the glamorous and exotic Dalisay (Franquelli), who happens to be "the voice of the Philippines" on the Japanese-controlled radio.[6] Madden succeeds in making sparks fly between these two nationalist symbols, one recalling the past, the other representing the current anti-Japanese resistance, with the memory of the Philippine-American War just at bay. Bonifacio's newfound potency revitalizes his commitment to Philippine nationalism. Thanks to Madden's expert manipulation of Bonifacio's libido, the Philippine nation rises up and bursts with gunfire onto the screen to defeat the Japanese. Rather tritely, the film offers a final scene in which the camera angles up to frame the ecstatic faces of the new Filipino couple. The American and Filipino flags behind them wave side by side. Bonifacio holds out his hand to Dalisay and exclaims: "Here. I've brought you something: Free Filipino soil!" Madden immediately enters the frame *between* the two to complete the neocolonial ménage as the broker of Filipino nationhood, masculinity, and heterosexual union.

If *Back to Bataan* cures flagging Philippine nationalism with a shot of American manhood, *The Real Glory* (1939), made immediately before the war, inoculates the archipelago against cowardice and cholera to show the United States in all its imperial glory. Like its wartime successors, *The Real Glory* also depicts flaccid Filipino nationalism requiring U.S. guidance and encouragement. Unlike *Back to Bataan,* it does not simply refer to the Philippine-American War (1899–1902). Instead, it is set in the aftermath of the war. Released five years after the passage of the Tydings-McDuffie Act, which promised independence to the Philippines in ten years' time, *The Real Glory* revisits the scene of imperial contact in 1906, when the last of the American troops withdrew from the war-torn southern islands. Before leaving, however, U.S. officers recruit native troops to form the insular police, the Philippine Constabulary, which formed the native arm of the U.S. military, along with the Philippine Scouts and the regular army.

The movie opens with the withdrawal of U.S. troops from Fort Mysang in Mindanao. The official withdrawal leaves a handful of officers and a band of frightened and unshod native troops to fend off devious and treacherous Moros (Muslim Filipinos) who threaten the peace in the U.S.-administered Philippines. A *civilian* doctor, Doctor Canavan (Gary Cooper), saves the day and the two nations by showing the more peaceful Christian Filipinos the error of their cowardly and superstitious ways. Combining military discipline with a dose of applied psychology, Canavan, managing borders and masculinity, hammers the native troops into a fighting force who later triumph over the savage Moros. Thus the movie recounts the birth of Philippine national unity and masculinity against an internal, racialized threat—the Moros—under the auspices of American psychomedical ingenuity.

The containment of disease, both psychological and physical, is a pervasive trope in the movie. Early-twentieth-century U.S. concerns with germs and disease mesh with the 1930s fascination with Freudian psychology to unlock a universe of knowledge about the Pacific wards. Interest in psychoanalysis entered American popular culture after World War I and had since infiltrated the movie industry. U.S. cultural historian Ann Douglas has revealed in her informative study how, much to Freud's consternation, the Hollywood mogul Samuel Goldwyn offered the Viennese psychoanalyst a hundred thousand dollars to write a "love story" for the studio.[7] Already irritated by the American simplification and popularization of his theories, Freud declined. Goldwyn had to wait fifteen years to see his Freudian "love story" unfold as a "romantic adventure" in the colonial Philippines. Movie-studio pop psychology could unlock (and wreak havoc with) the Filipino psyche, while showing American audiences the original "modernity" of American culture in 1906, before the definitive closing of U.S. borders to all Asians in 1934.

With the simmering threat of Japanese power in the region and the recent assignment of Douglas MacArthur as the commander in chief of the Philippine military, U.S. interest focused on the American democratic experiment in the Pacific. In this movie, the emergence of a fighting force, the Philippine Constabulary, which recruited from the locality that required pacification, depends not only on the physical preparedness of the natives, but also on their mental fitness. Having a civilian and not military doctor as the protagonist insists that the American presence heralds modernity for a primitive and superstitious people and underscores the ideological foregrounding of U.S. civilian, as opposed to military, rule in the imperial contact. Focusing on the lone efforts of a civilian medical doctor, *The Real Glory* proposes that the Filipino problem is not so much political as psychomedical. Such a prognosis ignores the long history of Muslim–Christian conflict since Spanish colonization in the region, even up to the movie's opening.

Central Mindanao, unlike the rest of the archipelago, was never dominated by Hispanic or Catholic influence during the Spanish colonial period. Both Islamic and non-Islamic groups of the southern islands resisted Spanish military and civil forces for three centuries. The conflict between Mindanao and the rest of the Christian-dominant Philippine Islands was further exacerbated when the island became a U.S. territory. Under U.S. occupation, the region was governed as an autonomous militarized zone, unlike the rest of the archipelago, which came under civil administration. Apart from the direct military rule of Mindanao, the Americans decided to create infrastructure in Mindanao to establish a ranch-cattle industry in the region reminiscent of the U.S. West, in order to encourage settlement from the other islands and facilitate the assimilation of the island into the rest of the Philippines.[8] This encouragement of migration of Christian Filipinos into the island to appropriate land resulted in increased tensions between the predominantly Islamic peoples there and the rest of the archipelago, tensions that continue to this day.

By dehistoricizing social issues, *The Real Glory* could glorify the lone efforts of one man in bringing about a final resolution to the Philippine question. By reducing the "Philippine problem" to a psychomedical issue, the narrative effectively occludes the political history of conflict among the various Filipino groups and the U.S. role in intensifying the conflict. If Filipinos could be made rational, then all would be well. Rationalization means the eradication of the supposedly irrational, therefore primitive, beliefs of natives, as well as the colonial restructuring of native social systems into manageable and knowable entities. The American Canavan is the doctor, and the Philippines is the mentally ill patient. His science and medicine would bring about the rationalization of the islands and lead the Filipinos into modernity and normalization.

The Real Glory presents Fort Mysang as a microcosm of Philippine–U.S. relations. The action is set not simply in the Philippines but in a far removed outpost, the frontier of the American imperial frontier. Indeed, the movie was previously called *The Last Frontier.*[9] Furthermore, ineffectual or "unmanly" nationalism imperils not only the Philippines but also the Philippines as an extension of U.S. domestic space. In this all-male world of the military, the American occupiers cannot achieve normative gender relations with the native populace. The welcome arrival of white American women, Captain Hartley's daughter, Linda (Andrea Leeds), accompanied by Major Manning's wife, Mabel (Kay Johnson), provides the white female presence necessary to transform the camp into a domestic rather than simply a military space. The younger, beautiful Linda, as her name denotes, becomes the center of the men's attention and ultimately Canavan's love interest. The budding romance in the jungle outpost between Canavan and the headstrong Linda promises a literal domestication of the colonial space and provides the requisite heterosexuality in the "romantic adventure."

The older Mrs. Manning adds the sentimental touch in this other scene of American domesticity when she reunites with her husband with an appeal for his return home. She describes the house she chose for them in Manila once his tour of duty is complete:

MABEL: I have the cutest little place fixed up in Manila right near the Luneta [Park]. Oh, darling, could you possible be as happy as I am?

MANNING: We're gonna have to change our plans a little.

MABEL: Don't tell me there's been another delay in your leave of absence?

MANNING: My leave is off. I've been assigned here indefinitely. Sorry, Mabel. It can't be helped. The C.O. died—Colonel Hatch, you never met him. So you see, that puts me in command.

MABEL: Well, it was a mighty nice little house, but I guess we can make this one do. Oh, George . . . [Fade]

The deferral of Philippine independence, whether in 1902 after the war or in 1934 with the Tydings-McDuffie Act, persists as a moral problem as it also defers the formation of a proper U.S. domestic space. Manila here serves as the surrogate American home as the administrative and most modern (Americanized) city in the colony. Mysang is the colonial outpost, and the American cannot come home until the outpost is in order. Duty to the Filipino people unsettles the U.S. household and relocates it at the very edge of the imperial realm and defers enjoyment of U.S. domestic bliss in the "mighty nice little house." In the meantime, the American couple must "make this one do."

On the other side of the problem, the movie proposes that Filipinos are not prepared to become a modern nation, wracked as they are by superstition, fear, and internal differences. The unshod Christian Filipinos are shown quaking in fear when confronted with a straw likeness of the feared Moro leader, Alipang. In fact, the movie uses this straw man to justify the continued presence of Americans in the archipelago and its remote regions. The movie shows the relatively peaceable Christian Filipinos expressing irrational and cowering fear of the presumably fierce and bellicose Moros. In pathologizing both Philippine nationalism and masculinity, the movie is able to formulate the archipelago's entry into modernity as a psychomedical question.

Science is cast as the cure for Philippine nationalist ills. At the root of the Filipino national dis-ease are both physical (cholera) and psychological (irrational fear) ailments. Thus Canavan rewrites the history of the United States in the Philippines as a scientific, not a military or political, conquest. One scene shows him vaccinating Linda and gives the doctor the opportunity to weave a metaphor about military campaigns and disease for the audience. What disease she is being vaccinated for is not explained: the notion of Westerners requiring some sort of immunization against whatever pathogen lurks in the unclean tropics is assumed. The scene allows Canavan to repudiate violence and military action in the colony and to attribute Philippine nationalism to the eighteenth-century father of immunization, Edward Jenner:

> CANAVAN: A man named Krag invented the repeating rifle. A man named Jenner invented vaccination. If the Philippines ever becomes a nation of its own, who'll get the credit? Krag. But who'll it belong to? Jenner. The whole post is in an uproar about a few Moros when all around them are billions of enemies. Whole regiments of disease. To a few of which you are now more or less immune.

Notably, 1906, the time of the movie's setting, was when the American Krag-Jorgensen rifle became the mainstay of insular police ammunition. Earlier, the Colt .45 revolver was invented under General Pershing specifically for use against Moro insurgents. For the civilian Canavan, the military concern over a "few Moros" is much less a danger to Philippine nationhood than "whole regiments of disease" threatening the mental and physical fitness of Filipinos for self-government. Therefore, for him the eighteenth-century Jenner and the question of immunity, not the Krag or the Colt .45, underwrite the future of the Philippines. Psychology and epidemiology as signs of modernity become the bases of a healthy nationalism.

At the turn of the century, the emergence of various scientific disciplines overlapped with U.S. entry into empire. Louis Pasteur's discovery of germs and disease melded with a distorted view of Charles Darwin's natural selection or survival of the fittest to enframe a world where species, from germs to humans, are in constant war with one another. Medical strategies were used to confine and define the colonial subject in order to fix and legitimize U.S. rule. Historian Reynaldo Ileto has argued that the strategies of the war of pacification continued with great overlap into the war against cholera in the islands.[10] American medical-administrative policies included quarantine, restricted access to food and land controlled by U.S. troops, interruption of local commerce and exchange, and the subordination of local knowledge about the treatment of cholera to Western medical practices.

This scientific turn transforms the U.S. project in the Philippines into a real "democratic experiment" in the scientific sense of the metaphor, which in the narrative has reverted back to its literal referent to obscure the violence that made the "experiment" possible. Germs and Moros are both symptoms of disease afflicting Philippine nationalism. The movie trailer highlights the figure of the Muslim *juramentado,* a suicide attack, and announces: "From the savage-infested jungle, an ominous warning of the tropics. Suddenly the war yell of the maddened Moro [is] raised by the primitive oath to kill." Savagery is an infestation embodied by the erratic behavior of "maddened" Moros. Thus the annihilation of Moros is conflated with the obliteration of germs invading the Philippines as a national body. Rewriting Philippine–American history as a triumph of science over "whole regiments of disease" obscures the real U.S. military violence visited upon Filipinos. In fact, war atrocities were most devastating as the campaign moved south. Before the pacification campaigns against fierce Moro resistance in Mindanao, General Elwell S. Otis ordered that Samar, an island just north of Mindanao in the central Visayas, be razed into a "howling wilderness." The movie's preoccupation with the shift from military to civilian-scientific logic redirects attention from the violent excesses of military occupation, associated with scorched-earth strategies and massive displacement, to the invisible traumas caused by psychological problems and "germs." Canavan's invisible army of germs and the spectacular threat of the Moros both act to obscure from view U.S. violence in the region.

Like disease, the Moros infiltrate the American domestic space in the guise of a friendly Datu, played by Vladimir Sokoloff, who arranges a *juramentado* during a welcome party for the newly arrived women.[11] A native posing as a vendor beheads Major Manning as he buys a silk scarf as a present for his wife, Mabel. This brutal attack violates the tranquillity of the American home. Tragically, the wife is widowed and any chance of happy domesticity is momentarily destroyed. The younger Linda and her romance with the doctor hold the promise for the future of American civilization in this outpost. In retaliation for the homicide, Lieutenant McCool (David Niven) suggests, "if a Moro can go *juramentado,* why can't a white man?" "Going native" to combat barbarism was not acceptable to the officers as this would bring the American to the level of the savage. Instead, Doctor Canavan, man of science, would use psychology against the Moros and for the Filipinos.

In line with his psychological view of Philippine social relations, Canavan renames the local belief system as native psychology. In one scene, Miguel, Canavan's young Moro valet and sidekick, asks Canavan if he kept mice in his tent for pets. Canavan explains to Miguel, whom he has renamed Mike, that the mice are for experiments. Then, Mike/Miguel mistakes Canavan's shiny brass buttons on his uniform as *anting-anting,* or talismans, which the natives wear to ward off evil spirits. Mike astutely points out that native belief in *anting-anting* to ward off bullets and malevolent spirits is similar to American scientific cures for diseases.[12] Both are attempts at solutions to problems with invisible causes—germs for Canavan, evil spirits and bullets for Mike/Miguel. Thus the boy draws an analogy between Western science and native belief. This leads Canavan to see the local problem in a different light. Like his renaming of Mike, the problem for Canavan is simply a question of translation. He must address the Filipinos' fears on their own terms. Now understanding the Filipino psyche, he must use psychology to undermine these fears. Psychology rationalizes the problem of difference. The U.S. military as a civilizing force has failed to take into account the Filipino psyche, which, according to Canavan, is half the battle. Science must take over this civilizing mission for the sake of Filipino development.

The local priest, Father Philippe, offers a further solution to the psychic dilemma. He reveals that the Moro is mortally afraid of being buried in a pigskin, believing that such a bodily desecration sends him straight to hell. Canavan exclaims: "Father Philippe, you've done it! You've isolated the germ for me. The pigskin might be the salvation of Mysang." The football metaphor notwithstanding, the discourse of science in isolating the source of disease provides the cure for Philippine nationalist ills. If Filipinos are "vaccinated against fear," they could overcome their primitive superstitions, defeat the Moros, and finally be psychologically prepared for modern nationhood.

To prepare a vaccination, Canavan captures a Moro and drags him to the fort. He orders the Filipinos to put the "genus *homo Moro juramentado*" in a pigskin. The terror-stricken Moro struggles and screams when he is forced onto the pigskin. Canavan has proven his point to the astonished group of native troops:

> This is your country, and if it's your country you've got to protect it. You never will if you're afraid of men like this. He thinks you're only fit for slaves. And that's because you act like slaves. Fear has made you slaves. Take a look at him. If we were to cut him open, we'd find one heart, one stomach, approximately twenty-five feet of intestine. No more, no less than you have. What makes him a better man? You. Because you're afraid of him.

The Filipino's own fears prevent him from standing up for himself as a man. By laying bare the vulnerable Moro, science delivers the Filipinos from their slave mentality. In the background, the Filipino soldiers are shown visibly realizing their native folly. Linda looks on admiringly, entranced by Canavan's scientific prowess and lesson in manliness. Her father, Captain Hartley, soon halts the humiliating scientific demonstration. Nonetheless, the Filipino soldiers seem to have gotten a much-needed shot in the arm, and begin hitting the straw effigy of the Moro leader, Alipang, which they have used for drilling exercises. The cure is a success, and they begin their journey to violent masculinity.

Scientific knowledge supplants military know-how as the American contribution to Philippine nationalism, thereby foregrounding the modern, civilized face of U.S. benevolent assimilation. With the eventual death of the American officers, the onus of military violence and protection of the American Tropics falls upon the Filipinos themselves. As if providing an equilibrium, on the American side, medical knowledge becomes more crucial when Canavan's "regiment of disease" in the form of cholera attacks the village. To lure Americans into a jungle ambush, the Moros dam the river, cutting off the village water supply and causing cholera. Cleansing and sanitary measures are taken. As the commanding officer slowly goes blind from a blow to the head by a *juramentado*'s bolo, he gives up hope of saving the Philippines and the United States:

> HARTLEY: You know what failure here means? Mysang is not just an isolated village. It's a test. If we can hold out here, our whole job in the Philippines is done. I've failed. I'm gonna send for the army.
> CANAVAN: What good would that do? It'd take days, maybe weeks. Maybe you can wait, but the cholera can't.
> HARTLEY: What can I do? Larsen's gone, McCool's sick. And I'm—
> CANAVAN: You're not blind yet. You're not a failure. You just quit. You're just as choked up with fear as those men of yours were. Afraid of blindness. Afraid of failure. Why don't you stop feeling sorry for yourself and do something? We don't need the army. We need running water.

The future of the Philippines and metonymically the whole American democratic experiment is at stake. For Canavan, Filipinos need less military and more science. U.S. military leadership has become literally blind to the needs of the Filipinos, he chides. Like that of the Filipinos before vaccination, the American fear of failure immobilizes the colonial project and its responsibility to Filipino independence. Canavan the modern (social) scientist needs to take over.

To rid the village of cholera, Canavan orders sanitary burning of infected houses and disinfection of the dead. Linda disobeys her father's orders to go back to Manila so she can help Canavan. While dancing with Canavan at the welcome party, Linda had confessed that she used to dream of becoming a soldier in her father's army, to which Canavan responds with charming alarm, "Oh, no!" Having run away from San Francisco to be with her father in the colony, Linda's gender-inappropriate dreams of becoming a soldier would be tested by the harsh conditions of warfare. During the health emergency, she gives orders in the native language to the confused and panic-stricken villagers, remarkable for someone who had been in the Philippines for only a few weeks. Later, as the last surviving American in the fort, she finds her girlhood dream fulfilled as a "soldier in my father's regiment" in battle with the Moros. While Canavan is in the bush, she remains behind as a loyal helpmate protecting the domestic hearth. However, like her father before her, she takes up arms in the American frontier as guardian of the imperial outpost. In this manner, she breaks out of her proper gender role as love interest to become a commanding officer over brown bodies in the colonial encampment after all the white men fall ill or are killed. Her entry into a leadership role and into "masculinity" is made possible also by the contrast to the villagers' helplessness and feminized hysteria, thus laying out the racial over gender hierarchy as regards Americans in the colonies.

Meanwhile, lone Canavan thwarts the jungle ambush set up by the Moros and successfully blows up the cholera-causing dam. In trite visual allegory, the water surges forth to cleanse the town of disease. The villagers rejoice, but not for long as the Moros have broken through the encampment by catapulting themselves over the fortress walls. Although the American hero has destroyed the dams as an initial step, the Filipinos must do their part to demonstrate their newfound immunity to this savage invasion. When all seemed lost in the encampment, the Filipino officer, Lieutenant Yabo, leading the rest of the native troops, comes in as reinforcement for the fighting Filipinos under Linda's leadership. In riveting hand-to-hand combat, Lieutenant Yabo kills the dreaded leader Alipang, giving the final blow to tyranny with the butt of an American rifle. Moros as internal difference and disease or pathogen have been eliminated from the body politic. The product of American training, the Philippine Scout, secures the well-being of the Philippine nation and proves his manly prowess at the same time with the use of the American prosthesis. Apart from these masculine props, Yabo's accession to violent masculinity is channeled through Linda's intermediate female leadership; that is, in the colonial race/gender hierarchy, white female masculinity precedes brown masculinity.

In this manner, Filipino masculinity only emerges after the establishment of imperial white heterosexual resolution.

American guns clear the jungles of savage infestation, but, more important, American psychology clears the Filipinos' mental jungles of fear and superstition to become proper men. When the remaining Americans—Canavan, Linda, and her blind father—prepare to set sail for Manila, well-dressed Filipinos give the Americans flower garlands. The village priest calls out, "We who are about to live salute you," and reverses his morose plea in the beginning when he begs the Americans to stay. Instead of a death sentence, the prognosis is good, announcing the recovery, if not the rebirth, of the Philippine nation. In good form, Lieutenant Yabo gives the Americans a twenty-one-gun salute as a token of appreciation. The last frame shows Yabo standing rigidly in respectful salute for American audiences to delight in as the new Filipino trained by Americans and to whom they can now bequeath the islands. Looking into the camera at attention in the final shot, Yabo gives the audience a clear view of the American legacy in the Philippines. The specular clarity of his rigid figure looking toward a Philippine future supplants that of blind Captain Hartley and his military rule. By arming the Filipinos with the medical and military knowledge to suppress, through violent means, their own internal difference—their allergens—the Americans have successfully vaccinated the archipelago from a seemingly disabling nationalism.

In another scene of transformation and development, what remains of the Moro disease is young Mike/Miguel, the remainder (reminder) of the Moro threat rendered harmless in the body of a teenager. Dressed in a white suit and donning an American straw hat, the excited adolescent boards the boat with his hero Canavan. Sartorially American and no longer a half-naked Moro, he is shipped off to the United States to put the last touches on his transformation as a brown American. Like Yabo, he too is civilized and domesticated, but without the instruments of warfare that were bequeathed to Yabo. Entry to the U.S. continent renders the boy harmless, as the legacy and instruments of state violence are left with Yabo. Whereas the Boy Scout novels foundered between ethnocide and genocide, the film marks a clear separation between state assimilation for the continental domestic space and state violence for the insular domestic space. With Canavan and Linda as the young couple who can now finally settle into domestic bliss, the adopted Mike/Miguel completes the American family as American rule in the film and in social history comes to a romantic and nostalgic end.

Popular publications were quick to point to Samuel Goldwyn's historical pretenses. *Time* magazine boldly introduced the film as the Philippine *Birth of a Nation,* recalling the controversial and racist 1915 D. W. Griffith film in which African Americans were represented as the domestic racial threat to pure-white American nationhood. In the insular American version, the movie portrays the moment when the Philippine Constabulary finally musters enough courage to squelch the purported roots of Filipino disunity—the savage and un-Christian Moros. A *New York Times* critic pointed to Goldwyn's hubris: "Considering there were national insurrections in the Philippines long before the Spanish-American War, Goldwyn may have let himself in for a bit of mild chaffing for his pretense, in 'The Real Glory,' at the Rivoli, that the history of the Philippines as a nation and a people dates from 1906 when the native constabulary found the courage to crush the Moro brigands led by an apocryphal Mohammedan called Alipang."[13] *Newsweek,* in its review of the movie, acknowledged that as late as 1933 Moros had annihilated a patrol of the Philippine Constabulary, thus giving the lie to the consolidation of U.S.-directed Philippine nationalism depicted by Goldwyn in the movie.[14]

Goldwyn's fantasy was not very original in the making of this movie. The studio took scenes from another lesser-known movie, *Zamboanga,* shot in the southern Philippines a few years earlier, in 1936, starring Fernando Poe, the mestizo father of FPJ (discussed in chapter 3) and Rosa del Rosario, and premiered in San Diego in 1937. The film dialogue was in Tausug, one of the local languages of the southern region. According to Nick Deocampo, who found a long-lost copy of the film in the Library of Congress in 2003, *Zamboanga* was directed by an American mestizo, Eduardo Castro, and produced by Americans Eddie Tait and George Harris under Filippine Films.[15] Made in the style of South Seas films like *Moana,* the film depicts the lush tropical isles as the backdrop for a love story between local Mindanao royalty, Minda (del Rosario) and Danao (Poe). *The Real Glory* three years later would take footage from a scene in which a neighboring Moro village raids another village to take wives. The raid is orchestrated by the cruel neighboring pirate chieftain to stage the kidnapping of the beautiful

Minda. The treacherous Muslim leader had been in cahoots with a sinister American privateer involved in the Chinese coolie trade, a marked contrast to the benevolent U.S. military. However, *The Real Glory* used the raiding scene in the beginning of its narrative, presenting the spliced scene as if it were a newsreel, thereby lending gravity and vérité to the movie version of Philippine–American history. Furthermore, the continental movie then adapts the island love story to focus on the white American couple; Goldwyn's formula did prove successful because *Zamboanga* was never seen again after it premiered, whereas *The Real Glory* had later screenings in Latin America.

Furthermore, on another level of fantastic disavowal, in a curious but revealing act of gestation, Goldwyn dared to set this analogous tropical birth of the Philippine nation in 1906. The movie fails to make mention of the war of pacification. The protracted Philippine-American War that ensued saw the Americans wage pacification campaigns against Filipino combatants, and later Muslim resistance, through 1911 in which atrocities were committed against civilian populations, especially in the Muslim south. In 1906, four years after the official end of what was called the Philippine "insurrection," the Jolo massacre saw U.S. soldiers kill nine hundred Muslim men, women, and children in the southern island. Twenty years later, the movie set in 1906 stages the pullout of the U.S. military at the moment of one of its bloodiest activities in the occupied islands. The movie's choice of national birth date produces a moment of U.S. imperial cultural forgetting and erasure. Goldwyn's fantasy of a scientific, civilian Philippine birth was in fact founded on very real and shockingly violent Filipino deaths.

However, such historical qualifications did not prevent Goldwyn from making his claims for the United States and its protector role in the Pacific. Japan remained a threat to U.S. interests in the Pacific in 1939. The film's making coincides with the moment that "U.S. Chief of Staff Douglas MacArthur is now training [Filipinos] to defend themselves against the Japanese."[16] However, Goldwyn displaces the contemporary Japanese as foreign threat onto the Moros as the domestic challenge to American Philippines in 1906. With this temporal and spatial shift, the 1930s Yellow Peril becomes, in time-traveling fashion, the turn-of-the-century Moro *juramentado*—the Muslim Filipino figure much feared for his religious fervor in his suicidal attacks against Americans and Filipino Christians. U.S. forces were needed to protect the Philippines from falling into the hands of irrational and culturally different savages, so the movie argues. The threat to U.S. order and civilization lay at "the heart of Moro country, the poison spot of the Philippines," implying fatally that Filipinos are not a united nation anyway.

When he was preparing troops to leave the fort, the colonel at Mysang stated: "from now on the little brothers will now stand on their own feet if they can," invoking William Howard Taft's reference to the newly acquired Filipino wards as "little brown brothers." The Americans felt that "sooner or later, [Filipinos] have to take care of themselves. If it works out here, it will work out for the rest of the islands." Thus, Americans would show Filipinos how to be manly men, and deem them fit for self-government. The production of violent masculinity in the service of nationalism is at stake in this democratic experiment. Notably, the film is dedicated to the Philippine Constabulary, the native arm of the U.S. colonial military whom the Americans trained to protect Filipinos from the Moro "brigands." The implication is that the creation of a national police force under the U.S. pattern guaranteed the "birth" of the Philippine nation.

The publicity and production of the movie in 1939 reinscribed racist assumptions about the Filipino national character and its inherent chaotic disunity. When the film was being shot, a *New York Times* columnist called attention to "the Filipino crisis in Hollywood."[17] Looking for Filipino extras, the studio grew exasperated as factions of Filipinos on the West Coast vied for space on the big screen. Replicating the movie's language, the *Times* article described Filipinos in California as full of disunity, factions of "chieftains" vying for the right of accession to American movie careers, if only for less than fifteen minutes of fame. For U.S. Filipinos, to be part of the American melodrama was at stake. Legionnaires, houseboys, elevator boys, and bellhops (most likely the fictional Mike/Miguel's peers), along with asparagus pickers from the Sacramento delta, fought to be in show business against the Philippine Volunteer Defense Corps, the Philippine American Legion Post, and the Houseboys' Protective League. The coverage conflated the disunity of these organizations with the viability of the Philippines as an emergent nation-state. Problems with the Filipinos on the continent spilled into perceptions of Filipinos in the islands. What the movie sought to represent about American-style nationalism was undone by representations of starstruck Filipino workers who had entered the continental United States as labor. The delicacy of Philippine nationalism was the media consensus and assumption.

Goldwyn's publicity-seeking studio played on this assumption, by hinting in the papers that scenes in the movie might endanger Philippine independence, perhaps to give the movie more international import than it truly possessed. Scenes that depicted the pusillanimous Filipinos in the face of Moro assailants, of course, offended the Philippine Commonwealth government. According to *Time,* shots of Filipinos as cowering natives were deleted "at the request of Commonwealth President Manuel Quezon."[18] However, Philippine resident commissioner Joaquin Elizalde, in an effort to lessen diplomatic friction, stated that "The matter is definitely not a diplomatic crisis. I represent the Philippine Government in this country and I can assure you that the government is not excited at all."[19]

The 1934 Tydings-McDuffie Act, rather than the 1924 Johnson Act, was the last of a series of immigration acts to stem the tide of immigration from undesirable spaces such as Eastern Europe and Asia. The movie's fiction relied on a definition of nationalism as guaranteed by violent masculinity, on the one hand, and as sanitarily hermetic and free of difference, on the other. American nationalism was at stake because of its potential to fail to reproduce itself correctly in the colony and thereby be unassimilable to its inhabitants. I have argued here that these two narratives of nationalism were divided at the film's conclusion between continental (U.S.) and insular (Philippines) America. In the film, nation building is intimately tied to creating two versions of masculinity: (1) making proper soldiers of the Filipinos in the islands, and (2) making proper heterosexual couples of the Americans on the continent.

If the continental United States is the exemplar of such pristine nationalism as represented by the heterosexual coupling of Linda and Canavan in sanitary white garb at the end of the movie, then the movie loudly disavows the internal difference the American mainland was already seeking so hard to control, whether through disenfranchisement of populations of color or the historic exclusion of Asian immigrants. The closing of U.S. borders makes possible Goldwyn's claims of nationalism as a closed system, much like immunization. American integrity and unity are achieved only by way of exclusion of foreign bodies and withdrawal from difference. By maintaining citizenship definitions (Asian and Pacific peoples were "ineligible for citizenship") and enacting immigration policies, the United States slowly made itself immune to foreign allergens or racial pathogens that threatened political unity on the continent.

Billed as "a great romantic adventure," *The Real Glory* leaves us with the question: romance for whom? The romance between Gary Cooper and Linda amid the struggle for independence is an allegory for the U.S. romance with its "democratic experiment" in island Southeast Asia. Romance and Philippine liberation seem to go hand in hand. As symbolized by Yabo, the establishment of homosocial fraternal nationalism in the colony paves the way for heterosexual, though sterile, nationalism at home, symbolized by Canavan and Linda. As Captain Hartley, Linda's father, recedes into the background, so does the old America governed by military rules. Linda is to marry a new type of American—the civilian doctor who will protect the world and the American home from pathogens. The story of the coming-of-age of the Philippines is therefore, in effect, the coming-of-age of the United States in the Philippines.

American Nobility and the Redistribution of Morality: Donovan's Reef (1963)

Modern America ruled by science and civic duty would not last long. After the Philippines was excised from U.S. geography proper, the Pacific theater in World War II offered another opportunity to renew the American eroticizing and exoticizing gaze toward the Pacific and Asia. Since Captain Cook's eighteenth-century accounts of the Pacific, the South Seas islands have been depicted as an idyllic paradise where Western sexual taboos could be suspended. However, because of U.S. military exploits after World War II, the Pacific shed some of its licentious image to become an ennobled place. The Pacific entered the American imagination and parlance when Pearl Harbor, Iwo Jima, Midway, and Guadalcanal became war memorials to American battles for democracy and freedom. Movies about the heroism of the soldiers continued past the war with such films as *From Here to Eternity* (1953), *Suicide Battalion* (1958), and *South Pacific* (1958). The heroism of Americans in the islands and atolls seemed to persist in justifying the U.S. claim on the fantasy spaces of the Pacific as part of what I have been calling the American Tropics.

The end of World War II brought radical changes to international, racial, and gender relations. U.S. postwar prosperity brought with it a rising civil rights movement. Europe, under reconstruction, was decentered, and the international scene was in the throes of decolonization. Amid these social transformations, Hollywood sought to memorialize the Pacific in order to construct a vision of the American Tropics as a place of pristine nobility and multicultural harmony, untrammeled by racial or national conflict. In this "elsewhere," Hollywood rediscovered "American" values that seemed to fuse perfectly with the mythically harmonious local cultural systems. The American Tropics was as malleable and welcoming as the locals who peopled it. Unconcerned with specifics, much less history, Hollywood's cinematic swathe blurred distinctions among the cultures and faces of various Asian and Pacific peoples to create an exotic undifferentiated Asian-Pacific mélange as the background to white American histrionics, escapism, and rediscovery.

To take a classic example, Nellie Forbush (Mitzi Gaynor) of *South Pacific* joined the navy as a nurse because she "wanted to meet different kinds of people and find out if I liked them better. I wanted to see what the world was like, outside of Little Rock." She trades her mainland Little Rock for another rock in the middle of the Pacific to find true love and to overcome her racism. Ironically, between the time of the stage musical's opening in 1949 and the film's release in 1958, her Little Rock, Arkansas, was the site of desegregation battles, the most prominent of which was the 1957 integration of Little Rock's Central High School when the National Guard was brought in to protect nine African American high school students. While Nellie was working through her prejudices in the Pacific, the conflict among "different kinds of people" raged back home.

However, Nellie's love object, Émile de Becque (Rossano Brazzi), is actually not a very "different" kind of person, but she did find that she liked him nonetheless after much soul-searching. The Frenchman is "different" only in that he is a sophisticated European and she is poised as an American "cockeyed optimist." In reality, Nellie wrestles not with an interracial relationship but with the ghost of one. She cannot marry him because he has a "dark past" and was once married to a Polynesian woman and has children by her. Her anxiety rests on the belief that Western men consorting with South Seas women are simply practicing immoral concubinage. He explains that the woman was his wife, but her anxiety only proves that Captain Cook's initial accounts continue to have a strong hold on her American imagination. The mixed-race children, adorably East Asian–looking and French-speaking, are dastardly reminders of this dark union. Nellie feels the responsibility of having to accept a nonwhite family and a brown predecessor. As Nellie admits about her inability to accept this interracial past: "It's not as if I could give you a good reason. It's emotional. This is born in me." She even turns to Lieutenant Cabel (John Kerr) to explain in verse why her racism is natural. Among "coconut palms and banyan trees / coral sands and Tonkinese," white Americans wrestle with their emotions in song and try to resolve their inexplicable racism.

Lieutenant Cabel refuses to admit such white racist solidarity. Having been seduced by his "special island," he is involved in an actual interracial relationship with Liat (France Nuyen). Uneasy about the prospect of interracial marriage and the fact that he has "a girl back home," he belts out that racism "happens to you after you're born. You've got to be taught to hate and fear, year to year / Carefully taught, you've got to be taught / To be afraid of people whose eyes are oddly made, and people whose skin is a different shade." Unfortunately for Cabel and Liat, he dies for his country while on a reconnaissance mission with Émile de Becque. However, his antiracist message is not lost on Nellie.

Once Émile de Becque, the exotic Frenchman and outlaw, is transformed into an American hero in the mission with Cabel, Nellie has a change of heart and takes her place as wife of a war hero and mother to miscegenated Polynesian children. *South Pacific* carries an integrationist message that Nellie internalizes in the name of American heroism. In this manner, the Pacific frontier, rather than "Philadelphia, PA and Princeton, NJ," paves the new "American way" where bravery and nobility overcome irrational race prejudice. Hollywood thus relocates in the Pacific the American moral compass to guide race relations for the mainland, using Asian and Pacific bodies to mark racial difference rather than African bodies, which might be more incendiary for a continental audience. In fact, the depiction of the Pacific and Asia as harmonious and peaceable, but racialized, spaces may be read as a way to discipline racialized bodies within U.S. borders. While the white characters learn tolerance in the narrative, most of the brown characters, except for Bloody Mary (Juanita Hall)[20] are depicted as docile and desirable like Liat or as children or as colorful background. As continental Americans have yet to come to their "special island" without racism, Hollywood created "one where they know they would like to be."

Another such production, John Ford's *Donovan's Reef* (1963), overturns the moral distribution between the U.S. mainland and the Pacific island space. *Donovan's Reef* is described by a *Time* magazine reviewer as Ford's worst movie and by the *New York Times* as his most tongue-and-cheek pleasure flick.[21] As with his other films, such as *The Man Who Shot Liberty Valence* (1962), released a year earlier, Ford the populist creates a Manichaean world where the powerless but tough guy representing democracy and civilization triumphs over the powerful and greedy.[22] However, Ford moves the western frontier where such triumph usually reigns off the continent and into the Pacific, following the U.S. military trail. Ford's fantasy envisions the Pacific as the last refuge of morality, decency, and duty.

One of Ford's favorite stars, the mainstay of U.S. cinematic masculinity, John Wayne, inhabits this Pacific frontier in a mythical, French colonial island (which looks like Hawai'i) called Haleakoloha. Unlike other John Wayne movies, the "Duke" does not go up against the Japanese or Native Americans in this light-hearted comedy but against a woman representing the eastern establishment. As "Guns" Donovan, he must tame an uptight Boston heiress, Amelia Dedham (Elizabeth Allen), who visits the island. In an effort to defraud her estranged father of his inheritance, Amelia Dedham goes to Haleakoloha to confirm her father's alleged immoral lifestyle. Years before, Doctor Dedham (Jack Warden) decided not to return home after the war and settled in the island. According to Boston reports, he has been cavorting with a "South Seas woman." While the "Doc" is away on a medical emergency in another island, Guns Donovan and Gilhooley (Lee Marvin), the Doc's best friends, welcome the daughter. They decide it best to hide the fact that the Doc has fathered half-caste children with his now-deceased wife, the island's hereditary princess. Donovan pretends that the three children are his, but in the process of feuding with the uptight Amelia, the latter falls in love with him, the children, and the island.

The comedy rests on the contrast between Amelia's eastern conservatism and the Pacific island's tranquillity, which she upsets. To introduce Amelia, the camera cuts from sunny Haleakoloha to snowy Boston in the boardroom of the Dedham Shipping Company ("est. 1763"). Clad in a dark suit, hat, and horn-rimmed glasses, Amelia presides over family members composed of eccentric senile ladies and gentlemen. The camera pans along the wall lined with the portraits of the dead Dedham men—a stern patriarch, a nineteenth-century ship's captain, a missionary, and, finally, a pirate. The panning mischievously traces the lineage of the Dedham family for the past three hundred years to a sinister privateer. Ending with the Dedham pirate unmasks the eastern establishment's pretense of propriety and moral superiority. At the root of old money and blue blood is rapacious greed.

The family has come together to discuss the redistribution of stocks among themselves, but Amelia's father stands in the way. The lawyer points to a clause that states:

> LAWYER: If anyone can prove that the heir is not of good moral
> character according to Boston standards, he may be deprived
> of his inheritance. Well, now, if this Dr. William Dedham has
> been living on some South Sea island with those native girls . . .
> Well, what I mean is the man has probably behaved in a way
> that wouldn't suit Boston. Now if you could prove that, you
> can cheat him out of stock and his money. Anyone object to me
> using the word *cheat*?

As in many of Ford's films, morality is a central theme, but "Boston standards" are placed into question and so is the concept of the American "blue blood," which has dubious pedigree. Boston as gauge of American morality is bankrupt and senile, as evidenced by the boardroom filled with vacuous-looking old people. Amelia's father has broken the line of white descent to run to the South Seas. There he becomes a naval war hero, and thus rescues the American relationship to the seven seas from its dark privateering past.

When Donovan and Gilhooley receive word of her arrival, they are unsure how Amelia would react to her father's interracial marriage and her interracial siblings, thinking that she might "get the wrong idea," much like Nellie's anxiety about concubinage. The "wrong idea" is the preponderance of bastardy as the vestige of the American military presence across Asia and the Pacific. Donovan

and the father's friends tell the three children of his plans to pass
them off as Donovan's own:

> DONOVAN: So you and the kids must move in with me and pretend
> you're mine.
> LELANI: But, Uncle Guns, I don't understand. First you tell me that
> I have a sister, and then you say that we are to leave our home.
> DONOVAN: Only until your father returns.
> LELANI: But, Uncle Guns, wouldn't it be proper for me and my
> brother and sister to welcome her here in the absence of my
> father? (Pause.) Oh, I understand. It's because I'm not white.
> (Runs off.)

The friends believe that knowledge about the children might tarnish the Doc's morally pure reputation. The preservation of moral
reputation depends on the preservation of white racial purity. The
nonwhite children would seem to evidence adultery because racist
discourse holds that brown women, especially in wartime, are con-
cubines to servicemen, not legal wives. The American establishment,
it seems, is not ready to accept that it might have brown offspring
and brethren at home or in the Pacific as a direct consequence of
its military colonizations. Although the children of the American
Tropics, along with other racialized groups and spaces, are fully cognizant of their (white) American heritage, cultural or genetic, white
Americans, protective of propertied whiteness and whiteness as
property, would prefer to obscure this fact. The children must pass
themselves off as Donovan's children so that the racist American nationalist imaginary might persist in trying to pass itself off as purely
white. And because wealth is at stake in the movie, the illusion of an
unadulterated white lineage would protect American property.

To prove that such hypocrisy is a moral outrage, Ford's liberal
film shows the children, under the strict supervision of the local
priest, to be paragons of charm, goodness, and propriety. Steeped
in French high culture and refinement, the mixed-race children are
equally at home with Mozart and French as they are with baseball
and rock and roll. Protocol guides the oldest child's every move as
the island princess, Lelani. She provides the warm contrast to her
cold, continental American half sister. The movie constructs the
island Dedham family as the legitimate one, possessing all the quali-
ties of true gentility that the senile, greedy Boston line could only
hope to have. However, the symbolic contrast between the tropical

tanned children as the noble future and the pale, old Boston fogeys as the vulgar past is Ford's unambiguous statement about where true American nobility and culture reside—in the insular space.

Because of the war, the mythical island is the refuge for decent, white American men who are noble, not by blood, but by character. Like Émile de Becque's ascent into America's noble ranks despite being a Frenchman with a dark past, nobility is attained through war. While out in the mountains with Guns, Amelia happens upon a plaque commemorating the valiant deeds of a group of Americans—Commander William Dedham, Michael Patrick Donovan, and Thomas Aloysius Gilhooley—presented by the Princess Manulani, the granddaughter of the last hereditary prince of the islands. Donovan fails to tell her that the princess is her father's wife and the mother of the children. Amelia realizes that her father, as a naval commander and doctor, is a war hero, an admirable combination also found in Gary Cooper's caregiving but manly character in *The Real Glory*. The narrative links the island's inherited nobility with the Americans' acquired nobility through military valor. However, the movie has still to legitimate to American audiences this war hero's interracial marriage and possible charges of bigamy and child abandonment.

When Amelia confronts her father about the past, he relates a sad but awesome story of duty and valor:

> DR. DEDHAM: I remember how happy I was when I heard that I was the father of a fine baby girl. That was early in the war. The months went on, the years, the letters got fewer and fewer, then none at all. . . . No one bothered to write. Then we were torpedoed. A lot of men were killed. A few of us managed to get to a raft. Ten days later we made it here. The sensible thing would have been to give ourselves up. The people who hid us fed us, nursed us; well, some even died for us. We owe them something for that. They didn't have a doctor on the island and, God knows, they certainly needed one. I didn't know about your mother until five months after it happened. I was discharged at Pearl Harbor. I just couldn't bring myself to go back to Boston. I wasn't needed there, but I was desperately needed here. I know I failed in my responsibility to you. But there were children here, too. Children that I had brought into the world, who might die if I wasn't around.

Throughout the explanation, the camera keeps Doctor Dedham underneath the royal portrait of his dead wife Manulani, referencing the early shot of Amelia under the Dedham men. His dead wife's noble portrait fuses with his heroic narration. His duty forced him to turn his back on the family he thought had abandoned him, thus reversing the charge altogether. He reveals that he received news of his American wife's death long after the fact. By then, he had taken it upon himself to care for the future of the island—its children. He played midwife to the life of the island, helping with childbirths, building a hospital, and naming it after his Polynesian wife, who herself died in childbirth. Not minding his irresponsibility to her, his own daughter, Amelia continues to admire her father as she spends more time on the island to observe her father's quiet dedication to the island's sick and poor.

As if the children and dutiful father were not enough to convince the audience of the moral uprightness of the island, a charming scene at a Christmas pageant transforms all of Christendom into the mixed Asia-Pacific world. The church choreographed a native adoration of the Magi in which the three kings bearing gifts are transformed into the "King of Polynesia," bringing fruits, the "Emperor of China," carrying a tea set, and finally, the "King of the United States of America," bringing a gramophone. In Ford's fantasy, the United States brings up the rear in this Pacific Christendom. The introduction of a new era with the birth of Christ is reconfigured in the American Tropics with a multicultural twist.

The purity and "nobility" of the islands challenge the piracy and immorality of New England. The values of the missionary past continue in the multicultural island in the person of Doctor Dedham. All families have secrets, but the Boston line is tainted with rum, pirates, and, most likely, slaves. Meanwhile, the Pacific lineage has secrets of its own, but its nobility is by way of native royalty and of American valor. Furthermore, as in *South Pacific,* the use of French colonialism foregrounds the high-culture element's having already displaced native barbarism. American bodies enter this reconstituted space, bringing heroism and the frontier spirit and new life to staid Old World high culture and the fast-disappearing ennobled native culture.

The reinscription of traditional gender roles accompanies the inscription of American lineage in the tropical isles. John Wayne makes a proper woman of the unsexed Amelia Dedham. Amelia is as sterile and cold as Boston upon her arrival. The shrew heiress, representing the eastern establishment, requires taming by Guns Donovan. The icy Boston princess melts when Donovan grabs and kisses her. He then goes offscreen to sing an old navy tune about the southern Philippines: "Oh, the monkeys had no tails in Zamboanga," a racist ditty popular in World War II, originating in the Philippine-American War.[23] While Wayne's masculinity manifests itself in slugfests, rough talk, and seduction, Amelia's femininity lies in the passive specularization of her body. When she challenges Donovan to a swim race, she performs a virtual striptease on the boat by shedding an early-twentieth-century woolen bathing suit to reveal a 1960s bikini, leaving no doubt as to her sexual identity and availability. At the end, holding out for a wedding ring, Donovan makes clear who "wears the pants" in the American home by giving Amelia a good spanking. She is literally disciplined as Donovan puts her over his knees to spank her as a condition of their marriage. She takes her place not as John Wayne's unsexed competitor, as at the beginning of the movie, but as wife to him and sister to the Polynesian children. Thus she regains her femininity as a subordinate partner in the new American royal family.

The Pacific as fantasy projection reproduces not only American values but also progeny. It is indeed a paradise, but one that is decidedly gendered male. Both *South Pacific* and *Donovan's Reef* contend with cultural and sexual miscegenation to offer integrationist resolutions. However, the integration comes at the price of disciplining white females and the obliteration of brown women. As the male's homosocial military image is shed to make way for his entrance into heterosexual domesticity, the violence in that militarism seems to be redirected to the female figures, all in a tongue-in-cheek manner, of course. In both movies, the white American woman eases into the role of stepmother to the Americanized (though still technically French) mixed-race children. Amelia's stay in the paradise finds her place in the Pacific American royal family, but first she is made to forgive her father for abandoning her and her mother to run off to the South Seas. Then her femininity is enforced by Guns Donovan's violent hypermasculinity. Soon thereafter, all her Boston iciness melts away, and she is a woman once more.

In *South Pacific,* Nellie trades her military duds for a husband, a French outlaw transformed into an all-American hero. Now that he is an American, she finds it in her heart to forgive him his dark past, his Polynesian wife. That she finds his dead Polynesian wife more disturbing than the fact that he had killed a man (in the name of liberty and equality, of course) in France leaves the viewer wondering whether she has truly overcome her racism or if her patriotism prevailed over her racism, thus evincing a collusion between nationalism and racism.

However, in both cases the Polynesian woman is dead. In *Donovan's Reef,* the Polynesian mother remains an absence, memorialized in a royal portrait, and remembered in names of places: a hospital, a monument, and a grave. The women leave as a legacy to their American successors well-mannered and adorable "half-caste" children. The American settlers not only recognize their royal brown children, but they have also provided them with proper white mother figures under whose care and tutelage they will remain as America's favored bastards.

Ford creates a multiethnic and gender-conservative haven on an island where the diversity of ethnic groups (Polynesian, Chinese, Japanese, French, and white Americans) and religions (Native, Buddhist, Christian, Jewish) coexist in unbelievable, heartwarming harmony.[24] For Ford, the island space becomes a funhouse mix of characters, times, and cultures without the problems of history, here represented by the eastern establishment. Amelia mocks her Boston aunts' pretense to propriety when they claim that "the Dedhams, Amelia, have never traded in rum. We refer to it as West Indies goods." Thus American identity looks not to its dark Caribbean-Atlantic past but to its noble South Pacific present. The latter is perceived not to have the former's taint of slave trade and piracy, despite the historical coolie trade and the devastation of native populations by disease. The Pacific is a purifying filter that retreats from the hypocrisy of ruling classes and reinvests American identity with a more noble line.

The film closes with Amelia and the children marching to the new Donovan home to relocate and redomesticate multicultural America. Amelia grew up without a father, and the children without a mother. Amelia regains her father, thus correcting the American lineage, and the children gain a mother figure in the older half sister. The traditional family is reestablished to correct the gender imbalance in which only men were raising the children, thus shedding yet again the military past and violence that made possible that domestic space. Amelia inherits a royal family, thus ennobling the capital-rich American line. American "nobility" is reconstituted in the tropics, having disavowed its dark, tumultuous Atlantic past to turn to a sunnier Pacific future.

Elvis and the Changing Tides of Capital: Blue Hawaii (1961)

Not all Hollywood movies needed a heroic excuse for white Americans to settle in the Pacific isles or even to make up protagonists to look like native half-castes. Films like *Blue Hawaii* (1961) simply claimed nativity by opening with white Americans "coming home" to the islands. While the United States was memorializing the war in the Pacific in the 1950s, it was also busy preparing to incorporate, transform, and domesticate Hawai'i as a full-fledged state. In 1962, a *New York Times* reviewer described *Blue Hawaii* as an "amiable, synthetic and blandly uneventful movie [that] is probably the brightest poster ever for Honolulu and pineapples—in about that order."[25] A postmilitary star vehicle to reenergize young Elvis's waning career with his trademark "rhythmical spasms" and provocative gyrations, *Blue Hawaii* is indeed a shameless advertisement for Hawai'i's booming tourism industry and its fast-fading pineapple agribusiness.

At the time of the movie's release, Hawai'i, the newest state in the Union, was in the midst of a radical economic transformation. The once-dominant plantation economy was being displaced by a tourism and land-development economy—part of the wave of development strategies sweeping the Asia-Pacific region after World War II. Dole Pineapple, the islands' major agribusiness corporation, suffered great losses because it was unable to compete with Libby and Del Monte, which used cheaper nonunion labor in Southeast Asia and Central America starting in the 1950s. Tourism and land-development strategies were a response to the downturn in the plantation economy and the multinationalization of the Big Five corporations (Alexander & Baldwin, Castle & Cooke, Amfac, C. Brewer & Company, Theo. H. Davies & Company). Hawai'i's first year of statehood in 1959 witnessed a 41 percent increase in tourism and 22 percent the year after.[26]

Two years before the movie's release, thirty-eight-year-old governor William Quinn was spearheading the way toward this new vision of a radically reconstructed Hawai'i, aggressively building infrastructure for tourism development and actively selling Hawai'i to tropics-starved continentals. Whereas the old Hawai'i depended on the plantation economy, the new Hawai'i would introduce a service economy with tourism at the forefront of its economic development. Elvis's film about a young man's Rock-a-Hula rebellion and coming-of-age frames and spotlights the analogous economic spasms and the capitalist gyrations of a Hawai'i and an Asia-Pacific in drastic transition from an old economic mode to a new one.

Blue Hawaii, directed by Norman Taurog, stars the Marvel of Memphis, Elvis Presley, as Chad Gates, a rebellious but beguiling young man determined to find his own way outside the confines of his plantation-manager class background. This lighthearted movie opens with Chad Gates returning "home" to Hawai'i after a two-year army peacetime stint in Europe.[27] As with the other two films, the movie brings up the memory of war only to retreat from it. The plot reveals that Chad's family moved to Hawai'i from Atlanta, Georgia, some fifteen years earlier, while he was still a little boy. Chad's father (Roland Winters) is the vice president of the Great Southern Hawaiian Fruit Company and his mother (Angela Lansbury) is a flighty Southern belle. To correct misapprehensions that her son had it easy in Europe, she insists to others that Chad has just "returned home from the war." Chad's girlfriend, Maile (Joan Blackman), is a part-French and part-Hawaiian girl of royal lineage. Rejecting the dictates of his domineering parents, Chad starts his own tourism business and, through various mishaps, misadventures, and musical numbers, manages to become an independent, self-made man.

When Chad "comes home," he avoids going directly to his parents and instead chooses to sing, dance, surf, and generally laze about with his local beachboy buddies for the first twenty minutes of the movie. While picnicking with his girlfriend, he announces his decision to grow up. Atop a hill with the camera framing a panoramic view of Honolulu, Chad comes to the realization that he's "got to get started and take a hold of things" away from his family. He finds support from Maile, who insists, reiterating a tenet of American individualism, that "we are not our families, Chad; we're what we make of ourselves." Chad's disaffiliation from his family is accompanied by a disingenuous disavowal of his class privilege. He refuses the "red carpet" treatment and prefers to "fly solo." This flight would be made possible by a more magical and more profitable carpet: tourism. Sounding like a spokesman straight out of a commercial for the Hawaiian tourism board,

Chad announces, "Hawai'i has a big future," and proclaims that he will be part of and riding the crest of this future's wave.

Chad rides this new economic wave to crash upon Hawai'i's shores and wash away with it the last remaining vestiges of the old order and regime of the plantation economy. The first scenes of the film waste no time in establishing his claim to be a virtual native "who knows every inch of the islands." Indeed, as part of his scheme to make it on his own in Hawai'i's brave new world of commercial tourism, he plans to share his intimate knowledge of the islands to cash-rich tourists coming in droves every day in search of their own tropical fantasies and pleasures. With no actual war or military exploit to invoke in making a man of himself, he now begins to rely on a new form of capital accumulation in which he refigures himself as exotic spectacle. A self-directed man charting a course for himself and "his" islands, Chad meets his (and America's) manifest destiny in this enterprising vision of the blue Pacific as a western frontier for a new ethic of self-development.

However, old Hawai'i insists on rearing its plantation-minded head in the guise of Chad's Southern belle of a mother. During his homecoming party at the Gateses' residence, Mrs. Sara Lee Gates first meets Maile Duval, whom she has earlier sneeringly referred to as "that native girl." The exchange between the two women is awkward as each is obviously vying for Chad's loyalty and affection. Luckily, Chad's rock-and-roll band decides to save Maile from further embarrassment by breaking into a rendition of "Rock-a-Hula Baby." Chad (Elvis, the Southerner) ends the scene with a traditional hula bow after throwing the *uli'uli,* a Hawaiian percussive instrument, at his mother.

His musical outburst plays a significant role in the scene by disrupting the uncomfortable and racialized confrontation between Mrs. Gates and her potential "native" successor, Maile Duval. Mrs. Sara Lee Gates, as caricature, symbolically revives the ghost of the plantation Old South and its racial hierarchies and conflicts. For the pretentious Southern aristocrat, to be potentially replaced by a native, mixed-race "Mrs. Gates," is unthinkable. Likewise, the time-warped Mrs. Gates fears her Chadwick's degeneration in this misalliance. She is still under the delusion that Chad had just returned from "the war," presumably the continuing U.S. Civil War, to take his rightful place with his own class in the

Southern Hawaiian Fruit Company. In a previous scene, she commands Chad:

> You're goin' to associate yourself with the finer elements on the
> island. And you're goin' to have a responsible position with the Great
> Southern Hawaiian Fruit plantation. And you're goin' to marry a girl
> of your own class and be a gentleman like your Daddy.

Here, of course, the word *class* is a code for unbreachable race and
color hierarchies. The maintenance of *haole* or white privilege in
the plantation economy depended precisely on a clear binary color
or racial division.

Here and in this context, it bears remembering that the
nonwhite—predominantly Asian, Pacific Islander, and mixed-race
(hapa)—population of Hawai'i produced great anxiety for conservative continentals when the territory entered the Union in 1959.
The National Origins Act limiting the entry of Asians and Pacific
Islanders into the continent was still in place. With this new political
status, Hawai'i would be free to engage in wanton commercial and
political intercourse with other states. Thus, when the Hawaiian
territory moved from being foreign territory to domestic space, the
nonwhite and mixed-race peopling of Hawai'i raised long-standing
concerns, anxieties simmering since Hawaiian annexation in 1898,
over the continued preservation of Anglo-American racial integrity
within the national and continental body politic.

Maile's impending infiltration of the domestic hearth, her candidacy for admission into the Gates household, allows the movie—in
the form of Mrs. Gates's lingering racist sentiments—to conjure
up and then represss these larger concerns or anxieties. Although
Mrs. Gates, as a vestigial reminder of the plantation establishment,
is depicted as a foolish and old-fashioned anomaly, her apprehension about her son's keeping company with beachboys and a local
girl (however Caucasian-looking) underscores the very real color,
caste, and class system that wove together Hawai'i's disparate
populations. Notably, during World War II, close to one-quarter of
Hawai'i's population lived on plantations.[28] The mother, as the reminder of Hawai'i's and the United States' plantation pasts, raised
contemporary fears of racial miscegenation and the nation's potentially unmanageable distension, whose possibility was alluded to
and subsequently closed in the Philippine case in *The Real Glory*.

Although Hollywood had earlier portrayed interracial romance with white actors in brownface, the industry did not allow actors of different races to kiss on-screen until 1954, seven years before *Blue Hawaii*'s release. Furthermore, although the state-by-state lifting of the ban on interracial marriage began in 1948, it took until 1967, with the Supreme Court case of *Loving v. Virginia*, to be completed. Against this historical backdrop of obdurate racial divisions, the film's Rock-a-Hula interruption covers over the racial tension between the North American continent and Hawaiʻi, as differently raced spaces, and between old Hawaiʻi and new Hawaiʻi as different types of social and racial relations. Thus, Mrs. Gates as plantation manager and Maile Duval as a mixed-race Native inescapably represent these two worlds. Although Chad acts as the mediator for the reconciliation of these two national figures, we know that he fails miserably, and can only break into song in lieu of any real resolution.

Athwart the contemporaneous context of the postwar (World War II and the Korean War) United States, Mrs. Gates's imaginary war in the movie failed to make Chad a man, but his entry into the new economy presents the possibility that he just might become one. Mrs. Gates, as the racialist gatekeeper, conjures up a plantation past and image—a past and image that could work to retard not only Chad's growth but also Hawaiʻi's profit-making potential as a tourist destination. Tourists, after all, want to see paradise, not a plantation torn by racial strife. To open the economic gates to Hawaiʻi's future, the narrative has to secure the heterosexual union between Chad and Maile (as well as that between the viewer and Hawaiʻi) in order to ensure Chad's ascent into a displaced and "rebordered" adulthood. The new tourist economy clearly is expected to reconfigure Hawaiʻi and its multiethnic inhabitants as desirably exotic and paradisiacal. Tourism marketing continues today to orchestrate the celebration of Hawaiʻi's ethnic plurality, purportedly free of conflict between locals and tourists, immigrants and native-born, settlers and indigenous, and among the various ethnic groups.

Contributing to this orientalist and primitivist discourse, *Blue Hawaii* eroticizes and feminizes Maile and Hawaiʻi as exotic spectacles. The movie figures Maile as the *proper* object of desire for Chad, the new man. Like the half-caste Dedham children in *Donovan's Reef,* Maile's own propriety hinges upon her presumably cultured French and royal Hawaiian background. Focusing on racial difference, as Mrs. Gates does in her plantation imaginary, does not serve Chad's purposes or that of the new economic formation. Under the new set of sociality, the "difference" between Maile's family and Chad's needs to be displaced as a matter of class, a seemingly more malleable category, and not of race. In an earlier scene, we witness Maile's aristocratic home setting with her regal grandmother and her French father. This contrasts significantly with Chad's overly anxious, class-conscious, and racially obsessed kin. Maile Duval's family offers to the continental agribusiness bourgeoisie not only a noble native heritage but also a cultured French one. The cultured French and royal Hawaiian lineage makes for a fine marriage with continental capital eager to be rid of its vulgarity and crassness. Chad, in a sense, "marries up." The Hawaiian wedding is not between different races, but between different classes, a more generally palatable miscegenation in American bourgeois democracy. Maile as part-French and part-native of royal blood is the perfect match for "the King" playing an enterprising self-made continental American man.

At the end of the film, Chad makes his final "declaration of independence," as he describes his business negotiation. Meeting with his father and the partner of the Southern Hawaiian Fruit Company, he proposes to contract his tourist services to the company, thus enabling him to work for himself and, indirectly, for his father. Chad's declaration marshals a new era of "capitalism." He guarantees the viability of the new economy with the cooperation of the old plantation managers. He collaborates with mainland capital, the old plantation managers. Interestingly, he chooses not to cast his venture as a subdivision of Southern Hawaiian Fruit Company, but as an independent contractor with monopoly rights to Southern Hawaiian's travel division. He thus refuses the old vertical integration strategy and opts for a more decentralized model of production of Hawai'i. According to his plan, he will sell Hawai'i vacations as a bonus to the father's salesmen on the continent, who in turn will sell more pineapples and more "Hawai'i" to mainland consumers. His strategy foreshadows "the flexible accumulation strategy" set in motion by the Big Five in the 1960s. The multinationalization of the Big Five effectively tethered the Hawaiian economy not only to the continent but also to the global economy.[29]

In the scene where he presents his economic plan, he proposes a partnership with Maile in the business as a way of proposing marriage. Maile thinks about the name of the travel agency:

MAILE: Gates and Duvall.

CHAD: Too long. Keep it simple. Gates of Hawaii.

MAILE: Don't I get any billing?

CHAD: Sure, Gates is plural. In case you didn't recognize it, that's a proposal. That has a better ring.

MAILE: You're sure?

CHAD: I suppose I could be romantic about it, but you'd say yes, anyway.

MAILE: You're pretty sure of yourself.

CHAD: Isn't it about time?

In one fell swoop, Chad incorporates Maile into his business scheme, appropriates her homeland, and then erases her name altogether from the "billing," with "Gates of Hawaii." The integrationist solution of partnership effectively erases Maile's heritage and name through marriage with no protest or even demurral on her part. This type of "pluralism" represented by "Gates of Hawaii" pretends to represent Maile's interests while effectively subordinating her as a silent and laboring partner. While depending on Maile's participation and local identity, the unequal partnership usurps not only island space but also origins, by claiming nativity with the name, Gates *of* Hawaii.

Hawai'i's tragic history of incorporation through the U.S. Marines–backed overthrow of Queen Lili'uokalani in 1893 and the kingdom's annexation as a U.S. territory in 1898, and into the sacred Union in 1959, not only suppressed and continues to suppress the archipelago's own nationalist desires or aspirations, but also preserved its difference from the continent as commodified spectacle. The juridical contract legally contained and domesticated Hawai'i within a particular placement within the Union, much like Maile's business marriage to Chad and integration into the Gates household. The movie's liberal message through the blurring of the color lines through the marriage contract refuses to acknowledge the complication of capital–labor relations in regard to race and nation. The integrationist narrative effectively consolidates U.S. power not by maintaining race and caste as the old plantation economy had done but by strategically co-opting them through marriage into the local elite. This consolidation, reinscription, and eventual denial of racial, gender, and economic dominance is accomplished with the supposedly cheerful consent of the subordinated figure. Chad's masculinity is secured by Maile's femininity and by the transfer of the gaze from him as a sexually available tour guide to Hawaiʻi as commodified spectacle. This also exorcises the possibility of Chad's remaining in a feminized position as tour guide for Hawaiʻi's service economy.[30] His ascent into manhood naturalizes the right of the white settler to control the tropical space as productive land and productive spectacle—all with local consent.

The seductive swivels and songs of the King in this movie, and the story of generational conflict and manly development gloss over (and make glossy) Hawaiʻi's actual traumatic transformation as a new economic battlefield or space for aggressive U.S. reinvestments. Lulled into imperial complacency by Elvis serenading us in his red convertible in *Blue Hawaii* and the seeming lack of resistance of Hawaiians to the intrusion of nonlaboring white American bodies in the tropics, the movie envisions a spatially and temporally distinct but economically incorporated Hawaiʻi, a modernized rock-and-roll Hawaiʻi now revisited as an American Tropics of tourist maps and handbooks. Chad is the mediating figure not only between the generations but also between plantation capitalism and corporate capitalism, between the continent and Hawaiʻi, between local musical tradition and invasive, modernizing rock and roll. In the end, it is Elvis as spectacle and his tropicalized rock-and-roll numbers that distract us from the underlying conflict between local and settler, between browns and whites, between Hawaiʻi and encroaching mainland capital. As the offspring of one economic formation, the dancing and surfing King becomes the harbinger of a new economy and a new set of social relations. While Sara Lee Gates tries unsuccessfully to maintain the gates and borders between native and white, between old and new, Rock-a-Hula opens the floodgates to a hybrid, culturally and racially miscegenated social formation in the service of a tourist economy for the reintegrated Pacific territory. Fiscal and libidinal economies intersect as we watch Chad develop his manhood and self through a realignment of U.S. imperialist desires, both economic and phantasmal.

The spectacle of the colonized space of Hawaiʻi provides a vehicle for America's heartthrob to seduce us with his singing and dancing prowess. But the spectacle also brings us a new way to envision ourselves in Technicolor. This consumable Hawaiʻi, as a new terrain for our viewing and visiting pleasure, is designed and offered to comfort us. By naturalizing the power of foreign bodies to appropriate and command the islands, the film secures Hawaiʻi not only economically to the United States but also libidinally to American fantasy production. The new economy (tourist, global) produces a new set of social relations (integrationist), which in turn produces a new man (Chad), a new kind of American, and therefore a renewed manifest destiny for his "generation."

The reproduction of Americanism in the tropics shifts from ideological dissemination in *The Real Glory* to insemination of white American blood into native lineage in *Blue Hawaii* and *Donovan's Reef* as solutions to integration by turning away from the stormy race relations going on in the mainland and toward a fantasy projection. The reproduction of American values and of progeny in the movies gave continental U.S. audiences the islands as part of their imagined home. The movies considered in this chapter offered imaginary new homelands, fraught with risks of racial miscegenation and unmanageability, it is true, but rife with opportunities for an enterprising kind of development and resettlement. The three fantastic visions of manifest destiny encoded in these films manage to clothe and shod native bodies for civilization even as white American bodies are given license to disrobe and appropriate Asian and Pacific spaces and identities. "Going native," however, did not mean descent into savagery. In fact, going native in the mid-century Pacific, for these films, becomes a way to revitalize American values and ingenuity. These created an image of Americans as rightful heirs and managers of Asian and Pacific island spaces abandoned by the European powers.

While the United States wrestled with the civil rights movement, the cold war, and the space age, these movie productions created a discourse of island Southeast Asia and of Hawai'i as multicultural havens where difference is managed through the infantilization or obliteration of local peoples. Through their subordination, the land is cleared and redeveloped so that the spirit of American heroism and moral values can be rediscovered time and again and assume their new incarnations. The filmic discovery of the American Tropics, a new New World exploration unabashedly undertaken in a series of Pacific and South Seas cinematic productions and made against the backdrop of significant global developments, constitutes a retreat not just from domestic racial and international conflict but from history itself.[31]

II
Toward an American
Postcolonial Syntax

5. Reconstituting American Subjects

Proximate Masculinities

> That's what they made me feel like—a mouse. Not like a smart house mouse but like a white house pet that ain't got no business in the middle of cat country but don't know better 'cause he grew up thinking he was a cat—which wasn't far from wrong 'cause he'd end up as part of the inside of some cat.
>
> —Piri Thomas, *Down These Mean Streets*

> "And I won't have a Filipino in my house, when my daughter is around," said one of the women.
>
> "Is it true that they are sex-crazy?" the man next to her asked. "I understand that they go crazy when they see a white woman."
>
> —Carlos Bulosan, *America Is in the Heart*

These instances of dislocation and disappearance in Piri Thomas's *Down These Mean Streets* (1967) and Carlos Bulosan's *America Is in the Heart* (1946) stage their respective problem of locating a narrative voice in the process of textual self-creation in the autobiography. While explaining the condition of being a dark-skinned Puerto Rican in the suburbs, Thomas faces not simply the discomfort of *not* belonging as a "house pet" but the possibility of disappearing entirely without knowing it. In the second instance, Allos, the protagonist, while working in his brother's employer's house, has disappeared entirely from the narrative for he is neither the subject of the conversation nor present in the text. Both protagonists have places *in* the house, but neither is *of* the house, and effectively disappears. The problem of narrating personal histories for the Filipino Bulosan and the Puerto Rican Thomas as heritors of the American Tropics, is not simply about their vexed relationship to the U.S. racial, national, and class order. More profoundly, the place allotted to them in this dislocation is also the site of their potential disappearance as speaking subjects.

The prose-poem prologue that introduces *Down These Mean Streets* and its protagonist opens with a young Piri shouting from the rooftop: "Halo, World—this is Piri . . . I wanna tell ya I'm here—you bunch of mother-jumpers—I'm here, and I want recognition, whatever that mudder-fuckin word means."[1] The difficulty for Piri lies neither in introducing himself before his narrative of development even begins nor in the "World" refusing recognition. Rather, Piri cannot articulate the manner of recognition necessary to bring himself into the world. His vexed demand articulates instead this recognition's inarticulability. This difficulty to write with integrity from a suspended subjectivity thwarts his *bildung* narrative. Lisa Sánchez-González argues that *Mean Streets*' "protagonist's apparent 'identity crisis' is a hermeneutical crisis that forces the narrator to establish his authority as an integral speaking subject in the autobiographical novel."[2] For Arnaldo Cruz-Malavé, the crux of Piri "dangling between two sticks" rests on the difficulty of meaning making in the zone of abjection.[3] In Piri's case, he is recognized as "black" *or* "Porty-Ree-can" but never both, for each designation fails him in its mutually exclusive binarism. To be a dark-skinned Puerto Rican in the United States forces him either to be "black" in order to become American but alienated from his lighter-skinned family members or to be "not-black" as a Puerto Rican but continue to be outside "America." The binarisms themselves—black/white and Puerto Rican/U.S. American—form another binarism between white racism and his friend Brew's black nationalism. Neither satisfies Piri as proper "recognition." His desire to belong is clear, but the terms themselves are inarticulable given the choices he is allowed in these identifications.

This self-narrating irreconcilability is also evident in the writing style of Bulosan's fictionalized autobiography with its fragmented and uneven narrative voice. Bulosan unrelentingly recounts a series of horrors and tragedies about his life in the continental United States: "I would like to tell the story of our life in America. It's a great wrong that a man should be hungry and illiterate and miserable in America."⁴ The prose recounting the violence continually visited upon Filipino bodies is distinct from the interior monologue, often cast in italics, when the narrator waxes poetic about his faith in "America." The separation of body and heart, the disintegration of one and the triumph of the other in melodramatic fashion is replayed throughout the text. Elaine Kim attributes this unevenness to the haste with which Bulosan wrote the work to meet his publisher's deadline, whereas Marilyn Alquizola proposes that Bulosan used the overdramatic assimilationist but naive voice to obscure the stinging critique of U.S. racism found in the rest of the book in order to reflect the antifascist, pro-American democracy demands of the post–World War II era.⁵ However, I would argue that this typographic and stylistic disconnect marks a condition of writing about occupying a disavowed subjectivity that can only be grasped by relating the different locutionary positions the narrative voices take.

Earlier chapters have demonstrated how the ambiguous national status of those inhabiting unincorporated territories creates not so much moving borders as enfolded ones. Given the enfolded borders that the protagonists' subjectivities occupy, one might read both Allos's and Piri's demands as desire for the recognition of an anomalous subject outside of facile oppositional or assimilationist stances. Toward the end of his novel, Bulosan reaffirms melodramatically his commitment to "America" as an emancipatory project:

> It came to me that no man—no one at all—could destroy my faith in America again. It was something that had grown out of my defeats and successes, something shaped by my struggles for a place in this vast land. . . . [I]t was something that grew out of the sacrifices and loneliness of my friends, of my brothers in America and my family in the Philippines—something that grew out of our desire to know America, and to become part of her great tradition, and to contribute something toward her final fulfillment. (326)

To make possible the logical leaps in this paragraph, several "Americas" are invoked—as place, as ideal, as faith, and as project. In this conflation of Americas, the very cause of the narrator's abjection is also what gives meaning to the pain. Once the object of the U.S. colonial project, the speaker seizes upon his projection of America to resignify and expand the American project itself. The former colonized subject makes it his own so that he plays a part, becomes a subject rather than an object, in its fulfillment as a historical process. When he discovers that he is able to "understand this vast land through our own [Filipino] experiences, I was sure now that we were at last beginning to play our own role in the turbulent drama of history" (312–13). The conflation makes possible the shift from an America as physical place *(topos)* to one that is a figure *(tropos)* for locating unfulfilled desire.

Allos's "struggles for a place," much like Piri's poetic insistence on being "here," is the pre-text of Bulosan narrative, its unwritten driving force, but one that does not surrender the materiality ("place" and "here") of its demand. For Bulosan, this faith that grows out of the desire "to know" and "to become part" of an America that had continually refused to give Filipinos recognition in the first half of the twentieth century governs the novel's writing as an event. The incorporation of the protagonist's collective tragedy and loss both "here" and in the Philippines makes them visible as part of the American literary tradition, in particular a radical literary tradition, as the narrator asserts while incapacitated in a hospital. Such literary incorporation serves to challenge the Filipino national unincorporation as well as the authority of this very tradition to dictate the network of meaning assigned to "America."

To "know America," for Bulosan, then, is to produce a relationship with the sign of America—a relationship prompted by an impossible desire given the disenfranchisement of the Filipino as colonial and racialized labor. Yet the kind of "knowing" Bulosan and Thomas privilege in this effort "to become part" of America, and the "turbulent drama of history" for both texts, depend on the violent destruction of the protagonist's corporeal and psychic integrity. Both narratives display for the reader the process of disintegration of the brown male body, and offer in its place, for Bulosan, a disembodied voice that makes claims upon a fantastical "America," and, for Thomas, the rhythms of his evocative prose poetry.

I want to draw attention to violence as repetition in these two texts. These violent episodes take place in obscured and neglected spaces of the American landscape. Both novels use nonnormative sexualities to stage this violence. In both works, violence and violation committed by and visited upon the protagonists precipitate their coming into a narrative voice culminating in the fictionalized autobiography as a moment of integration, as Lisa Sánchez-

González has suggested of Thomas's autobiography. Marta Sánchez has argued that Thomas's protagonist uses the abjection of women as "the guarantor of his ethnic and masculine difference."[6] Sánchez's argument signals how the racialized male's authority to speak depends on violation of women and transsexuals, eliding the two figures. Yet, this does not fully explain how in these narratives male bodies as sites of conflict *appear* whole in that moment only to disintegrate into spectacular violence in the next. This momentary authority signals at the very least an equally precarious relationship to masculinity and language.

Given this condition, both writers question the ease with which they could belong in order to narrate themselves smoothly into U.S. national time and space. The idea of "America" as a set of sexual, moral, and racial prohibitions precedes the entrance into their *bildung*. The law does not simply introduce prohibition, but also, as Priscilla Wald has signaled, legislates subjectivities into existence. Although desire for national belonging is clearly at stake in both novels, the performance of integrity and autonomy could very well be the very undoing of the same integrity because of these prohibitions. Thus this subjectivity produced by a series of violations creates multiple and often contradictory desires that may be read in any number of ways as a sign of irony at best, masochism at worst, or just plain bad judgment. The fragmented subject seems to desire the very delimitation—the desire to have integrity—that subjugates him. Both autobiographies struggle with a desire to belong to some sort of community, including, but not limited to, a national one.

Disintegrating Masculinities; Disintegrating Subjects

The white American's anxieties over race, empire, class, sexuality, and masculinity converge in the library scene quoted in the epigraph at the beginning of the chapter. The novel's young protagonist, Allos, overhears the conversation in the library of his brother Macario's employer, a movie director. Given entry into the American household, the educated native is feminized and elevated above his other racialized counterparts. However, this elevation and entry transforms his racial difference into a sexual threat as he crosses cultural and national borders. Bulosan dramatizes the anxiety in a highly condensed form to note the various positions "the Filipino" takes in the white American imaginary: docile native, American civilizing project, servile labor, racial other, and sexual threat. The transformation of docile object into unruly body occurs in the native's absence. With each line, the Filipino body looms larger and larger, becoming the screen on which the movie director and his friends project their anxieties. The Filipino figure morphs from a geographically separate abstraction to a dangerous bodily presence at home. The scene renders palpable the anxiety of the American empire and the threat the Filipino presents to the national, imperial, sexual, and racial order.

The dubious praise heaped upon the absent servant as colonial subject and cheap labor is later qualified by the discomfort caused by his suspect place in the U.S. racial hierarchy. Although the U.S.-educated native may not know his place in the American home, neither does the American imperial citizen in this anxiety of displacement. The anonymous white man observes that "niggers" and "Chinamen" "know their places," but Filipinos, by implication, do not. The invocation of this racial hierarchy informed by a history of slavery, segregation, and exclusion places Filipinos somewhere between the brutish and oversexed black man and the docile, asexual Asiatic.[7] The racialization of "the Filipino" oscillates between the two figures and takes on either or both characteristics, depending on the fears and desires of the speaker. "The Filipino" also offers a twist to the hierarchy in that he is an American colonial subject produced to replicate the American within U.S. territory. Unlike other Asian racializations, he was not excluded in terms of immigration. Culturally, he was not associated with cultures of antiquity like Japanese, Chinese, and Asian Indians. Rather, as Leti Volpp recounts in the testimony of the president of the University of California before the House Committee on Immigration and Naturalization in 1930, the Filipino was characterized "as having an enormous sexual appetite, as more savage, as more primitive, as 'one jump from the jungle.'"[8]

The racial other thought to be an ocean away is actually located closer to home in the uncanny presence of the educated Filipino butler, "who went to college here," producing an anxious dislocation in the imperial subject. The Filipino, imbued with the desires and demands of the American civilizing project, physically embodies American cultural training and proof of the culture's disseminable modularity. The success of U.S. education is now a threat as this portable American culture is contained in a racialized body now inhabiting a U.S. household. This anxiety reveals the blurring of both parties' geographic and cultural borders. The respective "places" of colonizer and colonized are not as securely defined as continental fantasy figures. The conversation displaces this cultural anxiety onto a sexual and racial map paved by racist narratives about brutish blacks and docile Asiatics more familiar to the white speakers. With this worry in mind, we can read the man's anxiety about the Filipino not knowing his place as a more radical threat to the American imperial subject himself. Unlike his other racialized counterparts in the American racial hierarchy, the Filipino's unplacedness is perhaps not so much owing to his ignorance of his station as to the peculiar place allotted to him. He is forced to inhabit sameness as an American colonial subject but is not recognized by the employer as such. Refusing contiguity with a racialized subject, the employer places him onto the domestic U.S. race–class hierarchy to inhabit difference.

The autobiographical text performs this anxious convergence for the reader through three narrative levels. First, the actual conversation discloses the anxieties of the white employers and guests about the Filipino's threatening unplacedness in the American domestic space. Second, the conversation takes place in the absence of the object of discussion, Macario, while disavowing young Allos's presence. Bulosan conceals Allos from the reader but strategically places him within direct hearing range, beside but not with the imperial speaker. Third, Bulosan recounts this overheard conversation about another person in a work that is subtitled "a personal history." Bulosan absents himself and his protagonist as a speaker in this scene. The meaning of the scene circulates and alters along the three narrative locations: the imperial speaker, the colonial object whose presence is disavowed, and the postcolonial reteller. Only by concealing the eavesdropping narrator in the story can Bulosan retell, reenact, and reveal this anxiety to readers. As readers, we bear witness both to the disappearance of the Filipino body and to the context of such abjection. In this way, the autobiography is able to narrate a disavowed presence.

These three narrative locations are at play throughout the novel. Retelling what he overhears in implied heterodiegesis frames the Filipino American "autobiography." Bulosan explains his project: "I would like to tell the story of our life in America . . . for all the world to see" (261). In contrast to the white employer's framing of the Filipino as a sign of sameness and difference, Bulosan's retelling of multiple anecdotal experiences and unofficial stories shapes the work into a composite sum greater than its parts.[9] As Oscar Campomanes and Todd Gernes point out, Bulosan distills the tragic story of the collective "Pinoy" to make sense and connect the individual isolation each feels in colonial dislocation and class displacement. This composite autobiography linking stories as a group event displaces the individual speaking subject and the purported object of the literary work and circulates events in a continual process of signification; that is, each articulation in the triangle—imperial speaker, absent colonized object, and reteller—refigures the Filipino American, his experience, his body, and his "place" in the text: the household, the nation, and the world. Beginning with the proper speaking subject of an autobiography, Bulosan orchestrates a series of disappearing acts to articulate a grammar of displacement, disavowal, and dislocation that reflects the Filipino experience in the United States. Thus, unlike the employer's facile placement of the Filipino as a servile object or sexual threat, Bulosan's "Filipino" is a composite narrative that interweaves thematics of race, imperialism, nation, class, sexuality, and masculinity. Each articulation produces the Filipino American body to shape the location and locution of "America."

This continual circulation refuses an easy production of meaning extractable from displaying the colonized male body. This imperial display begins before the scene when the protagonist Allos is a child in the Philippines. His first encounter with a white American is motivated by economic need and the American's voyeuristic desires. The small plots of land that his family cultivated are sold one by one to pay for his brother Macario's education in Manila, the administrative capital of the U.S.-controlled Philippines. The onset of industry and modernization accelerated by U.S. colonialism in the early twentieth century gradually destroyed the peasant economy and pushed out small farms in his small town. To earn money for his impoverished family, Allos goes from his family's little farming town of Binalonan in the northern Philippines to Baguio, a small, modernized mountain town that became the U.S. settlers' resort getaway, favored for its cooler temperatures. The pubescent Allos goes to the public market and performs odd jobs for the traders, surviving on the food his temporary employers offer or throw away:

> My clothes began to wear out. I was sick from eating what the traders discarded. One day an American lady tourist asked me to un-

dress before her camera, and gave me ten centavos. I had found a simple way to make a living. Whenever I saw a white person in the market with a camera, I made myself conspicuously ugly, hoping to earn ten centavos. But what interested the tourists most were the naked Igorot women and their children. . . . They seemed to take particular delight in photographing young Igorot girls with large breasts and robust mountain men whose genitals were nearly exposed, their G-strings bulging large and alive. (67)

Allos offers his young body to the white female voyeur. After the first request to disrobe before the camera, Allos decides to put his body on display for commercial exchange. Knowing the part he has to play in front of white visitors, he hopes for misrecognition by the addition of dirt to make him more *like* the Igorot "natives," a neighboring northern hill-tribe people. He performs the native for the colonizer's racial and erotic gaze. Campomanes and Gernes read this passage as "a visual metaphor for the definition of Pinoys as racial and historical others, exploitable and stripped of the habiliments of dignity."[10] Kandice Chuh reads the same passage as Bulosan's articulation of U.S. colonization as a sexualized project. She argues that the protagonist cannot fully disarticulate his distinction from the real native body as figured by the Igorots under the powerful imperial and touristic gaze.[11] At the time of the novel's writing, this steady gaze characterized the colonial relationship wherein the islands were displayed to the world as the American democratic experiment in Asia.

However, I would argue that Bulosan's description of the Igorots through the eyes of the white tourist offers the same sensual and erotic vision of the imperial gaze, as the writer highlights "large breasts" and "G-Strings bulging large and alive." His words replay the same ethno-pornography that the tourist camera produces. Although the protagonist cannot disarticulate himself from the imperial gaze, as Chuh suggests, he is also aware that he is in fact not the true object of desire; that is, he is not the "real" native. Although he cannot distance himself from the native in the tourists' eyes, neither can he stop himself from participating in the imperial articulation of the native who is deemed more authentic than he is. Earlier in the novel, when he first encountered non-Christian Filipinos, he would romanticize Igorots: "I had never before seen the Igorots. They were peaceful people, bent only on hard work, and religious in their own way" (40). He falls in line with Christian and U.S. perceptions of Muslim Filipinos: "The sudden contact of Moros with Christianity and with American ideals was actually the liberation of their potentialities as a people and the discovery of the natural wealth of their land" (47). Although he cannot disarticulate himself from the native body under the imperial gaze, neither can he disarticulate fully from imperial desires. He captures scenes and sensibilities as an observer imbricated within the relations of imperial subject and colonized object—a relation in which he is not quite the participant, but of which he is a product. His subjectivity is articulated alongside and parallel to the imperial looker but is never quite the looker's desired object either.

Allos's subsequent entry into the white American home to help his brother Macario as a servant creates the opportunity to replay this scene with a difference. After the aforementioned library scene in which the now sixteen-year-old Allos overhears the discussion by the movie director and his friends, he accidentally sees the lady of the house unclothed while serving her breakfast in the bedroom:

> She came back to the room without clothes, the red hair on her body gleaming with the tiny drops of water. It was the first time I had seen the onionlike whiteness of a white woman's body. I stared at her, naturally, but looked away as fast as I could when she turned in my direction. She had caught a glimpse of my ecstasy in the tall mirror, where she was nakedly admiring herself.
>
> "What are you staring at?" she said.
>
> "Your body, madam," I said, and immediately regretted it.
>
> "Get out!" She pushed me into the hall and slammed the door.
>
> (141)

The momentary expression of prohibited desire by the native servant across class and race lines is perceived by the mistress as impertinent and is immediately rejected. For this scene to follow the one that discusses predatory Filipino male sexuality is almost comical. The impudent stare of the young brown man intrudes upon the white woman "admiring herself" in the mirror. "Naturally," the narrator offers in weak defense, he stares, and the reader too gets a glimpse of the "tiny drops of water" gleaming on the lady's red hair—not on her head, one notes, but on her body. This "natural" stare focused on the painstaking and erotic details of the woman's "onionlike whiteness" is an uninvited one, to be sure, and he follows this intrusion by brazenly admitting to looking at her body. This gaze is as erotic and sensual as the imperial gaze on the Igorots' near-naked bodies. Unlike Allos's self-exposing performance for the lady tourist, the white woman here is completely disrobed, and not by request. In fact, Allos must steal a glimpse precisely because he knows it to be illicit. Indeed, he extracts pleasure, "my ecstasy," from the stolen glance, as the mirror reveals to the reader and to the mistress.

His voyeurism is, of course, contained by the social interdiction established by U.S. racial and class hierarchies. In the tropical resort, the American lady tourist desires to capture the erotic savagery of Filipinos, a desire sanctioned by imperial power. For the colonized body to look back, as Allos does to the movie director's wife, is unseemly and disruptive. The American lady tourist feels that she can without impunity gaze at the native's genitals and can request that the native disrobe for her. Like the mistress and her mirror, what the lady tourist captures in her camera is a narcissistic expression of her superiority, desire, and, most important, the privilege to *have* such a desire. Both white women's means of looking—mirror and camera—share this trait of imperial narcissism, a privilege to *have* desire not available to the colonized object, whose subjectivity, desire, and body are evacuated in the same process of imperial self-reflection.

The native under pain of violence or death cannot share in the imperial subject's desiring gaze. Allos's desirous but perhaps accidental glance also foreshadows the discipline he would later face as an adult for such transgressions. In order to take part in it, he must be concealed. He can only *steal* those glances and watch the looker watching herself. In the library scene quoted at the beginning of this chapter, Allos catches other people's conversation; in this boudoir scene, he surreptitiously catches a glance. In both spaces of the house, one more public than the other, he is concealed by virtue of his servant status, but this special status as part of the household yet wholly apart enables him to appropriate and collect narratives and images in which he is not meant to be a participant. The liminal space allotted to the Filipino in the household and in America at large prescribes a disembodied narrative voice emanating from a concealed body—a necessity dictated by laws, social hierarchy, and survival within this network of proscriptions. The consequence of evincing the physical signs of *having* desire, whether in the form of an impudent stare or a brazen response, ranges from ejection to harsh discipline, or worse, the violent destruction of that body. This is the critical difference between the imperial gaze and that which Allos imposes upon his mistress.

The outlet for Filipino male sexuality is limited by the prohibition of interracial liaisons with white women in many states, the paucity of Filipina women, and the abject state of the racially segregated Filipino homosocial spaces. The novel reveals the limited movement of the Filipino as it traces Allos's movement as a migrant worker from the Alaska canneries to Seattle and down along the West Coast. In search of a home, Allos travels in boxcars and finds himself in the harsh, lawless conditions of Chinatown ghettos and in the underworld of gambling houses, dance halls, prostitutes, and gangsters. This is the place the continent set aside for Filipinos, he discovers: a lonely bachelor society contained vigilantly in marginalized and criminalized spaces. He is invisible precisely because visibility comes at a dangerous price of brutal erasure. Outside these homosocial spaces, encounters with white men would result in violence.

As an adult, Allos encounters his first ambush by a white racist mob on a Filipino harvester campsite as a labor organizer:

> Then I saw them pouring the tar on José's body. One of them lit a match and burned the delicate hair between his legs.
> "Jesus, he's a well-hung son of a bitch!"
> "Yeah!"
> "No wonder those whores stick to them!"
> Why were these men so brutal and sadistic? A tooth fell out of my mouth, and blood trickled down my shirt. The man called Lester grabbed my testicles with his left hand and smashed them with his right fist. (208)

This castration scene unflinchingly portrays the violent consequences of crossing racial, class, sexual, and political borders beyond those set by the white, propertied social order. The implicit castration in burning José's pubic hair and the explicit one in crushing Allos's genitals assert white male control over the brown men's sexual and political agency but also evince the projection of white sexual and political anxieties. For the white racist, the disciplining of the brown body through violence keeps the Filipino in his racial and political place in the western United States, much the way the terror of lynching of the black body did in the U.S. South. The spectacular excess of a ravaged Filipino body, with genitals disfigured, serves as a cautionary tale for all other Filipinos and dissenting class voices to remain silent and unseen. The disavowal of the Filipino male body in the discursive realm in the earlier library scene takes on brutal materiality of negation in this castration scene. This socially sanctioned white lawlessness is a manifestation of the systemic dispensability of the Filipino and racialized others.

The hidden homosocial spaces the Filipino inhabits, in boxcars, bars, gambling houses, pool halls, and racial ghettos, are also sites in which the homosocial contract breaks down to make homosexual encounters possible. Bulosan uses these breakdowns as distinct from but part of the abject condition of Filipino masculinity in America. Allos would run away from these encounters, including one involving his own brother, Amado, who has been in the employ of a rich, white lawyer. Having been separated for months from his brother, Allos decides to find him to ask for help in caring for their ailing brother Macario. He finds Amado

> in a luxurious room. But it was actually rented by the lawyer; they always lived together when they were traveling.
>
> "In fact," Amado said proudly, "we sometimes sleep with the same woman."
>
> I did not believe him. How was it that successful lawyer would share a room with his servant?
>
> But Amado disappointed me: he was in a position to help Macario go to college but would not.
>
> I knew that he deserted us—even his speech was rapidly becoming Americanized. (201)

Amado, caught in an awkward situation, denies the implication that he is in a homosexual relationship by asserting the lawyer's and his heterosexual activities. The claim to "sometimes sleep with the same woman" becomes a way to shore up his heterosexuality and forestall the homosexual possibility with dispensable women. Allos curtly reacts in disbelief. Why, indeed, would a rich man share a room with a servant, much less share sexual partners? The living arrangement, Allos assumes, must be an economic and sexual one. However, Bulosan fails to pursue this question further, interrupting himself to introduce Amado's betrayal of his filial responsibility. The question remains hanging. I do not suggest that Amado is necessarily homosexual. More important, the narrative strongly implies a sexual and economic arrangement that is, at the very least, a nonnormative heterosexuality that crosses class and race, possibly involves more than two parties (if Amado is to be believed), and violates the opprobrium against homosexual relations. As Amado interrupts himself, so does Bulosan in exploring this aspect of Filipino American male sexuality in bachelor and impoverished communities. The narration instead shifts attention from the implied prohibited desire to another scene of abjection.

Immediately after taking leave of Amado, Allos recounts how he meets again a white woman named Helen, a known labor union infiltrator, who subsequently strikes up a romantic relationship with his brother Macario. Allos confronts her about her antiunion activities. When she denounces labor unions and calls Filipinos savages, Allos "struck her in the face with a telephone receiver. Something fell from her mouth. Now let her speak arrogantly about the Filipinos" (ibid.). Later, Allos tells of "unconfirmed reports that she had been beaten to death in Visalia" (203). The violent reintroduction of Helen after Allos leaves his brother Amado in the hotel room is unsettlingly sudden. Amado's betrayal of his family while possibly trading sexual services for economic gain is juxtaposed to Helen's comeuppance for infiltrating unions and Filipino organizations. The two acts of betrayal, both involving sex as a means to an impure end, undermine the integrity of the Filipino community in Bulosan's narrative. The proximate narration of the events seems to transfer the violence intended for Amado onto Helen. Allos attributes Amado's desertion to his assimilation as characterized by his speech "rapidly becoming Americanized," and he strikes Helen in the mouth as if the act might also render Amado's Americanized speech and ultimate betrayal inaudible. The encounter with his brother's nonnormative sexuality is recast into the disciplining of a white woman who had betrayed the Filipino labor movement.

Intense violence follows other fleeting episodes of attempted homosexual seduction. Having just arrived in Los Angeles from the Philippines, Allos finds himself wandering in a plaza "among drunks and jobless men" (127). While trying to sleep on a bench,

a young Mexican whose voice sounded like a girl's sat beside me. He put his hand on my knee and started telling me about a place where he could get something to eat. I was cold and hungry, but I was afraid of him. I walked away from him, watching the church across the street. (128)

Hunger, discomfort, and unwanted homosexual attention were Allos's introduction to the United States. When Allos walks away, his attention remains on both the Mexican and the "church across the street," as if the latter signaled a prohibition of the same-sex advance. A few paragraphs later, he walks aimlessly to the Filipino district, where he witnesses police detectives entering a Filipino poolroom and "[shooting] a little Filipino in the back." The bystanders "stopped for a moment, agitated, then resumed playing, their faces coloring with fear and revolt" as if resigned to such cruel but commonplace intrusions by white authorities. Soon, "the detectives called an ambulance, dumped the dead Filipino into the street, and left when an interne [sic] and his assistant arrived" (129). The ignoble display of the Filipino body cast off unceremoniously in the street is narrated alongside the unwelcome same-sex advance, and obscures the "fear and revolt" Allos expressed.

Later, under even more wretched circumstances in his jobless wandering, Allos finds himself among other homeless men:

I was terrified in this building of lost men. I tried to exclude myself from them, to shut myself off into a room of my own, away from their obscenities. . . . I heard an old man creeping slowly toward me. I thought he was looking for his place on the floor, but when he reached me and started caressing my legs, I sprang to my feet and flung him away. (155)

After escaping this unwelcome disruption, Allos wanders to another town. While eating at a restaurant, two policemen grab him and take him to a jailhouse simply for being Filipino: "I watched him stand boldly before me, his strong legs spread wide apart, his hands on his hips, showing me his menacing gun" (156). The emasculated perspective with Allos crouched between "strong legs" and "menacing gun" foreshadows the protagonist's degradation at the hands of the white authorities who brutalize him before driving him out of town. The undignified and frightful perspective seems to indicate a scene of possible sexual violation, but the humiliation subsequently narrated does not continue in this vein. Yet, Allos's lacerated hands and face and battered body, bloodied from the policemen's abuse, suggest that the intrusive and sadistic violations inflicted upon the Filipino by social and legal structures, as represented by the nameless white male policemen, produce similar emasculating effects.

Whereas the imperial speakers in the library scene mentioned above cast the racial threat the Filipino poses as sexual, the protagonist in these instances recasts the homosexual threat into racial violence outside of the scene of offense. The minor violence implied in his rejection of the seductions by the Mexican and the old, homeless man is displaced and intensified into more vicious scenes a few paragraphs later when the Filipino is shot, degraded, violated, and treated as a dispensable body. The series of misfortunes and violence within which these episodes are embedded portray the brutal conditions of racism that slowly tears away at the protagonist's body and interior: "were these Filipinos revolting against American society in this debased form? Was there no hope for them? . . . I almost died within myself. I died many deaths in these surroundings, where man was indistinguishable from beast. . . . Yet I knew our decadence was imposed by a society alien to our character and inclination, alien to our heritage and history" (133–35).

The ability for the male protagonist to occupy masculinity in America is a tactical problem.[12] Bulosan's male characters suffer the continual threat of violence and violation at the hands of white authorities. Antimiscegenation laws and sanctioned white lawlessness in lynching bounded the lives of Filipinos in the United States who lived in largely bachelor communities in the early decades of the twentieth century. Kandice Chuh identifies the nonsexual, almost idealized relations the protagonist Allos has with a series of white women as an alternative to the violent white masculinity that founds U.S. citizenship and that regulated the borders of race and (hetero)sexuality. The legal and extralegal prohibitions alongside the threat of violence force Allos to "imagine otherwise" in sexual relations. Bulosan indeed critiques nonnormative heterosexuality in racial terms, as Chuh points out. However, although Allos's masculinity, strictly speaking, may not follow normative heterosexuality as set by the law and extralegal discipline, I would suggest that heteronormative desire in gendered terms remains nonetheless. The imperial relationship, while expanding possibilities of sexual pairings, also offers another discursive avenue to revisit a resilient heteronormative desire. Whereas Chuh reads Allos's apotheosizing of the series of white women as a desire to make interracial union unremarkable, the protagonist's imagination and Bulosan's prose seem to posit encounters with the white female figures as being continually remarkable in the unattainable search for "America" in the heart. Both "white woman" and "America" come to figure as unfulfilled desire. Overcoming "the violent version of masculinity to allow for realization of the feminine ideal" (39), Allos refuses normative heterosexuality relations marked by white male violence and same-race relations within the confines of legal prohibitions. This disruptive masculinity, as Chuh terms this gesture, while offering an alternative to the violent normative heterosexuality that founds U.S. citizenship, also signals gendered heteronormativity refigured within colonial relations. More disturbingly, the narrative transfers violence onto homoerotic sites.

Of Machos and Maricones in Down These Mean Streets

Such performance and representation of masculinity is not so much disruptive as it is "proximate," to borrow from Arnaldo Cruz-Malavé. The discomfortingly close proximity between homosexual encounters and racial violence is notable in Bulosan's text. First, these instances are away from public view in boxcars or ghettos, marginal spaces that are not seen as part of the American landscape, but these are also sites of transient community with other Filipinos. Cruz-Malavé's reading of continental Puerto Rican literature as a process of meaning making in the zone of abjection sheds light on this politically difficult terrain in Bulosan's text. *Down These Means Streets* offers three instances of the protagonist's bodily presence as focal points in attempts to feel communal belonging. These moments signal questions about race, sexuality, and belonging in these novels.

Cruz-Malavé observes that in Nuyorican and Puerto Rican diaspora literature

> homosexual practices occupy that zone of reversibility where the Nuyorican author's struggle to emerge from the spectral state of abjection to which he is subjected by internal colonialism, by the "System," "the Man" always inevitably falls back on contested territory. One could say, the "queen" or the "faggot" are not so much the antithesis of the "macho" characters and poetic personae as that "proximate other" in whose likeness the latter see reflected the catastrophic condition of their own manhood.[13]

For Bulosan, the sexual encounter and the conditions of the sexual encounter are what discomfort the protagonist. Commercial sex with prostitutes reflects a debasement of Filipino men as much as fleeting same-sex passes in a boxcar.

In Cruz-Malavé's reading of Thomas, "macho" resides next to "faggot" to make the homosocial contract not so much broken as null and void in the first place. In a titillating chapter titled "If You Ain't Got Heart, You Ain't Got Nada," Piri and "his boys" go to a neighbor's apartment to score some marijuana by offering themselves for sex as "trade":

> I opened my eye a little. I saw a hand, and between its fingers was a stick of pot. I didn't look at the face. I just plucked the stick from the fingers. I heard the feminine voice saying, "You gonna like these pot. Eet's good stuff."
>
>   I felt its size. It was king-sized, a bomber. I put it to my lips and began to hiss my reserve way. (58)

This performance of fellatio with the "king-sized" joint precedes and then parallels Piri receiving oral sex from one of the *maricones*. Thus the intertwined nature of the faggot and the macho in this initiation blurs the line of receiver and giver of oral ministrations. They both disappear later in a cloud of smoke and in internal monologue. This high is interrupted and followed by screams from the next room where his buddy is beating one of the faggots. His initiation into sexuality via homosexual acts with "his boys" was constitutive of his "becoming hombre." One could read this vernacular Spanglish and the novel not so much as a development narrative in cultural translation; rather, "becoming hombre" is a refusal of equivalence with "becoming a man" to give the concept a different complexion. Thus, this American *bildung* signals "the precariousness of a norm that must be constituted compulsively in the expulsion, not of the radically different, but of the proximate other," the homosexual, Cruz-Malavé argues (134). Proximate masculinity does not disavow practices considered aberrant but posits them alongside other possibilities of masculinity, thereby problematizing the very category of masculinity.

In a subsequent chapter, "Learning Some New ABCs," Piri has a sexual encounter with a white woman in the subway that provides him a lesson in race and sexual subjectivity. Pushed against each other in the crowded train, Piri and the white female stranger start a flirtation with each other:

> We said nothing else. The great weight came back and pushed us close together again. I felt her breasts hard against me and my joint bursting its wide vein between her thighs. Pressed together, we let ourselves roll in that hung-up closeness, I looked at her. Her eyes were closed. I made my hips dance a slow grind, and I let my hand think for itself and bite those liberal breasts. The whole mother-fuckin' world was forgotten in the swingin' scene of stress and strain, grind and grain on a subway train.
>
> We were roaring into the 14th Street station. Hurry, hurry, our bodies urged, and swoom-ooo-mmm—girl and me and train got to the station at the same time. (136–37)

The joint between Piri's lips in the *maricones'* apartment now becomes his genitals, "my joint bursting its wide vein between her thighs." His buildup and orgasm here take the form of the whimsical rhyme and rhythm of his prose—"stress and strain, grind and grain on a subway train"—as the trill of his r's in the next paragraph rolls into a pleasurable "swoom-ooo-mmm." His poetics in this scene parallel that of his stream-of-consciousness monologue in the scene with the *maricones*. Yet, whereas the latter ends in violence against one of the faggots, the train scene is given another ending by Piri himself.

In a masturbatory scene following the train scene, Piri tries to relive the moment while he showers off at home. He takes the woman's place to imagine how she might have gossiped about the encounter to her friends: "*I felt myself tremble all over and that black boy pushing all his weight of his thing into me . . .*" (141; emphasis in original). In his imaginary replay of the event, he is refigured as a black man: "I'd thought 'black cock,' and that meant the broad was prob'ly sayin' 'nigger' instead of 'Porty Rican'" (ibid.). In his "mental production of 'Beauty and Black's Best,'" he becomes the stereotype of the oversexed, overendowed black man who cannot control his sexual urges. Race retroactively disrupts the lived poetic ecstasy on the train, and the heterosexual fantasy fails. Because he knows Porty Rican does not register in the public sphere, he finds himself strangely unable to control his own masturbatory fantasies and projection of his masculine prowess. His person and sexuality are reduced to a hypermasculine "joint," and without having realized it, he had already disappeared on the train: "inside me, I felt hot and real stink about this funny world and all the funny people in it" (ibid.). His self-production becomes his undoing, as his moment of pleasure is thrust so readily into a racial narrative not of his own making. He has learned the ABCs of racialized desire but there is no grammar to make sense of the simultaneous pleasure and repulsion that he felt after his fantasy and to articulate his own desires outside of race.

Piri realizes later that the rift race introduced into his sexual fantasy was already present in his family relations. The very public heterosexual encounter shifts to a more intimate scene with his brother in a painfully moving chapter titled "Brothers under the Skin" immediately after the train and shower scene. Piri's dark skin distinguishes him from his mother and brothers, James and José, who all have Anglo features and can "pass" for white. He has always felt less favored by his Poppa from whom he inherited his darker features. While in the bath, Piri observes his brother José urinating:

> I looked at my brother. Even his peter's white, I thought, just like James's. Only ones got black peters is Poppa and me, and Poppa acts like his is white, too. (142)

The color line runs through the family but a different system of color rules there; the meaning given to it by the U.S. racial schema disrupts familial belonging. Outside the home, at school, and in the streets, the three locations that comprise the novel's chapter schema, skin color determines his social relations. White peers, neighbors, and employers—"paddy people"—slight and reject him repeatedly. Racial difference and Puerto Rican family contiguity as ways to read color become irreconcilable sign systems: "Man, do you know what it is to sit across a dinner table looking at your brothers who look exactly like paddy people?" (124).

In the intimacy of the bathroom, the brothers discuss their color difference, with José denying the existence of "black blood" in the family and attributing the dark skin to *indio* blood, while Piri insists that the skin is evidence of an African heritage. While José and Piri were trying to articulate their brotherhood despite their color difference, wrestling with the issues escalates into physical violence out of frustration. Once Piri learns that the brothers had to "make excuses" for him in school, his anger could not be contained:

I made my self creep up a long sinking shit-hole agony and threw myself at José. The bathroom door flew open and me, naked and wet with angry sweat, and José, his mouth bleedin', crashed out of the bathroom and rolled into the living room. . . . I found myself on top of José. In the blurred confusion I saw his white, blood-smeared face and I heard myself screaming. . . . I saw an unknown face spitting blood at me. I hated it. I wanted to stay on top of this unknown what-was-it and beat him and beat him and beat him, and beat beat beat beat beat—and feel skin smash under me and—and—and—. (146)

The passage focuses not on the agents of violence but on its effects. José ceases to be a brother and becomes a "thing to be hit" (142), the "it" that separates Piri from his family. Piri describes the violence as an out-of-body experience as he hears himself screaming despite the excessive materiality of naked bodies sweating and bleeding. All familiarity and emotion disappears, replaced by an "unknown face" and "unknown what-was-it." The narrative voice ceases to offer diegesis and in its place is the rhythm of violence: "beat beat beat" and "and—and—and—." Prose fails to finish the sentence and gives way to the sounds of anguish. Bursting from the locus of shit and piss to the semipublic space, what was inarticulable owing to the incommensurability of understanding "blood" as metaphoric difference (race) and metonymic contiguity (family) becomes inarticulate violence. The rupture with his brother originates from his own abjection as he is unable to locate himself in either linguistic axis.

Poppa breaks up the fight and the exterior manifestation of the problem ceases to exist and is reabsorbed once again into Piri's body:

My fists were tired and my knuckles hurt at this Cain and Abel scene. As the hurting began to leave me, I slowly became a part of my naked body. I felt weak with inside pain. I wondered why. (147)

The internal pain returns as if the violence was simply the temporary second-order effect of the problem. Whatever Piri was hitting turns back to himself, and Piri's wet nakedness is testament to his abject state. Most important, this intimate pain is not locatable in the *maricón* fellating him, nor the white woman in the subway, but in his interior being torn apart. "I was trying to blame somebody for something that was hurting me," Piri cries, but he cannot name the "something." Whereas the previous poetic interludes evoked hazy ecstasy, the rhythmic cry after the fight signals the real breaking point for Piri. After the episode, he decides to leave his family and his neighborhood to travel down South with his African American friend, Brew, to explore what blackness means for him and to root himself in the U.S. nation-state.

Cruz-Malavé argues that "the novel confirms [Piri's] inability to acquire territory of his own through the performance of 'machismo,' racial affiliation, or a national romance" (144). With the train and bathroom scene in mind, I would suggest that the nature of masculinity, race, and nation in relation to the Puerto Rican positions the protagonist so precariously that he would be unable to hold on to any territory for more than a moment. Emerging from enfolded borders of race and nation, Piri's claim to a proper "turf" as a moment of triumph undoes him at the same time.

Thomas's novel, like Bulosan's autobiography, is a collection of these moments of disintegration in the *maricones*' apartment, in a sexual encounter on the train, or in his family's living room. In all these sites, as he had feared, he disappears without even knowing it, leaving him with a "hot and real stink" inside. He himself embodies what Cruz-Malavé describes as the "proximate other." Up to the moment when the reader sees Piri back on the rooftop after his release from prison at the novel's end, his narrative authority is founded upon the cumulation of these disappearing acts. In his reading of Puerto Rican Rafael Sánchez's poetry, Cruz-Malavé asserts:

> [T]he constitution of the community is not merely an act of expulsion but of cannibalism—literally an absorption. For the community here has been wise enough not to waste any of the abject's body parts, not even his dying breath, in order to found, in close counterpoint, its identity." (136)

Cruz-Malavé signals the absorption of the very parts expelled from a proper national community to create an alternative community that nonetheless remains attached to the dominant one. This proximity is what makes it a dangerous and tenuous place that Thomas signals—not knowing whether one has in fact disappeared. In Bulosan's collective text through Allos the witness, no story is wasted, including Amado's, retrieved once again to form this identity from abjection and reintegrated into a makeshift text.

Down These Mean Streets's integration of "proximate" masculinities in the act of expulsion-cannibalism renders a more productive reading of the difficult terrain in Bulosan's text. Bulosan figures moments of homosexuality and displaced homophobic violence as part and parcel of the disintegration of Filipino masculinity. The abjection of the colonized male body and male homosexuality shares the same origins of the Filipino's degradation and emasculation in American society. By the book's conclusion, the estranged brothers, Amado and Allos, reconcile after Allos publishes his first book of poetry. Amado leaves Allos a letter before going away to become a transporter in the U.S. Navy at the onset of World War II:

> I'm not as well read as you are, but I know that a little volume of poetry can give something to the world. I could have striven to raise myself as you have done, but I came upon a crowd of men that destroyed all those possibilities. However, I'm glad that I remained what I am, because it will give you a chance to see your own brother in darkness; in fact it will give you another chance to look at yourself when you were like me. My lostness in America will give you reason to work harder for your ideals, because they are my ideals too.
>
> I did not have a rich and easy life, but it was my own. I would like to live it over again. . . . You are my brother. (322–23)

Amado, the "brother in darkness," offers himself as the foil for the protagonist's own coming into public light with his newly published book of poetry. Amado does not apologize for his choices; on the contrary, his life becomes an offering to Allos to be integrated into his brother's literary corpus. Unlike the lady's mirror, the mirror Amado offers to Allos as his reflection is the abject origins of himself: "it will give you another chance to look at yourself when you were like me." Not only does the letter affirm their family ties, it also affirms their ties to each other through frustrated desires and shared abjection. As Allos promised in the beginning: "Yes, I will be a writer and make all of you live again in my words" (57). Allos's literary body made public becomes the repository for their shared abjection, to make possible the reintegration of masculinity, family, and community, beyond a bodily integration.

What type of erotic relations does Bulosan allow his protagonist? Cross-racial heterosexuality is represented as a nonsexual heterosociality. Unable to cross the color line except as servant and object, Allos is left with the homosocial and homosexual possibility. Both are figured as debased relations in the novel. The series of frustrated and impossible desires leads him to intellectualism: "This faith kept me from completely succumbing to the degradation into which many of my countrymen had fallen. It finally paved my way out of our small, harsh life, painfully but cleanly, into a world of strange intellectual adventures and self-fulfillment" (109). In this way, his masculine physical body disappears to achieve "self-fulfillment." The intellectual escape is the escape from the limits of his tubercular and physically abused body.

In the course of his work with the American labor movement, Allos learns that he has tuberculosis that will incapacitate him for years and require an operation to remove the ribs on one side of his body. His prolonged stay at the hospital affords him time to read, write, and later publish his poetry. Allos takes refuge in his books. His body is left in disintegrated tatters, only to be redeemed in the radical literary tradition. As the world contracts to apartments, hospital beds, and campgrounds precisely because of racial segregation, the body recedes and the immateriality of books and ideas moves to the fore: "these then were the writers who acted as my intellectual guides through the swamp of culture based on property" (266). Unable to work physically, he "catches up" on his reading. He reads and begins to identify with the Euro-American literary tradition. However, as a literary tradition he depends on a series of predominantly Euro-American writers to shore up a masculinity his body could not bear.[14]

What impoverishment, racism, and violence did to his fantasy of "America," a radical literary culture would render meaningful:

> There was something definitely American, something positively vital, in all of them—but more visible in Hart Crane, Malcolm Cowley, William Faulkner, and also their older contemporaries, Carl Sandburg, John Gould Fletcher, Vachel Lindsay. I could follow the path of these poets, continue their tradition. (228)

The tradition of proletarian American literature allowed him to "catch up," providing the philosophical and cultural lineage to which he could link his experiences and begin to give meaning to "all that was starved and thwarted in my life" (62). His frantic reading habits, and his compulsion to list repeatedly the authors he has to read, seek to ease his anxiety, while underscoring it. His intellectual pursuits and invocations would authorize and legitimate his own writing:

> I wrote every day and the past began to come back to me in one sweeping flood of memories. The time had come, I felt, for me to utilize my experiences in written form. I had something to live for now and to fight the world with; and I was no longer afraid of the past. I felt that I would not run away from myself again. (305)

By the end of his autobiography, Allos exorcises this haunting past by his ability to assign meaning to events in his life. By locating himself in a radical proletarian history and a literary tradition, he reconciles his subjectivity and gains access to a narrative of cultural and historical agency to counter the ahistorical stasis imposed by imperialism. Referring to the democratic aspirations of the American writers Jack London, Mark Twain, and William Saroyan,

> it came to me that the place did not matter: these sensitive writers reacted to the social dynamics of their time. I too reacted to my time. I promised myself that I would read ten thousand books when I got well. I plunged into books boring through the earth's core, leveling all seas and oceans, swimming in the constellations. (312)

America ceases to be a topos to become a site of universalism, "swimming in the constellations." His relationship to books is one of ecstasy, described in the same terms as his orgasm in an earlier chapter. The topos of America is in an unstable position, neither geographically locatable nor epidermally readable. "America" as trope is manifest through the narration of migration, daily survival, and, most important, the fantasy of the "desire to know America," an unfulfilled and unsignifiable desire. Yet this is also the production of a homoerotics acceptable to Bulosan—pure intellect, without physical sexuality.

Campomanes and Gernes suggest how the protagonist's love letters to Eileen Odell, the kind white woman who brings him books to his bedside, become Carlos's apprenticeship in writing: "writing fumbling vehement letters to Eileen was actually my course in English. What came after this apprenticeship—the structural presentation of ideas in pertinence to the composition and anarchy between man's experience and ideals—was merely my formal search" (235). Although his letter writing may have been preparation for his eventual entry into American letters, what precedes the formal structural presentation is in fact a heterosocial—that is, nonsexual—relationship with a white woman. This cloak of courtly address is the precursor to his *mere* "formal search" as constituted by his social criticism and this autobiography. Therefore, what comes before the social critique, the basis of the apprenticeship, is the series of frustrated erotics—"fumbling vehement letters"—and the *privilege to have desire* on which both are founded: "my long denied urge to feel a part of the life about me burst forth like a blazon of burning stars. This force annihilated personal motives, and again I began to feel stirrings inside me, coming out in torrents of poetry" (236). Again, the orgasmic gloss and displacement of the personal onto the greater social critique seem to have at their root the original prohibition against *having* desire. To know America was to belong in very erotic terms to America—characterized by a series of "fumbling" but "vehement" erotics that deny physicality. However, the disembodied critical copula—an unincorporated voice—offers a ravaged body of evidence on display for our gaze.

Bulosan evacuates his own personal voice and body to make room for other stories; his person disappears and is replaced by a composite collection of stories once rendered invisible and inaudible by the disavowal of American politics and letters. Importuned, even authorized, by those around him, Bulosan recollects sensational narratives of violation *for* the reader. Campomanes and Gernes's study highlights the epistolary form as a central metaphor of *America Is in the Heart* and Bulosan's other writings as the author's creation of a literary self that is "dialogic, collective and sentimental."[15] The epistolary form assumes at once an intimacy and a distance. A personal network of belonging mitigates this alienating distance, bringing with it a network of shared signs. As a letter writer, according to Campomanes and Gernes, "the narrator himself, and by implication, Bulosan, becomes figuratively translated so that he, in turn, can function as a translator, a cultural mediator and a spokesman for those rendered speechless by history."[16] In this light, Bulosan's autobiographical missive reaches beyond the intended reader to be overheard by others in a collective *bildung*. To extend the epistolary motif, Bulosan the writer and reteller of Filipino American experience acts as the cultural and locutionary copula among the variously dislocated Filipinos in the Philippines and the United States and between Filipinos and the greater American society. By articulating direct links of dispossession rather than subordinating them into a single metaphor, the network of shared signs stretches across half the world to reconfigure the location of "America" itself.

Autobiogaphy as self-writing and self-making takes a tortuous route, in that the speaker must disintegrate to appear as an integral whole. The narrative tactics Bulosan and Thomas employ are symptomatic of the structures of disavowal that govern U.S. imperial grammar. What is at stake is desire made inarticulable by the very structures that create it. Making central their precarious relation to masculinity in their autobiographical texts complicates the question of national belonging for Bulosan and national-racial belonging for Thomas. Both disavowed subjects—Piri, a U.S. citizen, and Allos, a U.S. national—belong differently to the nation-state. Yet neither work equates political citizenship with national belonging. The disavowal of enfolded political and cultural borders leaves no language for them to belong "otherwise," to echo Chuh's challenge, unless they reformulate the idea of America in the streets or in the heart. The narratives Bulosan and Thomas present express this inarticulable desire through the destruction of bodily integrity. The narrators insist on their bodily existence as being subject to and subject of U.S. nation-state politics. The narrative strategies themselves fragment the subject to enact a simultaneous self-making and self-destruction that operates in the structure of disavowal; that is, the body is made to appear in order to be destroyed. Yet what remains is an inarticulable desire to belong wedged between the state promise of belonging via political citizenship and the legal interdictions that precipitate the social destruction of that racialized body.

The abjection of other bodies in nonnormative erotic moments iterates the national seduction and abjection; it at once posits a moment of desiring and is rejected by it. The proximity of abjection casts the speaker's origins from such, but he cannot himself be articulated without it. This avoids the essentialist pitfalls of originary loss lamented by a nationalist argument that pits one nationalism over another—that is, trading one border for another. The enfolded borders in the subject create not only ambivalence and multiple belongings but violent proximate possibilities. The enfolding cannot allow easy excision without iterating the very violence that created the body in the first instance. Thus, narrating the development of these two protagonists is vexed because they cannot occupy an oppositional space but only a disavowed one. Entrance into language is already frustrated and dictated by social interdictions. Thus the frustrated desire here is the desire for the right to have desire.

Immigrant and coming-of-age narratives map the individual's route to reconciling herself to U.S. national time and space. If the nation-state within which the colonized subject resides refuses utterance or recognition of the word colony, what identities could be formed out of this simultaneous disavowed belonging? Furthermore, given the instability of time and space in the colonial order, the U.S. postcolonial ethnic emplots herself with much difficulty along these two narrative trajectories. The difficulty lies in the narrative demands placed on the colonized, then ethnicized, subject who must split herself between the assimilative subject of the immigrant narrative and the imperially disavowed other self that she must encounter in her "coming-of-age." American postcolonial narrative strategies are located between amnesia and anamnesis, forgetting and recovery of meanings, but also operate within U.S. imperial paranoia (difference) and narcissism (sameness) in relation to its other subjects. The immigrant and *bildung* narratives under the conditions of the U.S. imperium perform the same imperial amnesia. As narratives approach the fantastic but powerful force of any or multiple national subjectivity, the centripetal attraction of something like a "home," "identity," or "belonging" is thwarted. Rather than a cause of lament, I would suggest that national belonging's power of attraction offers infinite "elsewheres" at each parabolic turn for the American postcolonial imagination; that is, frustrated desire locates a focal point but each re-presentation or revision of "home" might offer different endings and recognitions. The recognition of subjectivities inhabiting multiple national chronicities and spaces creates multiple narrative possibilities, as we will see in the next chapter with John Dominis Holt's *Waimea Summer* and Jessica Hagedorn's *Dogeaters*.

6. Reconstituting American Predicates

Troping the American Tour d'Horizon

Let there be no mistake about it; it is to this zone of occult instability where the people dwell that we must come; and it is there that our souls are crystallized and that our perceptions and our lives are transfused with light.

—Frantz Fanon, "On National Culture"

In his essay "On National Culture," Frantz Fanon underscores the psychic transformations in the colonized subject who is forced "to recognize the unreality of his 'nation,' and in the last extreme, the confused character of his own biological structure."[1] Fanon does not argue that culture in some form distinct from the colonizer's ceases to exist. The evacuation of the colonized subject for the colonizer's presence may fracture national and bodily borders to make them confused and unrecognizable, but this site also seems to be the source of reanimation of a different system of understanding. How is the "zone of occult instability" recognizable only in its movement and its destabilizing force in meaning making? The spatial and kinetic trope is provocative in that it insists on the existence of a place "where people dwell" as material and social but without defined borders.

The previous chapter offered a model by which to understand the narrative strategies employed by continental Puerto Rican Piri Thomas and Filipino (American) Carlos Bulosan to articulate alternative subjectivities occupying states of disavowal and abjection.

As enfolded borders create a precarious locutionary condition for the speaker, the question remains how these subjects make sense and meaning of the world around them from which they are estranged. If the subject herself cannot appear at all times in her own narration, can she sustain meaning long enough to tell a story?

In *Imagined Communities,* Benedict Anderson argues that the novelistic fictions of nationalism create for the reader a system of shared horizontality to delimit shared borders with the narrator. Of the Mexican novel *El Periquillo sarniento,* he observes:

> Here again we see the "national imagination" at work in the movement of a solitary hero through a sociological landscape of a fixity that fuses the world inside the novel with the world outside. This picaresque *tour d'horison [sic]*—hospitals, prisons, remote villages, monasteries, Indians, Negroes—is nonetheless not a *tour du monde.* The horizon is clearly bounded: it is that of colonial Mexico. Nothing assures us of this sociological solidity more than a succession of plurals.[2]

Yet, I would argue that the American horizon is not so clearly bounded precisely because the condition of the American colonial is one of enfolded borders wherein articulation could easily undo the subject. The "succession of plurals" that Anderson describes refers, I would argue, not only to objects within national borders, but to the meanings assigned to those objects. The multiple systems created by multiple colonizations also create multiple systems of signification. Thus, the task before the reader is not only the recognition of plurality of objects in the horizontal sense, but the hierarchy of signification with which those objects are imbued.[3] Thus, the postcolonial parataxis would demand interpretative techniques that interrogate the conjunctions that link (extra)national signs together, as well as the plurality of significations assigned to them.

John Dominis Holt's *Waimea Summer* (1976) from Hawai'i and Jessica Hagedorn's *Dogeaters* (1990) from Filipino America use narrative strategies to expand the spatial *tour d'horizon* suggested by Benedict Anderson to extend to a more sedimented semiotic and sociohistorical *tour d'horizon.* They reconfigure the enfolded *tour d'horizon* of the American Tropics to reveal the sedimentation of a range of possible meanings wherein various readers recognize not only the familiar national objects but also the meanings alienated or subordinated by colonization. Bulosan and Thomas underscore the complicated and dangerous relation of unincorporated narrators to the enfolded borders of the American landscape. How, then, does this tenuous subject relate to and make itself signify among its surrounding objects? How does the unincorporated speaker read?

Holt's *Waimea Summer* was one of the first novels by a Native Hawaiian writer to articulate the negotiations of being a Native Hawaiian caught in changing Hawai'i. Set against the backdrop of 1930s Hawai'i before the American territory's entry into statehood, the novel remaps the history and culture of Hawai'i through its multiple Hawaiian, British, hapa haole, and American heritages. Ostensibly a coming-of-age novel, the story follows fourteen-year-old Mark Hull during his summer at his Uncle Fred's ranch in Waimea on the Big Island. The novel is also a return narrative in which the protagonist goes back to his ancestral home to reread Hawaiian national space and time through the various strands of the hero's genealogy in order to lay claim to a different manhood and national identity.

Hagedorn's *Dogeaters* returns one of its many protagonists to the postindependence Philippines of the 1950s and the neocolonial Marcos era of the 1980s and weaves several narratives out of displacement and unstable memory to recount life in Manila. These memories are awash in Technicolor, shattered in the Hollywood film collage and Filipino radio melodrama that flow across Manila's postcolonial horizons. Hagedorn challenges the reader's interpretative practices by orchestrating various narrative forms to complicate the easy conjunction of the "Philippines" as sign of origin and "America" as sign of destination.

Waimea Summer and Initiations into Reading

Waimea Summer opens with Mark, a Honolulu denizen accustomed to the city life, wandering through the old family home in Waimea. An eerie sense of foreboding makes the present unreadable to the protagonist:

> At four in the morning, three days after I arrived on the Big Island to pay my first visit to Waimea, I awoke and was gripped by a sense of doom and apprehension, even before I could shake off the lingering remnants of sleep. All the things I'd heard about Waimea being a place ridden with ghosts and black magic seemed now to be true. Before this, the excitement of being at last in this place my

father had so endlessly extolled, my exploration around the once handsome house and garden, and exhaustion had successfully kept back the age-old sensitivity Hawaiians have to the world of spirits. But this morning, in my darkened room, a chilling sense of portent and unseen things being everywhere had complete hold of me. The fourposter in which I'd felt quite comfortable for three nights now seemed forbidding. The handsome quilt of the breadfruit design, which had been specially granted, felt now like a shroud.[4]

Fraught with spirits and portents, six periodic sentences with elaborate clauses delay our entry into the story of this adolescent. Although apprehension might rightfully accompany adolescence, the sense of doom and death overpowers the opening lines. Mark's uncanny awareness of a world beyond renders the opening overfull from the beginning. Breadfruit, traditionally a symbol of sustenance and life in Hawaiian culture, has turned to a death shroud. With these hauntings from the past, Mark becomes embroiled in the act of deciphering his ancestral home to allay his fears by reading these signs and making sense of them. After three days, his world has begun to disintegrate into seeming and sense, not yet articulable, but the portents demand to be read nonetheless.

Waimea seems like a throwback to the unspoiled and untouched beauty of "old Hawai'i," a place that seems to both fascinate and appall Mark. At first miserable in Waimea, he pleads to his father to send him a first-class ticket back to Honolulu, but he is soon embroiled in the inescapable specters of his family history, his family genealogy, and his aptitude for reading omens and signs:

> I lay awake, plotting an escape from Waimea. Spirits did not thrive in my world of bright lights, clanging streetcars, and modern plumbing, where scientific education continually refuted the lore which still clung, like coral clusters on reef, at the outer edges of memory. (48)

His modern upbringing might reject "spirits," but the signifying power of these myths "still clung . . . at the outer edges of memory." As science and lore compete for his development, his spatial metaphor for memory is a reminder of how national borders not only delimit and exclude but also mark history, time, and meanings. Away from modern Honolulu, Mark's experience of Waimea begins to reconfigure the relationship between past and present and the spiritual and the material plane.

The experience of the uncanny, as Susan Najita suggests, overwhelms young Mark and physically manifests itself through his palpitations, retchings, and numerous panic attacks. His gut-wrenching reactions are not just the ordeal of a young man grasping for a sense of identity but of one who must reconcile significations that have been alienated from objects, people, and relationships. Critic Stephen Sumida sees Holt's novel as a city boy's search for the pastoral, its stability and timelessness, through a "dead" history distilled in a distant and romanticized past.[5] For Susan Najita, history, far from dead, loops in and out to disrupt the development narrative and to destabilize categories of gender and race in order to carve out different pathways for this colonial Hawaiian *bildung*:

> [The] *hapa haole* protagonist's identity is constructed through an engagement with this uncanny and traumatic history, producing a particular type of hybridity, specifically, a multiple dialectics of race and gender that, while a direct result of colonial contact, look toward the postannexation "future" of the novel.[6]

As with Thomas's "becoming hombre," Mark's Hawaiian *bildung* refuses equivalence or translation with "becoming a man." Like the circulating narrative locations in *Down These Mean Streets* and *America Is in the Heart,* Najita describes Mark's position as a self divided between observer and observed: "the detached tone and use of objectifying terms such as 'indigenous habitat' and 'observing' suggest that Fred [his older cousin] is, in Mark's view, an ethnographic specimen."[7] Indeed, both the habitants and the land are specimens of difference for Mark, but it is within this network of difference that he must relocate himself. Therefore, his development is tied intimately to honing his perceptions and reading skills in order to connect with his family and Hawai'i's history. Holt ushers us into old Hawai'i, during a period when it was simultaneously a colonial outpost of *haole* intruders and the disputed sovereign nation of native Hawaiians. The boy from Honolulu brought up to be a proper gentleman is taken aback by the eroticism and spirituality of Waimea and its inhabitants that offer him another route to manhood.

The feud between Fred, Mark's cousin, and Julian Lono, Fred's brother-in-law, is driven by the legacy of racism and colonization in a changing Hawai'i. Both men are mixed-race Hawaiians: Fred is phenotypically white and Julian is phenotypically dark-skinned.

Related to each other by marriage, both men offer Mark rival models of masculinity. Fred is a brash rancher who performs a violent masculinity, is at ease with womanizing, drinking, and hunting as pastimes, and holds native Hawaiians and their "old" ways in utter disdain. He tries to warn Mark against Julian from the beginning and suggests that Julian is a *mahu* (inadequately translated as homosexual) and a kahuna (misunderstood as a kind of sorcerer, though in the indigenous tradition a spiritual teacher). Such a double but hierarchized valence is symptomatic of conventional and alienated meanings vying for Mark's (and fast-changing Hawai'i's) understanding of his place in this world. Yet, young Mark is forced to wrestle with issues of masculinity and the consequences of racism and colonialism as configured in the web of interpersonal family relationships.

Fair-skinned himself and "nearly one-half Polynesian" and raised in urban Honolulu, Mark is ambivalent not only about traditional beliefs but the possibility that he might possess the gifts of a kahuna. He is drawn to Julian and his overt sensuality. In contrast to Fred's brashness, Julian is emotionally expressive, especially in his love for Puna, Fred's young, sickly son whom many believe to be Julian's. Seemingly coarse, uneducated, and from "old Hawai'i," his masculinity is the "Hawaiian" kind—erotic, open, and spiritual. He protects young Puna by reciting a chant to keep him out of evil's way, and he later mourns Puna's death so deeply that his wails drive Mark away from the funeral gathering. By virtue of being raised Anglo, Mark is more familiar with prohibitions and propriety than with the florid excesses of his Waimea relatives; "mine was not Fred's world, nor Julian's" (48), he proclaims.

Contrary to Sumida's reading, the past is not distant and haunts the protagonist in his attempt to place himself in his family's and, in turn, Hawai'i's history. As "simultaneously both ethnographic historian observer *and* primitivized native," Najita underscores, the protagonist must articulate his multiple relationships to the once familiar objects in different terms:[8]

A night heron flew overhead. I was instinctively fearful. They were night birds and brought bad luck to those who saw them by day. I cursed myself for being afraid. Hawaiians see omens in everything. I cursed myself for being Hawaiian. Look at me, I thought, sitting here imagining I'm surrounded by spirits, that they will reveal things to me in the shape clouds take, in the particular rustle of trees when a breeze passes through their foliage, or in the pattern of water as it passes over rocks. And I was helpless for I could not sort out the good from the evil portents. . . . Would I spend the rest of my life being pushed by the need to interpret *signs* as they appeared? Is this the way Hawaiians live? (136–39; emphasis added)

Mark cannot find a way out of a racial and cultural incommensurability. His remarks have the detached tone of one outside, yet this detachment is his very undoing as "I cursed myself for being Hawaiian." He at once desires to live as an untouched observer, and is also compelled to read signs in his environment from clouds to wind to water.

"Hawaiian," then, signifies not so much a racial identity as a relationship with the world around him that allows him another interpretative lens. The strange doubleness in the beginning is not so much about the otherworldy seeping into his world as it is the revelation of multiple histories in the island space. His query— "Would I spend the rest of my life being pushed by the need to interpret *signs* as they appeared? Is this the way Hawaiians live?" (139)—expresses a fear of the burden of reading as a way of living. Being Hawaiian is a defined position of relationality within the texts around him; that is, he reveals the very position of observer as a particular engagement with the text that itself becomes part of the aesthetic object.

Even though he continually wakes from nightmares, suffers chills, sweats, and vomits, he continues to thrust himself into every family conflict between cowboys and *mahus,* into the family narrative of gentlemen and chieftains, into the family legacy of kahunas and matriarchs. He proves his aptitude for tracing the complex web of family relations. One day, he receives a gift of spurs from his great-aunt, Mrs. Warrington, the clan's matriarch, who delights in his talent. Mark accepts the spurs with great apprehension because they belonged to a cousin who died. He feared the evil spirits that the dead man might bring into his life if he accepts the gift. His reading rested on the object itself and its association with, rather than the sign within, a web of relationships. Soon

the silver spurs regained their original significance: a source of strength and joy. Eben had actually given up his ownership in order that I might have them. Anything belonging to him could not be steeped in bad *mana*. . . . I was linked now to Eben as I had been since childhood to Uncle Tony Stevenson. Years later it came to me that the connection was an aesthetic one. (140)

Recalling the Hawaiian practice of chanting one's genealogy, for Mark, to belong to a network of relationships redefines his personhood.[9] As a patriarch later informs him: "People don't *believe* in spirits here, Sonny. They *live* with them. They're a part of life!" (172). Understanding the sign as not having a singular meaning, but rather as a linkage to a web of interpersonal connections, extends genealogy to the aesthetic. Mark begins to see his fellow Hawaiians as "aesthetic objects, as repositories of music, art and poetry" (118). The wretching and anxiety attacks are symptomatic not only of Mark's being turned inside out or being beside himself, but, more profoundly, of the fact that these moments of bodily, psychic, and emotional instability signify a reconfiguration of his bodily signifiers—sounds, chants, bodies, genitals, thoughts, *mana*—and their relationship to the Hawaiian world to form a different aesthetic living within multiple sign systems.

Given the sign systems at work in the novel, Mark goes through two initiations, both erotic, one heterosexual and the other homoerotic and spiritual. His intiation into heterosex occurs in the middle of the novel. Mark rescues Kimiko Moriyama, the wife of a family friend, from a potential rape by a drunken guest after a party. Later, she thanks him and leads him in a surreal masquerade as a prelude to sex:

> She began to fondle my hair. She ran her fingers over my cheeks and neck. She unbuttoned my shirt, wheeled round, and, still sitting, reached for something under the shelf. She turned back, holding masks. She put one over my face and covered hers with the other. I accepted mine with misgivings, but they were not those about what *mana* or signs it contained. She wheeled round again, lifted her mask, and blew out the lantern. (156)

His heterosexual initiation is notable in that he mentions his participation only once in accepting the mask. The sentences begin with her as the subject and him as the passive object of her not-yet-sexual ministrations. There is no tone of intimacy. In fact, the whole encounter is mediated by masks, as if in a theatrical performance. Moreover, he accepts this mask—this role—with "misgivings," but not about its meaning or aesthetics. Rather than as a sign of disavowal, adultery, or pretense, one could read this masking as multiplying possibilities of heterosex. However, unlike his other apprehensions, this one about heterosex was not a result of his misreading its signs, but of participating at all.

The heterosexual initiation in the middle of the novel functions as a prelude to the "real" initiation later, and lends the latter, by comparison, a more profound eroticism. He meets Abraham Hanohano, a patriarch and kahuna. He spends the night talking about Hawaiian history and spirits, and later watches the dawn on the beach. Later, Hanohano has a confrontation with his local adversary, who insults and curses them. To Mark's surprise, Hanohano, to ward off the curse, "unbuttoned his trousers, pulled out his penis and began to urinate. He caught the yellow liquid in his hand, and rubbed it in his hand and rubbed it on his shoulders, over his torso and on me" (180). He comforts Mark afterwards:

> He embraced me with a gentle certainty. I sank my nose into his chest muscles and drank in the smell of the sea, clinging still to his silken skin. He pressed me closer as though to give me the strength of his *mana*. I pulled away, memory of the early morning intimacy at the beach made me tremble. (181)

Although Mark experiences both initiations with ambivalence, he describes this encounter in more intimate and impassioned terms than the first. He trembles, and the sentences alternate subjects between "he" and "I." Unlike the first encounter, Mark is an active participant. The reader is not quite clear about the "early morning intimacy," yet the scene is an unmistakable same-sex embrace in a continuum of the range of masculinities that he has encountered.

He later runs away from this scene, but upon leaving Waimea, he has a vision. Past chieftains appear to take their place around a sacred gathering ground, and he sits among them. His vision and initiation into the *ali'i* or royalty transport him into a timeless place and provide him with another ancestral home apart from the Victorian one shrouded in death. In this gathering place in Waimea, he recovers not only the alienated meaning of his genealogy as connected to British, American, and hapa haole heritages, but also his (and John Holt's) relationship to Hawai'i's royal past.

Dogeaters and Other National Obscenities

"I need my own movies, with their flexible endings. Otherwise, it's just shit," says Joey about his "johns" in *Dogeaters*. Whereas Mark in *Waimea Summer* envisions new life sentences for himself in his initiations, Joey in *Dogeaters* advocates for multiple predicates to these life sentences. Like *Waimea Summer, Dogeaters* hesitates to begin. The novel starts and stops three times in 1956:

> 1956. The air-conditioned darkness of the Avenue Theater smells of flowery pomade, sugary chocolates, cigarette smoke and sweat. *All That Heaven Allows* is playing in Cinemascope and Technicolor. . . .
>   1956. Long before my mother Dolores leaves my father Freddie and takes me to North America. . . .
>   1956. My Lola Narcisa Divino's room is filled with the sweet gun-powder smell and toxic smoke of Elephant brand katol, a coil-shaped mosquito repellent incense.[10]

Each invocation of 1956 takes a different generational and spatial perspective: first, Rio and her cousin, second, her parents, and third, their grandparents. Each one frames a different generation in national time, locating "America" differently in each. The first is a received Hollywood version of America in a mediascape, connoting the excess of color, smell, and scope. The second is America as destination on a world scale, along with other possible destinations for the father. Only in this dependent clause, a fragment sentence, is there mention of immigration in the novel. The rest of the section relates the father's multiple passports and allegiances. The third recalls Rio's intimate memories of her grandmother, who married an American, "leftover from the Spanish American war." The year 1956 as the calendrical marker is shot through with intersecting narratives that range from a "guest room by the kitchen" to a Manila theater with English-only movies, to the triangulation of Spain, the United States, and the Philippines in the family history. However, at the end of the novel this marker of stability is removed by Pucha's complaint: "*Puwede ba?* 1956, 1956! Rio, you've got it all wrong. Think about it: 1956 makes no sense" (248). What remains is the web of narratives that locate the novel's characters, with each chapter introducing a character whose story is interwoven with that of another.

The father of another narrator, Joey Sands, is an unknown African American soldier from a military base, part of the enduring U.S. neocolonial presence in the Philippines. Unlike middle-class Rio, young Joey is a gay prostitute, part of the socially invisible but massive Manila underclass, living in the city's slums as expendable labor. Hagedorn connects the lives of these two characters separated by social class through their genetic connection to the unyielding history of U.S. imperialism. At the same time, through these characters, she traces the unbroken line of American descent and colonial legacy from the late nineteenth century to the present.

Joey is the unromantic product of the imperial encounter, one of the many children born all around the Pacific Rim where U.S. military bases and the attendant sex trade proliferate. Joey marks the excess, the bastard product of U.S. military occupation. Offspring of a Filipina prostitute and an African American soldier, Joey introduces himself and addresses the reader directly: "Joey Sands. Do you like it? Like a crooner, don't you think? That's where I got my last name. 'The Sands.' A casino in Las Vegas" (72). Without a proper patronym, he creates an identity for himself culled from the elements of the U.S. mediascape that permeate Manila. His self-naming is determined by U.S. fantasies and his American genealogy: "GI baby, black boy, I am the son of rock'n'roll, I am the son of R and B, I can dance well, you can all go to hell! *Putang Ina Ko* [My mother's a whore]!" (205). Joey is doubly racialized as Filipino and African American. In bitter irony, he takes possession of the stereotypes attending the Filipino GI baby and the African American, which, along with Las Vegas, is yet another marker of Joey's own fantastic America.[11]

Hagedorn complicates the critique of U.S. imperialism by her choice of an African American father for Joey. She signals the multiple and echoing power relations visited upon various racialized bodies and spaces, and complicates the image of occupying U.S. forces as white and privileged. Rather than paint a simple picture of the "imperial American," she illustrates how American bodies entering the colonized space vary in time of arrival, class, and race, producing a wide range of legacies. These are not easily categorizable or recognizable using the colonizer/colonized binary. Less privileged Americans, often from minority groups and the poor, fill the rank and file of the U.S. military today. Although marginalized in the United States, they gain a different privilege when representing the United States as an occupying force in countries throughout the Pacific. Their Filipino offspring, located across different class strata, inherit the social stigma or admiration associated with their phenotype, thus adding another layer to racialization in the American Tropics.

Joey's story defies the romance that the imperial encounter is supposed to engender. An illiterate callboy, deejay, hustler, and heroin addict, the GI baby lost his mother when he was six years old. Joey's only family consists of another street kid, Boy-Boy, and a man he calls "Uncle" with whom he lives in a shack. Uncle had taken Joey into his home after paying for his mother's burial and introduced him to Manila's informal economy first selling "cigarettes, boiled peanuts, Chiclets, *sampaguita* garlands, the Metro Manila Daily, and movie magazines" (43). Joey later graduated to pickpocketing and sex work.

He makes a living at the dance club where he deejays: "Coco Rico is home for me too—a safe place, cool, and dark and easy on the eyes" (32). Coco Rico is a commercial establishment where entertainment and sexual favors may be bought. For Joey, home is the commercial space where imperial encounters ease into a sexual and economic exchange. Coco Rico is a tropical paradise for Western tourists. For a price, tourists and the well-heeled can fall in love with their tropical fantasies. Joey, cognizant of the imperial delusion, diverts and converts this desire into an exchangeable commodity. The recognition of the commodity fetish as such drives his imagination. He seems to offer what the men desire. He brags:

> I learned early that men go for me; I like that about them. I don't
> have to work at being sexy. Ha-ha. Maybe it's my Negro blood. . . .
> I take advantage of the situation, run men around, make them give
> me money. For me men are easy. (44)

Like Bulosan's protagonist disrobing for the camera, the moment of recognition in the other's dreams is also a moment of appropriation. He realizes that the combination of his youth, color, class, and milieu is an eroticized commodity in the international tourist market. Joey becomes a fantastic commodity, in the form of a sexually available brown boy: "I could tell he was fascinated, just like the rest of them. Joey Taboo: my head of tight, kinky curls, my pretty hazel eyes, my sleek brown skin" (73). Joey's beauty is an American inheritance; Joey's African features make him marketably more exotic to international sex tourists but also mark his genealogic American heritage, a heritage in turn marked by its history of slavery and internal colonization. Rather than creating a fantastic rupture between the U.S. dark Atlantic past and the muticultural Pacific future as in Hollywood cinema, these histories converge in Joey's character to suggest their imperial and racialized linkages.

Potential clients are eager to consume these "othering" markers. However, these very inscriptions also serve to shape Joey's self-perception, desires, and fantasies. He recognizes that because of his difference, desire and bodies are commodities that he can possess, use, and perform to create a prelapsarian fantasy. In a chapter titled "Paradise," Joey meets a client, Rainer, a German filmmaker:

> "I hope you fall in love with me," [Rainer] suddenly says, just loud enough for me to hear. "Why should I, rain or shine?" I chuckle. "Because I am the most corrupt human being you will ever meet," he says, in that soft voice of his. "Are you bragging?" I challenge him, rolling my eyes to show him I've heard it all before. (132–33)

Rainer has already prescripted a fantasy for himself and Joey, the powerful "corrupt" man seducing Joey's boyish innocence. He errs in thinking that the tropical fantasy before him could respond freely to his invitation: "I hope you fall in love with me." Like the American tourist's camera or the movie director's wife's mirror in Bulosan's text, imperial desire is a narcissistic undertaking, investing in the colonized space its fantastical version of itself. As with Narcissus, the tourist mistakes the colonial surface of his making for depth of reality.[12] For Rainer, the economic exchange does not negate the hope that the desired object might actually return his affections. He takes his own fantasies literally. Literalness, then, is the corrupting force, not fantasy.

Joey rolls his eyes, refusing to play the role. He knows better. Although illiterate, Joey, like Mark, has learned to read people and cultural signs. Besides, he has his own fantasies to draw upon to make the encounter with the older men more bearable:

> That's when I imagine I'm in my own movie. I'm the strong young animal—I'm the panther. Or else I'm the statue of a magnificent young god in a beautiful garden. The old man with the elephant skin drools. Maybe he's God the Father, lost in paradise. He can't get over how perfect I am; he can't get over the perfection of his own creation. He falls in love with me. They always do. I'll admit, I can get off with some old man that way. (132)

For Joey, the movies cushion the stark economic exploitation under which he must make a living. "Mister Heartbreak," as he likes to see himself, fashions movie scenarios for himself as an act of self-pleasuring. Joey's ironic readings and performances make a mockery of his role as the "perfect creation." God the Father, like other Western tourists to follow, is "lost in paradise" and "can't get over how perfect I am." He falls in love with what he believes is his own creation. Joey's own scenarios with old men reverse, at least temporarily, the economic power relationship. The client's desire for a young brown boy makes possible this temporary power. According to Joey, "it's just shit. Most sex is charity, on my part. I'd rather dance alone" (ibid.). For both sides, desire is but an act of self-pleasuring.

The commodity fetish, therefore, is not the perfect romance the client would wish, but a mere performance. Yet, the spectator would continually seek evidence of "reality" behind the performance. Rainer later interrogates Joey about erotic shower dances, when boys soap themselves up onstage for paying onlookers. He voyeuristically asks:

> "Are they hungry or greedy?" "Hey, man. How should I know? Boys are hungry, so they perform. Audience pays to sit there greedy to watch—"
>
> "Do they do it slowly?" The million-dollar question: "Are they hard? Do they come onstage?"
>
> "Some."
>
> The German is incredulous. "Some? Not all? What about your friend, Boy-Boy? Does he like it? Such a wonderful name, Boy-Boy." (142)

For Rainer, "hardness" and "coming" evidence real desire rather than its performance. Undergirding Rainer's question (if they "come onstage") is to ascertain the spectacle's complicity in his own specularization and commodification. Rainer wants to believe that the performer derives sexual pleasure from being looked at. Thus, the looker becomes the provider of pleasure, rather than the reverse. Secure in the performer's agency, the spectator is absolved of any need to consider the limitations of this agency. Again, the visual consumer mistakes the spectacle's performed desire for mutual desire.

Exasperated with Rainer's questions, Joey exclaims: "That's what's it's all about. The dance. That's what the greedy audience pays to see" (ibid.). For Joey, the economic exchange makes possible the relationship between the desiring spectator and the spectacle. The boys are hungry, which is why they dance and the audience is greedy, which is why they watch. The sexual performance seems to hinge upon the convergence of lack and excess. Rainer mistakes the boys' physical hunger for sexual greed, but what actually fuels the spectacular relationship blurs the line between hunger and greed, and, by extension, lack and excess.

While Rainer continues to pose his voyeuristic questions, Joey recognizes himself in Rainer's eyes: "I recognize myself in the absence of light in his eyes, the junkie in him" (ibid.). In this moment of reflection, Joey recognizes Rainer's desire as hunger and addiction. Behind Rainer's eyes is hunger that has to be continually sated, verging on greed. Addiction is but excessive and insatiable hunger. Like Joey's heroin addiction, Rainer's greed requires a fix. Knowing that he himself is this fix, Joey knows how "to get to" his clients, to get under their skin. At its root is a frustrated and insatiable desire that hinges on preserving the unequal power relationship.

The reader is also complicit in this power relationship. Hagedorn destabilizes the reader's position as spectator of this scandalous sexualized figure. When Joey as first-person narrator gives a tour of the slums where he lives, he plays with the reader's First World notions of Third World squalor and then disrupts the privileged voyeuristic gaze: "I sleep right next to chicken, pigs, goats and dogs. Hey, I'm just kidding. Uncle has one mongrel, that's all" (38). Joey's character continues to destabilize the reader as a tour guide. As Joey himself admits: "Maybe I'm lying. Uncle says I was a born liar, that I can't help myself" (45). First the reader is treated like a tourist in Joey's Manila. Joey, once the spectacle, turns the table on the reader, challenging us to reexamine First World assumptions about Third World squalor and its prescripted narratives, *our* tropical fantasies. Robbing us of comfortable fantasies, whether of pity or repulsion, he treats us like one of his johns: "I like to let them know how little their trinkets are really worth. . . . It's a warning, my philosophy of life—keeping things slightly off-balance. It's how I survive" (37). This doubt keeps the reader's own assumptions "slightly off balance," underscoring how the power relationship between viewer and viewed informs and constructs the vision and narration of "reality." Thus, the "familiar" of Anderson's national *tour d'horizon,* "made strange" or unfamiliar in *Waimea Summer,* is shattered once more in *Dogeaters* by the plurality of perspectives within a nationally bounded horizon.

The sexual exchange figures one way the Philippines and other underdeveloped nations enter the international imagination. The imposition of the Western developmental model brings about an economic dependency, as dominant political economies dictate what and how the developing nation should produce and want. Those in the center, like Rainer, misrecognize survival strategies such as prostitution, tourism, crime, and mass emigration, not as a result of an asymmetrical power relationship resulting from this demand but as natural to the subject sites, and proof of the sites' inferiority, need for help, and bad development.

Each is addicted to different objects, though the end result—sex—might be the same. What Joey desires is to leave his dismal conditions in Manila: "I'll hit the jackpot with one of these guys. Leave town. I'll get lucky like Junior. Some foreign woman will sponsor me and take me to the States. Maybe she'll marry me. I'll get my green card. Wouldn't that be something?" (40). As Rainer lives off his abstract tropical fantasy, Joey's focus is starkly material. While in another client's hotel room, Joey luxuriates in the lavish surroundings. He begins to collect the hotel room toiletries and amenities:

> I stuff the plastic shower cap and slippers with the Manila Hilton insignia, complimentary robe and two bars of Cashmere Bouquet soap into one of Neil's SPORTEX shopping bags. He hates it when I do that. . . . He just doesn't understand. I love the newness and cleanness of my little souvenirs, the smell and touch of the glossy plastic. I would live in a hotel room forever, if I could. (75)

If Coco Rico is the Western tourist's paradise, then a modern hotel room is Joey's dream palace. His "little souvenirs" and material goods give him a "fix." The sexual performance itself holds nothing erotic for Joey, but the material goods for which it is exchanged contain the erotic charge. The manifestation of desire when he orders room service is more sexual than when he performs onstage or in bed:

> I am still naked. We both pretend not to notice how hard I'm getting. "Cheeseburger deluxe," I say dreamily. "French fries with ketchup . . . Mango ice cream . . . and a coke." (77)

Joey is genuinely "hard" for his Western fantasies, the material goods this dream conjures. He savors and makes love to the words, "French fries . . . Mango ice cream . . . and a coke." Contrary to Rainer's belief, the source of sexual excitement is not the client, but the "cheeseburger deluxe." Each "deluxe" food product and its enunciation brings him closer to orgasm. Deluxe conjures up visions of America, as bits of America may be delivered via room service and consumed. Through sexual labor and money exchange, he gains access to and ingests the signs of America and all the comfort and luxury with which they are associated.

Such an eroticization of U.S. cultural detritus goes against a vision of a "proper" nationalism in which an independent Philippines severs all ties to the imperial center. The novel "quotes" underground accounts of Philippine history that emphasize the colonial sedimentation of the Philippine imagination:

> The underground circulates a pamphlet . . . "The Suffering Pilipino." He describes us as a complex nation of cynics, descendants of warring tribes which were baptized and colonized to death by Spaniards and Americans, as a nation betrayed and then united by our hunger for glamour and our Hollywood dreams. (101)

The pamphlet condemns the nation's past disunity and a unity forged out of colonization and desire. Disavowing any notion of unified origins, the account describes Filipinos as descendants of "warring tribes," who were then reborn and reconstructed ("colonized to death") by the Spaniards and Americans. The "glamour and our Hollywood dreams" are the remains of the U.S. culture industry, but it is precisely the unfulfilled dreams and images that unite and tether the people to one another. Addiction to the signs of the imperial center may be an obstacle to a "proper" nationalism, but the simultaneous desire for *and* repudiation of imperial culture give shape to the postcolonial imagination. Hagedorn is not much concerned with depicting "proper" nationalism, but instead demonstrates the creative reimagining of national signs.

Performing their versions of "America," Joey and Rio may be read as practitioners of the postcolonial imagination. Their reconstitution of "America" culled from various sources, real and imagined, is bricolage. Like Claude Lévi-Strauss's description of the *bricoleur,*

His universe of instruments is closed and the rules of his game are always to make do with "whatever is at hand", that is to say with a set of tools and materials which is always finite and is also heterogeneous because what it contains bears no relation to the current project, or indeed to any particular project, but is the contingent result of all the occasions there have been to renew or enrich the stock or to maintain it with the remains of previous constructions or destructions.[13]

Joey's "tools and materials" for transformation are the images in movies and romances. His vision is informed by "previous constructions or destructions" of his body, and he uses these representations in exchange for material goods. Contrary to the nationalist vision, he is not simply a passive consumer of popular culture. To endure his living conditions he uses popular signs to make and remake relationships with the colonial other. In the process, the signs become his own.

This retailored America Joey performs has no actual original, but rather is the received idea already transformed in the colonized space. In a study titled "The Power of Appearances," anthropologist Fenella Cannell examines how drama and signs of "America" are circulated in Filipino gay beauty contests. Cannell sets local notions of beauty within the larger context of Southeast Asian culture where "beauty" is associated with voyages, the outside, and a cultivated style. In Philippine historical experience, that "outside or distant place [is] the imagined America[,] . . . a place of power, wealth, cleanliness, beauty, glamour and enjoyment."[14] According to Cannell, imitation of icons as self-transformation is a means of accessing these traits and elevating one's status in the community. Notions of beauty are derived from the unequal relationship between city and country, metropole and periphery, but the appropriative act demonstrates the intricate agential process of transformation by which received notions of "America" are themselves transformed in the performance of "America."

Hagedorn does not offer an easy victim/victimizer paradigm to tell Joey's story. Although Joey's disempowered position is made clear, she allows him an interior life independent of tourist fantasies and imperial whimsy. His imagination serves as a source of pleasure and creative survival amid exploitative relations. He navigates the physical Manila landscape as well as the intangible mediascapes that shape his life and imagination. Las Vegas, rock and roll, movies, music, dancing, and sex are all part of this post-colonial landscape. Hagedorn does not offer the reader a local indigene as passive spectacle, but a vibrant character able to produce pleasures for himself in his self-fashioning.

Joey's local story of survival crosses paths with another narrative in this landscape. He witnesses the murder of Senator Avila, the opposition leader. He takes refuge in Uncle's shack but realizes that Uncle has betrayed him to the authorities. His only home taken away, he hides out with Boy-Boy, who arranges his disappearance. When Boy-Boy delivers him blindfolded in the car with strangers, the reader is unsure if Boy-Boy, too, has betrayed him. After traveling for a day and a half concealed under blankets on the floor of a car, strangers take Joey to a jungle clearing. There he meets Daisy Avila the daughter of the slain senator and beauty queen turned revolutionary.[15]

Daisy's story has been interspersed throughout the novel alongside Joey's and other stories. The simultaneity of Manila's horizon stages both their narratives, but renders them invisible to each other because of the class divide maintained by the colonial legacy under the Spanish and American rule. Their seemingly unrelated stories converge when state violence under martial law threatens both their lives. Both disappear "underground" to escape.

Of Beauty Queens and Revolution

Daisy Consuelo Avila is a beauty queen turned revolutionary. The shy daughter of the president's political adversary, Senator Avila, Daisy has unexpectedly won a national beauty title over the beautiful daughters of other prominent politicos. She was the "dark horse" contender. However, like the other contestants, she is young, female, educated, and from a respectable middle-class family, characteristics necessary to embody a sanitized nationalism. Rumors circulate that the general together with the first lady has rigged the pageant so that the daughter of her husband's adversary would win. By making the senator's daughter a bourgeois nationalist symbol, the first lady could co-opt the main opposition. She would silence the opposition by casting the daughter in an image that appeals to mass nationalist desires. Thus Daisy's aesthetic image would eclipse and drown out the political oppositional voice. Described only as demure and solitary, Daisy is thrust into this convenient web of nationalist representations. After winning the contest, however, she disappears.

When Hagedorn first introduces the reader to Daisy, the beauty queen has in fact already disappeared from the novel's world. Daisy's story begins thus:

> Before her twentieth birthday, before she marries a foreigner in haste and just as hastily leaves him, before she is given the name Mutya by her guerrilla lover in the mountains, Daisy Consuelo Avila is crowned the most beautiful woman in the Philippines, our tropical archipelago of 7100 known islands. (100)

The sentence is followed by descriptions of real and mythical beasts and spirits that populate the islands. Hagedorn proceeds to describe an enchanted but deadly archipelago inhabited by "humming locusts," predatory vampire bats, sleeping giants, and serenading gecko lizards. As she condenses narrative time, Hagedorn draws the reader into a mythic space and simultaneously ironizes tourist brochures that turn "our tropical archipelago of 7100 known islands" into a menacing jungle. Into this strange and overwrought jungle our Mutya, or Muse in Tagalog, has disappeared.

The passage itself is, to say the least, a strange and overwrought sentence, made up of three subordinate clauses preceding the main clause, which, in turn, is weighed down by a descriptive phrase. In this thicket of a sentence, a whole life passes before the reader's eyes. This condensed life is layered, sedimented with three eventuations, one more absurd than the other, to lead us to one frozen moment: "Daisy Consuelo Avila is crowned the most beautiful woman in the Philippines." This dominant image grammatically and literally subordinates the other dramatic events as afterimages, or, in this case, before-images. Yet, Daisy appears in the main clause only as a passive subject embedded in multiple narratives. Her crowning glory is immediately eclipsed by the descriptive addendum of the Philippines, as if to weigh down the passive subject even more, with the onus of representing the "7100 known islands." In the syntactic enactment of one paragraph, Hagedorn reveals the narrative layers to unfold. This proleptic approach—this "will have been"—to Daisy's story figures the subsequent narration as a ghostly trace.

Before Daisy or the Muse disappears into mythic time and space, she is made into a national symbol—a beauty queen. Despite the personal victory, a profound unhappiness overtakes the senator's daughter. She locks herself in her bedroom and refuses to face the media. To the dismay of fans, corporate sponsors, and the first lady, she has declined to do interviews, appear in movie musicals, tour the provinces, and perform the functions expected of a beauty queen. Waiting for the national symbol to come out, "the hungry pack of journalists, photographers, and fans maintain a twenty-four-hour vigil on the sidewalk outside the gates of the Avila property. . . . Who will capture her tarnished image with the powerful zoom lenses of their Japanese cameras?" they ask (107). The function of beauty as spectacle here is to be captured and framed. Her refusal tarnishes the very image she is expected to perform. Surrounding the house, fans and the media imprison the family, but the hidden beauty rejects their demand to be their queen—the repository of nationalist libido, myths, and fantasies.

Although she has taken herself out of visual range, her disappearance as spectacle only generates a flurry of gossip that circulates without her participation. The *spectacle* becomes the object of *speculation*. Fantasies and scandals—pregnancy, an illicit affair, criminal acts—converge on the absent image of Daisy Avila proffered for public consumption. Inside and outside seem to lose distinction, as her public image is fused with her absent and imprisoned person. Inside the house, she sleeps and cries incessantly. Coffee and amphetamines do not prevent her from dozing and waking up, and crying involuntarily. Daisy is unable to maintain the physical and imaginary boundaries of her body. Like the overwrought and overfull sentence that introduced her, she can no longer contain herself as a physical body or as an image. With the imposition of the national and royal title, the boundaries that define Daisy's selfhood—both physical and imaginary—have been erased. The media star collapses under the weight of representation.

One day she submits to her dreaded sleep, but nothing happens and "no tears fall" (108). She finally agrees to appear in a television interview with Manila's leading gossip reporter. Before the interview even begins,

> Daisy seizes the opportunity to publicly denounce the beauty pageant as a farce, a giant step backward for all women. She quotes her father and mother, she goes on and on. . . . The segment is immediately blacked out by waiting censors. (109)

The once "sleeping beauty" uses the hungry media against itself to "break the spell" (ibid.). Using her mythic status, she attempts to sabotage the interview, but her plan to short-circuit the media backfires. To her dismay, "Daisy becomes a sensation, almost as popular as her father" (ibid.). The spell in fact remains unbroken and no prince is in sight for the sleeping beauty. When a wealthy, publicity-hungry foreigner in the guise of a prince does appear, she causes further scandal by marrying him. She abdicates her title and the tabloids dub the couple "The Rebel Princess and Her Playboy" (110). Unable to escape the incessant media production of her life, she divorces the foreigner and retreats back to her home.

As beauty queen or "rebel princess," Daisy's gendered body is immediately absorbed in preset narratives either as a symbol of Madame's neocolonial nationalism or of her parents' nationalist opposition. As a mouthpiece against the government, she simply *quotes* her father, the political opposition, and her mother, an ultranationalist professor at the university. Daisy cannot escape the representations heaped upon her body, which is made to be the site of competing nationalisms. Neither the lack she introduces in her self-withdrawal nor the excess of beauty as spectacle allows her voice to be heard.

She retreats to her cloister once again, refusing further consumption through her self-imposed entombment. Through a letter from her cousin, "An Excerpt from the Only Letter Ever Written by Clarita Avila" (115), the reader learns secondhand that Daisy has run away to the mountains with her guerrilla lover, Santos Tirador. Through this secondhand account, the Muse recedes farther away from the reader's view. She goes underground, rejecting both nationalist symbolizations, beauty queen and rebel princess. However, her descent underground makes her vulnerable to the equally obscured extension of state discipline—the military. Pregnant with her guerrilla lover's child, she is detained by the military for her alleged Communist activities. As we can see, her off-site and unseen guerrilla activities outside of co-optable state narratives (as pawn or opposition) have their counterparts in equally off-site and off-scene, indeed obscene, state-sanctioned terrorism.

Daisy is taken to an interrogation room in the "recently renovated military complex" (211) in a secret and distant location. The general shows Daisy a picture of a torture victim's mutilated body whose brain has been replaced by a styrofoam cup. The general warns, "Even I can do nothing about my men's excesses" (215). This threat of excessive violence is the state's military response to her refusal to be disciplined in the public arena. The image itself as excess situates the terror not in the victim's death, but rather in the spectacle of mutilation as sign of state power (symbolized by the military) over citizens' physical bodies. As part of the government's repressive tactics, the mutilated spectacle terrorizes and disciplines the individual and the public for whom it serves as a cautionary tale. This terrifying photograph of torture echoes and displaces the photographs *not* taken of Daisy earlier. Daisy's material body, once forced to symbolize neocolonial nationalism, is now rendered vulnerable to rape. Once wielded and destroyed as a public image, her body is now reduced to a violable physical object subject to the state's violent excesses.

Hagedorn recounts this gruesome scene in a peculiar format: the eerie narrative alternates between Daisy's interrogation and torture and a local radio drama, *Love Letters*. On the physical pages of the novel, the torture scene is in boldface and enclosed in parentheses, set off from the radio script as if to announce and underscore its very concealment:

> (Daisy's tears flow hot down her cheeks; she tastes the salt in her mouth. She tries in vain to stop crying, but her tears keep streaming down. "Look—" the General shoves the last snapshot in front of her averted face. "Look—my men rearranged him totally. A styrofoam cup where his brains should be—isn't that ingenious?")
>> (A knocking sound at the door. There is tension in the music, percussion and a taut plucking of strings.)
> MAGDALENA: (alarmed) Who could that be at this time of night? (More knocking sounds, this time more urgent.) (215–16)

The use of boldface *and* parentheses highlights as it obscures the violence. The radio drama playing in the background provides the distraction to the screams and rape in the bolded torture scene set off in parentheses as if it were script instructions. Part of the discomfort in reading this chapter is the tension between the hypotactic parentheses subordinating the torture to the radio drama and Hagedorn's paratactic fragmentation of each narrative thread. The surreal juxtaposition of the radio drama and the torture scene marks not only the horizontal relationship between disciplinary productions but also the state-enforced invisibility of one to the other; that is, the state produces spectacles of national dramas as blinders. The entertainment industry creates fantasies of drama and spectacles of beauty queens to mask and muffle state crimes and violence occurring alongside them. Hagedorn seems to suggest that these paratactic strategies lie on a continuum of state discipline in order to produce docile national bodies. The relationship between the two has been erased as a necessary part of their respective productions.

Daisy reappears later in the novel as a conclusion to Joey Sands's narrative. Their seemingly unrelated stories converge when state violence under martial law threatens both their lives. Both disappear "underground" to escape. In a chapter ironically titled "Terrain," Hagedorn presents an ambivalent utopia, a literal no-place, outside of spectacular Manila. Joey and Daisy descend into the untraceable path of resistance, into a terrain untouched by spectacular productions. Only upon their meeting does the reader learn that Daisy has been released from detention with a presidential pardon and a sentence to exile. However, she returns immediately to the Philippines to her refuge in the mountains. Daisy's and Joey's stories conjoin and end on this murky and invisible terrain:

> They will get drunk together on cane liquor one night. She cries while Joey describes his mother, what he remembers of her. She reproaches herself, and apologizes for being sentimental. She will not cry when she describes how her lover was captured while she was in detention, or how her unnamed baby girl was born premature and dead. They are together all the time. She teaches him how to use a gun. (233)

Out of sight and underground, the two are extracted from their respective spectacular circuits to form a new but undefined coupling. Hagedorn uses the future tense as if viewing the hazy scene from an ever-increasing distance. She maintains the ambiguity of this future by simply listing the said eventualities in nonhierarchical order. Syntactically, this contrasts radically with Daisy's overwrought and elaborate introduction: the description of the meeting is pared down, stripped of adornment, simplified in staccato phrases: they will get drunk; she cries; she reproaches herself; she will not cry; she teaches him how to use a gun. The sentences are terse, no longer weighed down, ungrounded, leaving the reader with a continuing future: all action, no spectacle. Again, this paratactic conjoining offsets the initial frozen moment of her spectacular introduction.

Daisy's story began as an overwrought future perfect: this will have been. It ends in a hazy future tense. The future perfect is an overwrought and contradictory tense, looking to the past and the future simultaneously. It is a teleological tense, offering only predetermined endings. By contrast, the future tense does not yield such a telos, but is literally unpresentable. The two characters meet at this vanishing temporal and spatial point somewhere in the mountains. While seeming to offer a utopic closure in this zone of occult instability, Hagedorn refuses to offer the reader a proper "nationalist" ending. Drawing away from the temptation of narrative and nationalist closure, she chooses instead to maintain an asymptotic relationship with a definitive "national" telos to suggest one as yet unimagined.

If one were to read this narrative thread as an allegory, the narrative lines and their syntactic enactment thematize the sedimentation of erasures—the palimpsestic and contradictory nature of narrating an American postcolonial nation. Daisy as a beautiful object becomes visible only when wielded for nationalist narratives; that is, simply as a place filler for preset narratives. Yet she cannot contain these competing nationalist narratives; she collapses under their weight, and even disappears. The gleaming spectacle of bourgeois nationalism is tarnished and layered with these other unreconciled stories. Only outside of time and space, in the no-place of utopia, is she able to appear, and that only as a fleeting afterimage, a sign of erasure. By the time we read her story, she will have been, a future perfect, but certainly no perfect future is in sight.

In the same way that Daisy disappears from sight, the novel as a whole too seems to fall apart. Hagedorn undoes her own narrative in the end, raising doubts about the nature of narrative and nation itself. The novel closes with Rio Gonzaga's cousin challenging the accuracy of Rio's recollections, protesting: "*Puwede ba?* 1956, 1956! Rio, you've got it all wrong. Think about it: 1956 makes no sense. It must have started around 1959, at the very least! You like to mix things up on purpose, *di ba? Esta loca, prima*" (248). The cousin accuses Rio Gonzaga of tending to "mix things up on purpose"; the same may be said of Hagedorn's narrative style. Its terrain, its grounding, has been destabilized by flawed memory, as memory reveals at once too much and too little. Assimilation into a singular thread will always have remainders and reminders of what the narrative fails to recover.

This story of the disappearing muse that allows the reader only to view her trace is intriguing for its ability to encapsulate the legal and political fictions that legislated colonial subjectivity explored in chapter 1. Geographic and legal fictions shaped the relation of the colonies to the United States to create the uncanny "unincorporated" double, the colonial *national,* the other American subject ineligible for representation under "We, the people." Yet, this is not a story of failed nationalism but rather a challenge to imagine a different type of community, forged out of competing and incommensurate national narratives. Furthermore, it reveals the processes of both politics and aesthetics as practices in invention and misrecognition. Like Daisy, the nation as object of fetish is made visible only through set narratives that leave the sediments of undelineated eventualities as afterimages, as a ghostly trace, as unincorporated elements. The vision of the nation as spectacle and object of speculation is a homogenizing project that ignores the tensile pluralities of spaces and temporalities inherent in a locality. The beautiful distraction of a pristine nation seduces and subordinates the sedimentation of history, leaving only a trace.

The same may be said of the U.S. memory of empire and its relation to the American Tropics. The assimilation of empire's ghosts wreaks havoc on a properly linear narrative. The novel wrestles with the difficulties of nationalist and personal identity formation in a world where geocultural borders fuse, enfold, and clash. Hagedorn orchestrates alternative histories as mutually articulated but not readily assimilable into a developmentalist, emancipatory, or nationalist narrative. She gives texture to "reality" by layering "simultaneous narratives" that rub up against and shape each other, perhaps to reveal untold stories and imaginary spaces. This paratactic strategy forces the reader to interrogate the justifying conjunction that refuses to appear.

This rhetorical inelegance leads us to interrogate the unjustified conjunction between nation and colony. What, indeed, justifies the tethering of the Philippines to the United States in the once official designation of the Philippines as "United States of America, Philippine Islands," a curious conjunction separated by the breath of a comma?[16]

The nonlinear movement of the novel is dispersed across time and space through personal histories, letters, news accounts, gossip columns, statements by President William McKinley, observations of mid-nineteenth-century anthropologist Jean Mallat, movies, soaps, and untrustworthy narrators. Hagedorn's non-universalizing, but catholic, compass of the Philippines fragments representation to parallel the layering and disjunctures in American postcolonial identity formation. As Rachel Lee observes of the dismantling of the narrative voice:

> Hagedorn takes seriously the perspectives of the watched, the gazed upon, the icons of spectatorial pleasure (and contempt) who offer counternarratives to the official "information" produced about Filipinos by political and intellectual authorities such as nineteenth-century Jean Mallat and the American president William McKinley. Rather than offering a single perspective on "reality," Hagedorn presents several conflicting and simultaneous narratives that exist in a horizontal relationship to one another.[17]

Past and current colonialisms converge to mark the horizontal connections among the denizens of the Philippines. Jessica Hagedorn's and Carlos Bulosan's novels, read alongside novels from other parts of the U.S. empire, Hawaiʻi and Puerto Rico, articulate the Filipino (American) postcolonial convergence and contestations with their constitutive "American" national identity. The image of "little brown brothers" eagerly following on the heels of their Western leader, replicating his every step, or the white parent caring for a mixed-race brood, or the Western lover and his feminized love object, are all part of this imaginary forged out of orientalism, primitivism, and imperial narcissism. Indeed, escape from these institutional representations is an almost impossible task. The texts reread the place and time of America to disrupt imperial desire and law by recognizing the Filipino specular image as a (mis)recognition, without necessarily discounting it as a narrative constitutive of Filipino (American) identity. The novels thus fragment and dislocate imperial desire and its projections from its privileged position. The colonial relationship between origin (the Philippines) and destination (the United States) is recast as a shifting sedimentation of temporalities and landscapes.

Before immigrating to the United States, Rio tells her boyfriend, "I'm going to make movies, Tonyboy. Not act in them!" (241). She partakes in the creative reproductions taking place in the peripheral landscapes of the American Tropics. Like Joey's narrations, her stories constitute her "own movies, with their flexible endings." The characters take pleasure in the irony of self-fashioning. As Paul de Man observes in "The Rhetoric of Temporality":

> By avoiding the return to the world, by reasserting the purely fictional nature of its own universe and by carefully maintaining the radical difference that separates fiction from the world of empirical reality. . . [irony] serves to prevent the all too readily mystified reader from confusing fact and fiction from forgetting the essential negativity of fiction.[18]

With irony comes the knowledge that symbolization fails at every turn. Rather than subscribing to the notion of "America" as the ultimate determinant of the characters' stories, the reappropriative weavings and creative junctures produce "flexible" endings. These productions provide room for competing visions of cultural narrative along the lines of Bulosan's trope of America and Holt's recovery of subordinated meanings. For Holt, the cultivation of a different reading practice unpacks multiple and lost meanings in the island nation to take its place alongside its American and British heritages. Hagedorn's appropriations of popular culture allow for an open-endedness that thwarts the sententiousness of imperial desire in the colonized space.

Dogeaters opens in an American movie theater in the Philippines of the late 1950s and ends in the late 1980s in the United States with a *kundiman,* a Tagalog love song dedicated to "Our Mother" in heaven. The interposition of the two national spaces and two localized narrative modes suggests the novel's sedimentation of multiple cultures that make up and complicate notions of Philippine America and American Philippines. The *kundiman* in the form of a Catholic prayer to the Virgin Mary is also a lament for *Inang Bayan* or the motherland:

> I would curse you in Waray, Ilocano, Tagalog, Spanish, English, Portuguese, and Mandarin; I would curse you but I choose to love you instead. *Amor, amas, amatis, amant,* give us this day our daily bread. (251)

By invoking the curse in multiple languages, Hagedorn defies the notion that cultural unity or a unitary voice might fix the Philippines as a place of origin. Furthermore, the multiple points of origination are never lost in time or in transit to the United States. Instead, they seem to be in continual play alongside other chronicities and spaces, much like Holt's Hawaiʻi. The prayer also oscillates between contempt and love for the imperial markings of "motherland." In Hagedorn's Manila, Clarita Avila brings to her mother a collection of books: "Novels in Spanish and English, anthologies of Tagalog poetry, spy thrillers, westerns, historical romances, and biographies. The Brontë sisters and José Rizal were Delia Avila's current favorites" (113). Such an array reveals contiguous histories and cultures that constitute the reader's world.

Like Holt and his multiple heritages, Hagedorn captures not only the more obvious American elements translated and reappropriated by Philippine culture but also the enduring Hispanic and international European presence in cosmopolitan Manila. Notably, this excess of available signs does not impoverish or displace the subjects' imagination, but in fact constitutes and enriches it. The markings seem to provide sustenance, "our daily bread." The ambivalence—the love–hate sentiment—expressed in the curse–prayer finds articulation in the use of irony by the different narrative voices. Irony pervades the novel and disturbs the complacency of the reader, who is forced to interrogate continually the ever-shifting borders of fact and fiction, literature and history, the Philippines and the United States, origin and destination, and spectator and spectacle.

Coda

The readings of various American texts across the twentieth century are testament to one fact: 7,100 islands did, in fact, float away
from Latin American shores to settle for the moment in Asia, only
to shuttle back and forth across the Pacific and the Caribbean.
Such a critical mass has left a trace along the equatorial axis of the
Americas. This isthmian connection marking insular tropes and
multiple American identities issues from the initial misrecognition
of the Philippine archipelago.

Hagedorn and Bulosan illustrate the contradictions and difficulties that obtain in the term "Filipino American," its "ethnic"
formation in relation to the United States, and its diasporic formation in relation to the Philippines as home. The improper and non-
existent hyphenated appellations "Puerto Rican–American" and
"Hawaiian American" render visible a historical nonpossibility
that reveals the disruptive incorporation of nations and identities
to a nation-state that disavows their existence as fully sovereign
entities. These impossible appellations in turn make visible the violent intercultural, national, and historical contradiction in the very
term "Filipino American," currently rendered as a subset descrip-
tor within Asian America. The term cannot be viewed simply as
an ethnic marker, another hyphenated multicultural Americanism,
but as a mark of an exilic and disavowed identity.[1]

These colonial and postcolonial subjects in (trans)formation
trouble a facile American nationalism by complicating the American "ontopology." Homi Bhabha defines ontopology as "the spe-

cific binding of identity, location, and locution/language that most commonly defines the particularity of an ethnic culture."[2] U.S. imperial ontopology, then, is the easy conjunction of U.S. terrestrial space with the self-projected myths and meaning of Americanness. However, this signifying conjunction is sanctioned by imperial disavowal, historical exclusions, and cultural fantasies. My turn to a heterogeneous view of Asian American cultural politics seeks to complicate that signifying conjunction with other American colonized spaces. Such a refractory vision breaks from an identity politics of reflection. Discourse about ethnic pluralism obscures the workings and ways by which different groups cathect to national projects and identities. If, like the American project, one views "Asian American" as a political project, this study attempts to explore the type of "nationalism" or extranationalism that Filipino Americans and other colonized peoples bring to Asian America as a political and cultural project. If Filipino nationalism is characterized by incomplete decolonization, then the ambivalent relationship to the imperial developmental model obtains in this understanding of Americanness. In turn, this relationship informs the fissures in the complex of Asian American differences.

Yet, not all misreadings and misrecognitions are productive. In October 2003, George W. Bush flew to Manila seeking to justify U.S. occupation of Iraq and to strengthen ties with Philippine president Gloria Macapagal-Arroyo.[3] She had been a staunch ally in Bush's global counterterrorism campaign by increasing military measures in the Islamic south of the Philippines. Speaking before a joint session of the Philippine Congress, Bush described the U.S. role in Iraq as a liberatory project similar to that undertaken in the Philippines a century earlier in the Spanish-American War. U.S. soldiers alongside Filipinos fought to overthrow the tyranny of Spanish colonizers, he asserted. This was the highlight of his eight-hour visit to Manila amid quiet walkouts by legislators and vocal protesters in the thousands outside burning U.S. flags and Bush in effigy. Many scholars and opinion makers on both sides of the Pacific took issue with Bush not only for characterizing the situation in Iraq and U.S. military activity there as a liberatory project, but also for misreading U.S. policy toward the Philippines in the aftermath of the Spanish-American War. The protracted war of pacification, the Philippine-American War, resulted in a conservative count of a hundred thousand Filipino dead, U.S. congressional hearings on torture and other atrocities committed by the U.S. military in the archipelago, and occupation of the "unincorporated territory" for a half century. Amy Kaplan wrote of this historical revision in the *Los Angeles Times*: "If the story of democracy in the Philippines is a model for Iraq today, how ironic that the president of the United States, more than 100 years after the end of 'hostilities,' found it too dangerous to stay the night. Filipino protesters in the streets of Manila last week have a very different interpretation of his history."[4] Bush returned to a site of U.S. imperialism to establish similarities between the two imperial wars through an infuriating disavowal of historical facts.

Two years later, Bush's narrative returned to the U.S. continent in the form of dead bodies back from wars in the Middle East and a domestic battle over the term "American." In May 2005, the American Gold Star Mothers, Inc., an organization for mothers who had lost a son or daughter in military service, denied membership to a Filipina mother, Ligaya Lagman, who had lost her American son, Anthony, twenty-six, a year earlier in the invasion of Afghanistan. Her application for membership was rejected because she was not an American citizen. The fallen soldier was born in the United States, but his mother was not. The organization is meant to celebrate a patriotic motherhood and sacrifice and was founded for the purpose of "perpetuating the ideals of Americanism for which their children had so gallantly fought and died." It wanted to preserve the "American character" of the organization by excluding noncitizens. The group's president claimed that Gold Star Mothers "cannot go changing rules everytime the wind blows."

Newspapers, conservative organs, opinion makers, and bloggers alike picked up the story to criticize the organization. Hillary Clinton weighed in to remind the organization that there are currently thousands of noncitizens serving in the U.S. armed forces. Unable to withstand the press attention and the rejection, Lagman withdrew her application for membership. At the Gold Star Mothers' annual meeting, the members voted unanimously to do away with the citizenship requirement for membership. In September 2005, the organization welcomed its first noncitizen mother, a Jamaican whose son, a marine, died in the war in Iraq.

One wonders about the force of this "wind" blowing to which the former president alluded. The protection of borders is contingent upon the sacrifice of American lives, yet the conjunction of the

Caribbean and the Philippines in this story reveals the character of these sacrificed American lives. The military recruits mainly from the ranks of immigrants, people of color, and the poor segments of society. An estimated thirty-one thousand U.S. troops fighting in the Middle East are foreign nationals. After service they may apply for citizenship under an 1894 statute providing an accelerated process. Filipino volunteers, then U.S. nationals, fought in Europe during World War I. Looking at Asian American history, Japanese American males were drafted from the internment camps to serve as translators in the Pacific theater and to fight in European front lines in World War II, but the racial bar to naturalization in effect until after the war meant that many had noncitizen parents. Many military personnel today also come from immigrant families in which not all members share the same nationality or citizenship status.

For the Gold Star Mothers, a private organization, the rejection of Lagman was an exercise in creating difference in order to preserve the "American character" of the organization. But this difference was founded on an elision of U.S. citizenship, a nation-state affiliation, with Americanness, a more complicated geocultural form of belonging. This metaleptic error was rectified with the applicant from Jamaica, but not until after creating a symbolic rift between the Filipino mother and her American son. Anthony's death bound him to a space of Americanness constructed by patriotic death, but one that his noncitizen mother was not allowed to inhabit. The rejection of her application in this instance implied not so much a rejection of the son's death as American, but rather her mourning and sacrifice as somehow less American than the Gold Star Mothers'. While political citizenship cannot be transmitted in reverse from one generation to the preceding one, does Americanness as a complex affect of belonging work in the same way? The "American" character seems to circulate differently when talking about political citizenship and when nationalism is tied to death and mourning.

Bush's metaphor of sameness and the Gold Star Mothers' metalepsis of difference are exercises in U.S. imperial grammar as a tropical malady that subordinates bodies and histories. The spurious denial of membership to Lagman together with Bush's equally spurious misreadings of the Philippine-American War signal the serviceability of Filipino bodies and Filipino history to a closed narrative of the "ideals of Americanism" that disavows the very violence that founds it. One can also point to the machinations of historical and cultural forgetting in these two seemingly unrelated events. The offspring of U.S. empire in island Southeast Asia at the turn of the twentieth century were sent to fight another imperial war in West Asia at the turn of the twenty-first. Bush's misreading and the Gold Star Mothers' misrecognition were practices in creating sameness and difference through the disavowal of U.S. imperialism's continuity from Manila to the Middle East, separated by five thousand miles and a hundred years of forgetting. The conjunctive readings of two seemingly unrelated news stories refuse this hypotactic disappearance to bring out the contiguity of events and speech acts that constitute the American Tropics.

If American colonies themselves are in excess of U.S. national boundaries, then the American postcolonial imagination exceeds national-imperial fantasies. In *Dogeaters,* the Filipina narrator's white American grandfather and veteran of the Spanish-American War, Whitman Logan, has been lying sick at the American hospital in Manila for weeks. The grandmother is sure that her husband suffers from a native sickness called *bangugot*:

> My *Lola* Narcisa claims that her husband is the first white man stricken with *bangugot*. She seems almost proud of his nightmare sickness, a delirious fever in which he sweats, sleeps, and screams. Most *bangugot* victims die overnight in their sleep. It is a mysterious illness which usually claims men. . . . *Bangugot* is ruled out of the picture by the chief of staff, Dr. Leary, who dismisses the tropical malady as native superstition, a figment of the overwrought Filipino imagination. (14)

Debilitated by an inexplicable "tropical malady," Whitman Logan, "a leftover from recent wars," is a remainder of the imperial Spanish-Philippine-American War and part of the Filipina narrator's genetic and cultural heritage. Throughout the novel, Rio tries to reconcile her hazy American heritage with her Philippine landscape through fantasy and speculation. Rio asks, "And where was my maternal grandfather from? Somewhere in the Midwest, my mother shrugs and tells me. I am ashamed at having to invent my own history" (239). Part of her history, this delirious "leftover," is a ghostly reminder of empire, but it is also a site for her narrative reworking. In this uneasy incorporation, they become embodied in the lives and imagination of the Filipino characters. These imperial ghosts are the persistent but constitutive elements that have to be incorporated, however uncomfortably, into the novel's many story lines.

For Filipino Americans, legal discourse and cultural representations have created enfolded borders and disavowed subjectivities that have constructed dangerous and endangered postnational subjects with which nation-states must grapple. Thus, recognizing such a unique colonial formation complicates the notion of "community" represented by "Asian America," a community that even in its initial moment of self-naming was never so transparent. Recognition is itself a reading practice, and the "community" as recognition is the negotiation of interpretative authority over such readings. The mimetic character of literature, I would suggest further, is neither about recognizing the familiar nor about the repetition of proffered knowledge. Rather, such a destabilized entry serves to familiarize us with our more complex and unrecognizable selves. As Kandice Chuh has forcefully argued, such recovery of unrecognized ground enables creative connections with subjectivities other than identity or difference with nation.

A past of disjointed and sedimented histories of colonialism necessitates invention and creativity on Rio's part. If by "overwrought Filipino imagination" the American doctor means "elaborate," "excessive," and "overdone," perhaps this tendency signals the multiple national and extranational spaces and chronicities that the Filipino postcolonial imagination must inhabit to piece together inelegant histories. If so, then the tropical malady itself might also represent the Filipino *American* postcolonial imagination that claims American bodies, spaces, and culture so that the sign of "America," like Whitman Logan, "sweats, sleeps, and screams." To fit its needs and reality, the American Tropics must continually deform and disfigure "America" to the breaking point in order to tell its stories.

Notes

Introduction

1. See Richard Slotkin, *Gunfighter Nation: The Myth of the Frontier in Twentieth-Century America* (New York: Atheneum, 1992).

2. I do not intend to engage in an exhaustive review of all national and Filipino American media coverage of Andrew Cunanan. I look at mainstream coverage in those few weeks to determine the themes and stories that emerge from the news.

3. Other books include Gary Indiana, *Three Month Fever: The Andrew Cunanan Story* (New York: Cliff Street Books, 1999); and Maureen Orth, *Vulgar Favors: Andrew Cunanan, Gianni Versace, and the Largest Failed Manhunt in U.S. History* (New York: Delacorte Press, 1999).

4. The "I Love You" computer virus reported on May 4, 2000, was less fatal but brought dubious attention to the Philippines.

5. "Cunanan Mourned and Reviled by Fil-Ams," *Filipino Reporter* (Jersey City), July 25–31, 1997, 12.

6. *Amok* is a Malay word meaning to engage furiously in battle, adopted into English "to run amok," a pathology of frenzied violence.

7. "Killer on the Loose," *Filipino Express,* July 21–27, 1997, 1.

8. "Publicity on Cunanan Tarnishes FilAm Image," *Philippine News* (San Francisco), July 23–29, 1997, 1.

9. "Cunanan Commits Suicide," *Filipino Express* (Jersey City), July 28–August 3, 1997, 1.

10. "No Philippine Burial for Cunanan," *Filipino Express,* August 4–10, 1997, 1.

11. Richard Alleman, "Glamour after Dark," *Newsweek,* July 28, 1997, 28–29.

12. Jeffrey Toobin, "The Bench: Did South Beach Want to See the Soap Opera End?" *New Yorker,* August 4, 1997, 25.

13. Lizette Alvarez, "Jittery Public Sees Cunanan in All the Wrong Places," *New York Times,* July 21, 1997, A12.

14. Emil Guillermo, *Amok* (San Francisco: Asian Week Books, 1999), 104.

15. See Philip Brian Harper, *Are We Not Men? Masculine Anxiety and the Problem of African American Identity* (New York: Oxford University Press, 1996). For a study of the prerequisite cases looking at the racial bar to citizenship, see Ian Haney Lopez, *White by Law: The Legal Constructions of Race* (New York: New York University Press, 1996).

16. Alvarez, *"Jittery Public Sees Cunanan in All the Wrong Places,"* A12.

17. Vicente Rafael, "Introduction: Writing Outside: On the Question of Location," *Discrepant Histories* (Durham, N.C.: Duke University Press, 1995), xxvii.

18. *Downes v. Bidwell,* quoted in Efrén Rivera Ramos, "The Legal Construction of American Colonialism: The Insular Cases (1901–1922)," *Revista Jurídica de Universidad de Puerto Rico* 65:2 (1996): 250.

19. Arjun Appadurai, "Sovereignty without Territoriality: Notes for a Postnational Geography," in *The Geography of Identity,* ed. Patricia Yaeger (Ann Arbor: University of Michigan Press, 1996), 42–43.

1. American Tropics

1. Hayden White, *Tropics of Discourse* (Baltimore: Johns Hopkins University Press, 1978).

2. There are also more than three hundred independent Native nations that share U.S. geography.

3. Edward Said, *Culture and Imperialism* (New York: Vintage Books, 1993), 61. Said argues that in the nineteenth century the "interpellation of culture by empire" intimately links European imperialism and the transnational project of comparative literature.

4. In the current "war on terror," this jurisdiction has extended even farther from the Philippines to connect the Islamic south of the archipelago with western Asia in Afghanistan and Iraq, as home for Al-Qaeda training camps and cell groups.

5. For a thorough delineation of each territory's organic act, see Julius Pratt, *America's Colonial Experiment: How the United States Gained, Governed, and in Part Gave Away a Colonial Empire* (New York: Prentice Hall, 1950).

6. Neferti Tadiar, *Fantasy Production* (Hong Kong: Hong Kong University, 2004), 9.

7. Amy Kaplan quoted in Oscar Campomanes, "Filipinos in the United

States and Their Literature of Exile," in *Discrepant Histories: Translocal Essays in Filipino Histories,* ed. Vicente Rafael (Philadelphia: Temple University Press, 1995). The increasing body of work on American imperialism owes a debt to past historians such as William Appleman Williams, Walter La Feber, and Julius Pratt, who much earlier attempted to make visible American empire to itself. Writing against the historiographical disavowal of an American "Empire as a Way of Life," Williams revisited American foreign policy by tracing U.S. history of police power from the 1840s and the navy buildup in the 1880s to Wilson's global intervention and Roosevelt's New Deal. A revisionist historian, he argued that U.S. foreign policy has attempted to control and maintain a system of global market rules fusing industrial and government interests since the mid-nineteenth century. He refutes the thesis of Amerian imperialism as a historical aberration and frames imperialism as very much part of U.S. Pan-Americanism and foreign policy since the mid-nineteenth century. See William Appleman Williams, *Empire as a Way of Life: An Essay on the Causes and Character of America's Present Predicament, along with a Few Thoughts about an Alternative* (New York: Oxford University Press, 1980).

8. Amy Kaplan, "'Left Alone with America': The Absence of Empire in the Study of American Culture," in *Cultures of United States Imperialism,* ed. Amy Kaplan and Donald Pease (Durham, N.C.: Duke University Press, 1993), 15.

9. Ann Laura Stoler, *Race and the Education of Desire* (Durham, N.C.: Duke University Press, 1995), 99.

10. Michel Foucault, *Difendere la societa,* quoted in ibid., 75.

11. Lisa Lowe, *Immigrant Acts: On Asian American Cultural Politics* (Durham, N.C.: Duke University Press, 1996); David Palumbo-Liu, *Asian/American: Historical Crossings of a Racial Frontier* (Stanford, Calif.: Stanford University Press, 1999).

12. Gilles Deleuze, "Coldness and Cruelty," in *Masochism,* trans. Jean McNeil (New York: Zone Books, 1991).

13. See Neil Gotanda's critique of color blindness as a decision-making technique that institutionalizes disavowal of race in his oft-cited critical race essay, "A Critique of 'Our Constitution Is Color-Blind,'" in *Critical Race Theory: The Key Writings That Formed the Movement,* ed. Kimberlé Crenshaw, Neil Gotanda, Gary Peller, and Kendall Thomas (New York: New Press, 1995).

14. Natsu Taylor Saito, "The Enduring Effect of the Chinese Exclusion Cases: The 'Plenary Power' Justification for On-Going Abuses of Human Rights," *Asian Law Journal* 9 (May 2003): 13ff.; idem, "Asserting Plenary Power over the 'Other': Indians, Immigrants, Colonial Subjects, and Why U.S. Jurisprudence Needs to Incorporate International Law," *Yale Law and Policy Review* 20 (2002): 427.

15. Homi Bhabha, "Of Mimicry and Man," in *The Location of Culture* (London: Routledge, 1994), 91.

16. William J. Pomeroy, *American Neo-Colonialism: Its Emergence in the Philippines and Asia* (New York: International Publishers, 1970), 132.

17. In contrast, Cuban–U.S. relations had been intertwined since the late nineteenth century, when a colonial bourgeois elite emerged who had resided or been educated in the United States, held U.S. citizenship, and were also involved in the Cuba Libre movement. It was an elite with North American cultural preferences. In war-devastated Cuba, U.S. investments expanded with Cuban cooperation. The Cuban economy was integrated into the U.S. economy. U.S. interests included sugar, tourism, banking, retail, transportation, utilities, and infrastructure. Cuba became an economic frontier for big and small U.S. enterprises with cheap labor from Jamaica, Haiti, and Spain.

18. Pomeroy, *American Neo-Colonialism,* 210. According to Pomeroy, because of concern over capitalist speculation and pillage of the new territory, the administration imposed a limit of sixteen hectares of land acquired by one person and 1,024 by a corporation.

19. Quoted in Howard Zinn, *A People's History of the United States* (New York: Harper, 1980), 306.

20. Glenn May, *Social Engineering in the Philippines: The Aims, Execution and Impact of American Colonial Policy, 1900–1913* (Westport, Conn.: Greenwood Press, 1980), 92.

21. Pomeroy, *American Neo-Colonialism,* 142.

22. Several educational textbooks for dissemination in the archipelago were produced during the era written by Americans for Filipinos, among them Prescott F. Jernegan, *The Philippine Citizen: A Text Book of Civics* (Manila: Philippine Education Publishing, 1908), and H. C. Theobald, *The Filipino Teacher's Manual* (New York and Manila: World Book Company, 1907).

23. Bienvenido Lumbera and Cynthia Nograles Lumbera, *Philippine Literature: A History and Anthology* (Manila: National Book Store, 1982), 110.

24. Renato Constantino, *A Past Revisited* (Quezon City: Center for Nationalist Studies, 1975), 313.

25. Stanley Karnow, *In Our Image: America's Empire in the Philippines* (New York: Random House, 1989).

26. Diana Fuss, *Identification Papers* (New York: Routledge, 1995), 146.

27. Ibid.

28. Stuart Hall, "Cultural Identity and Diaspora," in *Identity,* ed. Jonathan Rutherford (London: Lawrence & Wishart, 1990), 225.

29. Slavoj Žižek, *Mapping Ideology* (London: Verso, 1995), 21.

30. Bhabha, "Of Mimicry and Man," 91.

31. Gayatri Spivak, "Teaching for the Times," in *Dangerous Liaisons: Gender, Nation, and Postcolonial Perspectives*, ed. Anne McClintock, Aamir Mufti, and Ella Shohat (Minneapolis: University of Minnesota Press, 1997), 469.

32. Frantz Fanon, *The Wretched of the Earth*, trans. Constance Farrington (New York: Grove Press, 1968), 236.

33. Fuss, *The Identification Papers*, 141.

34. Fanon, *The Wretched of the Earth*, 227.

35. Ibid., 245, 247.

36. Quoted in Bhabha, "Of Mimicry and Man," 87.

37. Benedict Anderson, *Imagined Communities: Reflections on the Origin and Spread of Nationalism* (New York: Verso Books, 1999), 30.

38. Homi Bhabha, "The Other Question: Stereotype, Discrimination and the Discourse of Colonialism," in *The Location of Culture*, 67.

39. Samira Kawash, *Dislocating the Color Line: Identity, Hybridity and Singularity in African American Literature* (Stanford, Calif.: Stanford University Press, 1997), 21.

40. Ibid., 48.

41. Palumbo-Liu, *Asian/American*, 91.

42. Kandice Chuh, *Imagine Otherwise: On Asian Americanist Critique* (Durham, N.C.: Duke University Press, 2003), 149.

43. Ibid., 56.

44. Anders Stephanson, *Manifest Destiny: American Expansionism and the Empire of Right* (New York: Hill and Wang, 1995), 28ff.

45. Roman Jakobson and Morris Halle, *Fundamentals of Language* (Paris: Mouton, 1971), 90.

46. Ibid., 95.

47. Ibid., 77.

48. Paul de Man, *Blindness and Insight: Essays in Rhetoric of Contemporary Criticism* (Minneapolis: University of Minnesota Press, 1983), 209.

49. Reference to "geocultural" is from Frances R. Aparicio and Susana Chavez-Silverman, *Tropicalizations: Transcultural Representations of Latinidad* (Hanover, N.H.: University Press of New England, 1997). Aparicio and Chavez use the term "geocultural" instead of "geophysical" to encompass places beyond the Caribbean. I use it similarly here to underscore the cultural and geopolitical reach of U.S. imperialism into Asia and the Pacific.

2. Disappearing Clauses

1. See Juan R. Torruella, *The Supreme Court and Puerto Rico: The Doctrine of Separate and Unequal* (Río Piedras, Puerto Rico: Editorial Universitaria, 1985), 240.

2. Gerald L. Neuman, "Constitutionalism and Individual Rights in the Territories," in *Foreign in a Domestic Sense,* ed. Christina Duffy Burnett and Burke Marshall (Durham, N.C.: Duke University Press, 2001), 185.

3. *Downes v. Bidwell,* quoted in Efrén Rivera Ramos, *The Legal Construction of Identity: The Judicial and Social Legacy of American Colonialism in Puerto Rico* (Washington, D.C.: American Psychological Association, 2001), 83.

4. I wish to acknowledge my many discussions with Oscar Campomanes for this insight.

5. See J. A. Hobson, *Imperialism* (Ann Arbor: University of Michigan Press, 1965 [1902]), and V. I. Lenin, *Imperialism: The Highest Stage of Capitalism* (New York: International Publishers, 1990 [1939]).

6. See Martin Sklar, *The United States as a Developing Country: Studies in US History in the Progressive Era and the 1920s* (Cambridge: Cambridge University Press, 1992). Sklar argues that the contending forms of capitalism—corporate capitalism and proprietary capitalism—were vying for dominance along with the corresponding modes of social stratification and production. Changes in the modes of production also called for new strata of managers, teachers, and other professions.

7. However, Secretary of State John Hay studied carefully the British colonial system in Hong Kong and South and Southeast Asia to inform the Schurman Commission's course of action in the Philippines.

8. Emily S. Rosenberg, *Spreading the American Dream: American Economic and Cultural Expansion, 1890–1945* (New York: Hill and Wang, 1982), 7.

9. Rosenberg argues that the search for new markets was not so much caused by overproduction as by a shift in the making, marketing, and consumption of products. The turn of the century witnessed, for example, the introduction of "planned obsolescence, mass advertising and annual model change" in the mode of production.

10. I thank Anita Mannur for this nuance.

11. Jacob Bromwell (R-Ohio): "We propose in this way to establish a precedent for the Filipinos, the unruly and disobedient, by disciplining and punishing Puerto Rico, the well-behaved and well-disposed"; quoted in José A. Cabranes, *Citizenship and Empire* (New Haven: Yale University Press, 1979), 34.

12. Hazel McFerson, *The Racial Dimension of American Overseas Colonial Policy* (Westport, Conn.: Greenwood Press, 1997), 122. The Jones Act for the Philippines was passed in 1916, a year before Puerto Rico's Jones Act, promising eventual independence to the archipelago to allay continental domestic fears about its inhabitants being U.S. citizens.

13. Carl Schurz, "No Colonies for the United States," in *The Nationalizing of American Life,* ed. Ray Ginger (New York: Free Press, 1965),

289 (originally, "American Imperialism: The Convocation Address Delivered on the Occasion of the Twenty-Seventh Convocation of the University of Chicago," January 4, 1899).

14. The naturalization act passed on June 29, 1906, considered Filipinos ineligible for naturalization. U.S. citizenship was not extended to Guam (acquired as part of the Philippines) until 1950.

15. William J. Pomeroy, *American Neo-Colonialism: Its Emergence in the Philippines and Asia* (New York: International Publishers, 1970), 122.

16. Ibid.

17. Torruella, *The Supreme Court and Puerto Rico*, 55.

18. *De Lima v. Bidwell*, quoted in Rivera, *The Legal Construction of Identity*, 114.

19. Ibid., 265–70.

20. Quoted in Julius William Pratt, *America's Colonial Experiment: How the United States Gained, Governed, and in Part Gave Away a Colonial Empire* (New York: Prentice Hall, 1950), 158.

21. Priscilla Wald, "Terms of Assimilation: Legislating Subjectivity in the Emerging Nation," in *Cultures of United States Imperialism* (Durham, N.C.: Duke University Press, 1993), 60.

22. Ibid., 79.

23. *Downes v. Bidwell*, quoted in Rivera, *The Legal Construction of Identity*, 83.

24. Samira Kawash, *Dislocating the Color Line: Identity, Hybridity and Singularity in African American Literature* (Stanford, Calif.: Standord University Press, 1997), 8–18.

25. Wald, "Terms of Assimilation," 68.

26. *Congressional Record* 1901, 330.

27. Salvador P. Lopez, "The Colonial Relationship," in *The United States and the Philippines*, ed. Fred Golay (Englewood Cliffs, N.J.: Prentice Hall, 1966), 8.

28. The twenty-year delay of Philippine independence between 1912 (end of the Taft administration) and 1934 (Tydings-McDuffie) may be understood as a time of political negotiation and reconfiguration of the outmoded European model of empire to give way to American neo-imperialism.

29. For a fuller account of this history, see Neuman, "Constitutional and Individual Rights in the Territories," 2001.

30. Much of the criticism I use here is indebted to Avelino J. Halagao Jr., "Citizens Denied: A Critical Examination of the *Rabang* Decision Rejecting United States Citizenship Claims by Persons Born in the Philippines during the Territorial Period," *UCLA Asian Pacific American Law Journal 5* LJ 77 (spring 1998).

31. *State v. Manuel* (1838) held that "sovereignty" in the United States has been transferred from one man, the king, to the collective body of the people, to mark the shift from subject to citizen.

32. Kandice Chuh, *Imagine Otherwise* (Durham, N.C.: Duke University Press, 2003), 52.

33. In 1902, Theodore Roosevelt declared the Philippine-American War over on the same day, July 4.

34. The assumption is that the United States was free to withhold citizenship emerging from *Afroyim v. Rusk* (1967) regarding naturalization. That case decided that the government could grant but not withhold citizenship, and therefore barred "collective denaturalization."

35. Philippine Supreme Court Case, G.R. nos. 161434, 161634, and 161824, March 3, 2004, *Maria Jeanette C. Tecson et al. v. COMELEC, FPJ, et al.* Many thanks to Mona Katigbak for her help with these documents.

36. The definitive reversal of the Roa case concerning a Chinese Filipino in *Tan Chong v. Secretary of Labor* (1947) established the *jus sanguinis* principle as the sole basis for natural-born citizenship.

37. This is the case in the United States after *Nguyen v. INS* (2001), in which a young Vietnamese man who had lived with his American father for more than ten years in the United States, charged with misdemeanors, was deported because the citizen father did not file proper papers for recognition. Legal scholars have criticized this ruling as not only legislating compulsory motherhood for citizen females but also giving license to citizen male promiscuity abroad.

38. Joaquin G. Bernas, S. J., position paper submitted for *Victorino X. Fornier v. Commission on Elections and Fernando Poe, Jr.* (2004) 8.

39. Richard Chu, "Chinese Filipinos and the Making of the Philippine Nation," lecture delivered at the University of Santo Tomas, Manila, June 2004. Here, I would add to Chu's list Moros or Filipino Muslims of Mindanao.

40. I thank my colleague Sean McCann for suggesting this insight.

41. At the time of this writing, FPJ has passed away, Gloria Macapagal Arroyo is under fire for voter fraud, and rumors abound that FPJ's widow, the screen legend Susan Roces, might step in if Arroyo is ousted.

3. Moral Sentences

1. "Kiser's Sturdy Brown Boy Scouts of Moroland," *New York Tribune,* 1914.

2. Alan Trachtenberg, *The Incorporation of America: Culture and Society in the Gilded Age* (New York: Hill and Wang, 1982), 126–27.

3. Apart from the three novels treated here, other titles include *Boy Scouts on Old Superior; or, The Tale of Pictured Rocks* (1913), *Boy Scouts beyond the Arctic Circle; or, The Lost Expedition* (1913), *Boy Scouts in*

Belgium; or Under Fire in Flanders (1915), *Boy Scouts on the Hudson Bay; or, the Disappearing Fleet* (1914), *Boy Scouts on the Open Plains; or, The Round-up Not Ordered* (1914), *The Boy Scout Camera Club; or, The Confession of a Photograph* (1914), *Boy Scouts on Motorcycles; or, With the Flying Squadron* (1914), *Boy Scouts in the Northwest; or, Fighting Forest Fires* (1911), *Boy Scouts in an Airship; or, The Warning from the Sky* (1912), *Boy Scouts under the Kaiser; or, The Uhlans in Peril* (1916), *Boy Scouts with the Cossacks; or, Poland Recaptured* (1916), *Boy Scouts in a Motorboat; or, Adventures on the Columbia River* (1912), *Over There with the Marines at Chateau Thierry* (1919), *Over There with the Yanks in Argonne Forest* (1920).

4. James Fenimore Cooper popularized stories about the frontier and Indians in the early decades of the nineteenth century. Popular among the working class, by the last quarter of the century, dime novels as a genre included adventure stories written for boys and girls.

5. David Lloyd, plenary lecture delivered at "Performing Ethnicities" conference, City College of New York, October 2004.

6. George Harvey Ralphson, *Boy Scouts in Mexico; or, On Guard with Uncle Sam* (Chicago: M. A. Donohue & Co., 1911), 8. Subsequent references are given in the text.

7. "These Boy Scouts like Knights of Old," *New York Times,* December 17, 1910, 5.

8. Waldo Sherman, "The Boy Scouts 300,000 Strong," *The World's Work* (November 1912): 14859ff.

9. Richard Hofstadter, *The Age of Reform* (New York: Vintage Books, 1955), 148ff.

10. Ibid., 163–64.

11. For a thorough account of the Boy Scouts movement and its progenitors, see David Mcleod, *Building Character in the American Boy: The Boy Scouts, YMCA and Their Forerunners 1870–1920* (Madison: University of Wisconsin Press, 1983).

12. James E. West, "The Boy Scouts: Socialist's Attack on Organization Ignored Its Expressed Purpose," *New York Times,* March 12, 1911, 12.

13. "Boy Scouts on Fair List," *New York Times,* December 8, 1912, 20.

14. Richard Slotkin, *Gunfighter Nation* (New York: Atheneum, 1992), 162–63.

15. Oscar Martinez, *Troublesome Border* (Tucson: University of Arizona Press, 1988), 39.

16. Timothy J. Dunn, *The Militarization of the U.S.–Mexico Border* (Austin: CMAS Books, University of Texas at Austin, 1996), 9.

17. "Society Men Aid Boy Scouts," *New York Times,* January 30, 1911, III-6.

18. Theodore Roosevelt, *The Strenuous Life: Essays and Addresses* (New York: The Century Co., 1911).

19. George Harvey Ralphson, *Boy Scouts in the Canal Zone; or, The Plot against Uncle Sam* (Chicago: M. A. Donohue & Co., 1911), 242. Subsequent references are given in the text.

20. William J. Pomeroy, *American Neo-Colonialism: Its Emergence in the Philippines and Asia* (New York: International Publishers, 1970), 166.

21. Charles D. Ameringer, *U.S. Foreign Intelligence: The Secret Side of American History* (Washington, D.C.: Lexington Books, 1990), 83.

22. George Harvey Ralphson, *Boy Scouts in the Philippines; or, The Key to the Treaty Box* (Chicago: M. A. Donohue & Co., 1911), 10. Subsequent references are given in the text.

23. There are, in fact, more than 7,100 known islands.

24. For an insightful analysis of imperial tropes in discourses of domesticity, see Amy Kaplan, *Anarchy of Empire in the Making of U.S. Culture* (Cambridge: Harvard University Press, 2002).

25. Pomeroy, *American Neo-Colonialism,* 87.

26. Ralph D. Blumenfeld, "The Boy Scouts," *Outlook,* July 23, 1910, 617. The Christian magazine surveyed the political goings-on of the American social arena with Theodore Roosevelt as a contributing editor.

27. Ibid.

28. Daniel Beard, letter to *Outlook,* July 23, 1910, 697.

29. Amy Kaplan, "The Birth of an Empire," *PMLA* 114 (October 5, 1999): 1071.

30. Ronald K. Edgerton, "Americans, Cowboys, and Cattlemen on the Mindanao Frontier," in *Reappraising an Empire,* ed. Peter Stanley (Cambridge: Harvard University Press, 1984), 172.

31. Quoted in Julius William Pratt, *America's Colonial Experiment: How the United States Gained, Governed, and in Part Gave Away a Colonial Empire* (New York: Prentice Hall, 1950), 203.

4. Imperial Romance

1. Luis Reyes, introduction, in *Made in Paradise: Hollywood's Films of Hawai'i and the South Seas* (Honolulu: Mutual Publishing, 1995), xxiii. For discussions of film shorts made in 1903 depicting the Philippine–American War by the American Mutoscope & Biograph Company, see Amy Kaplan, "The Birth of an Empire," *PMLA* 114 (October 5, 1999): 1067–79; and Oscar Campomanes, "Casualty Figures of the American Soldier and the Other: The Imperial Nation in Love and War," in *Vestiges of War,* ed. Angel Shaw and Luis Francia (New York: New York University Press, 2002).

2. White actors have often played mixed-race or racialized roles in

Hollywood: for example, Elvis in *Flaming Star* (1960), Joan Collins and James Woods in *Island in the Sun* (1957), Jeanne Crain in *Pinky* (1949).

3. Viet Nguyen, *Race and Resistance: Literature and Politics in Asian America* (New York: Oxford University Press, 2002).

4. Bill Ong Hing, *Making and Remaking Asian America through Immigration Policy 1850–1990* (Stanford, Calif.: Stanford University Press, 1993), 32.

5. War brides from Asia were the exception to these laws. See Robert Lee's reading of *Sayonara* in his *Orientals: Asian Americans in Popular Culture* (Philadelphia: Temple University Press, 1999), 161ff.

6. She is an elegantly romanticized "Manila Rose." I thank Anita Mannur for pointing this out.

7. Ann Douglas, *Terrible Honesty: Mongrel Manhattan in the 1920s* (New York: Farrar, Straus and Giroux, 1996), 123.

8. Ronald K. Edgerton, "Americans, Cowboys, and Cattlemen on the Mindanao Frontier," in *Reappraising an Empire,* ed. Peter Stanley (Cambridge: Harvard University Press, 1984), 172.

9. "Screen News Here and in Hollywoood," *New York Times,* June 17, 1938, 25.

10. Reynaldo Ileto, "Cholera and the Origins of the American Sanitary Order in the Philippines," in *Discrepant Histories* (Durham, N.C.: Duke University Press, 1995), 51ff.

11. Sokoloff was again in brownface as a Filipino school principal who gave his life resisting the Japanese occupying forces in *Back to Bataan* (1945).

12. For an insightful account of the role of native belief and *antinganting* in grassroots revolutionary and millennial movements during the Philippine-American War, see Reynaldo Ileto, *Pasyon and Revolution* (Manila: Ateneo de Manila University Press, 1979).

13. Frank Nugent, "The Screen: Four Films in Review," *New York Times,* September 15, 1939, 30.

14. "Gore in the Philippines: 'Real Glory' a Hair-Raising Tale of the Constabulary," *Newsweek,* September 25, 1939, 42–43. The tragic and violent "pacification" of the Islamic south to create an integrated archipelago continues until today, with Philippine armed forces engaging Muslim liberation factions in the region.

15. Nick Deocampo, "'Lost' RP Film Found in US Archive," *Philippine Inquirer,* February 5, 2004, excerpted from *Film: US Colonization and the Emergence of Cinema in the Philippines* (forthcoming).

16. "The Real Glory," *Time,* September 25, 1939, 33.

17. Douglas W. Churchill, "The Filipino Crisis in Hollywood," *New York Times,* April 16, 1939, X5.

18. "The Real Glory," 33.

19. Douglas W. Churchill, "Hollywood and a Roosevelt Hoax," *New York Times,* August 27, 1939, X3.

20. Juanita Hall, an African American actress, also appears in *Flower Drum Song* (1961; opened on Broadway in 1958), which, along with *South Pacific* and *The King and I,* makes up Rodgers and Hammerstein's Oriental trilogy.

21. "Men Will Be Boys," *Time,* August 2, 1963, 82:50; "Screen: Excitement on Haleakoloha," *New York Times,* July 25, 1963, 14.

22. Gerald Mast, *A Short History of the Movies* (Chicago: University of Chicago Press, 1981), 240.

23. Wayne's role and the tune recall Wayne's previous war movies, but the tune is also fascinating historically. The "Monkeys" tune is known in the Zamboanga region of the southern Philippines and was learned from the U.S. military occupiers at the turn of the century when *gook* was first used against Filipinos, along with other racial epithets. Filipinos as tailless monkeys is a disturbing reminder of American racism during its military occupation of the area in the early twentieth century (from a commentary at www.zamboanga.com).

24. Mythical "Haleakoloha" is administered by a French governor (Cesar Romero) and his trusted Amherst-educated Chinese valet (Jon Fong).

25. "'Blue Hawaii' Opens," *New York Times,* February 22, 1962, 20.

26. See Noel J. Kent, *Hawaii: Islands under the Influence* (Honolulu: University of Hawaii Press, 1983).

27. Elvis Presley himself had just finished his army stint in Germany, where he met his future wife, Priscilla. To revive his career after his absence from public view, his manager compelled him to make rock-and-roll romp movies.

28. Beth Bailey and David Farber, *The First Strange Place: Race and Sex in World War II Hawaii* (Baltimore: Johns Hopkins University Press, 1992), 24.

29. On Fordist and post-Fordist regimes of capital accumulation, see David Harvey, *The Condition of Postmodernity* (Cambridge: Blackwell, 1989).

30. As a tour guide in a service economy, Chad is in a subordinate and feminized position. The fact that he is escorting teenage girls does not do away with the specter of his being a gigolo. His feminized position is also apparent in the song-and-dance sequences in which he is half-clad. True to the codes of propriety, women and Elvis do not reveal navels, but the local brown men are allowed to show theirs. To redeem his masculinity, he manages to get into a bar brawl to protect one of his teenage charges, whom he later spanks for running away. This spoiled girl, Ellie, is later thankful that someone cared enough to discipline her.

31. William A. Callahan and Steve Olive, "Chemical Weapons Discourse in the South Pacific," in *Asia/Pacific as Space of Cultural Production,* ed. Rob Wilson and Arif Dirlik (Durham, N.C.: Duke University Press, 1995), 61.

5. Reconstituting American Subjects

1. Piri Thomas, *Down These Mean Streets* (New York: Knopf, 1967), ix. Subsequent references are given in the text.

2. Lisa Sánchez-González, *Boricua Literature: A Literary History of the Puerto Rican Diaspora* (New York: New York University Press, 2001), 107.

3. Arnaldo Cruz-Malavé, "'What a Tangled Web!' Masculinity, Abjection, and the Foundations of Puerto Rican Literature in the United States," *Differences: A Journal of Feminist Cultural Studies* (1996): 44.

4. Carlos Bulosan, *America Is in the Heart* (Pullman: University of Washington Press, 1973 [1946]), 261. Subsequent references are given in the text.

5. Elaine Kim, *Asian American Literature* (Philadelphia: Temple University Press, 1982), 43–57; Marilyn Alquizola, "Subversion or Affirmation: The Text and the Subtext of *America Is in the Heart*," in *Asian Americans: Comparative and Global Perspectives,* ed. Shirley Hune, Stephen S. Fugita, and Amy Ling (Pullman: Washington State University Press, 1991).

6. See Marta Sánchez, "La Malinche at the Intersection: Race and Gender in *Down These Mean Streets*," *PMLA* 113 (January 1998). Sánchez points out that "faced with the trauma of racial oppression, Thomas's protagonist, Piri, compensates for the racialized and feminized abjection of black men in the United States by making the abjection of women the guarantor of his ethnic and masculine difference" (118).

7. See Leti Volpp, "American Mestizo: Filipinos and Anti-Miscegenation Laws in California," *UC Davis Law Review* 33:4 (summer 2000): 795ff.

8. Ibid., 810–11.

9. I concur with the many critics who have commented on the composite nature of this fictionalized autobiography. Elaine Kim *(Asian American Literature)* has surveyed Bulosan's career as one of the few prominent Asian American men of letters along with Younghill Kang. Unlike the Korean-born Kang, Bulosan sought in his work a collective identification with other dispossessed Filipinos rather than Kang's more individualized approach to achievement of a place in America. The autobiographical "I" in the work is a collective one that bears witness to Filipinos' abject state in America and the unfolding of American promise. Oscar Campomanes's research and interviews conclude that the protagonist is "more

likely a composite character drawn from autobiography, family history and the experience of the typical Pinoy" (Oscar Campomanes and Todd S. Gernes, "Two Letters from America: Carlos Bulosan and the Act of Writing," *MELUS* [fall 1988]: 17).

10. Campomanes and Gernes, "Two Letters from America," 21.

11. Kandice Chuh, *Imagine Otherwise: On Asian Americanist Critique* (Durham, N.C.: Duke University Press, 2003).

12. See David Eng's illuminating work on Asian America and masculinity using a Lacanian psychoanalytical framework in his *Racial Castration: Managing Masculinity in Asian America* (Durham, N.C.: Duke University Press, 2001).

13. Cruz-Malavé, "'What a Tangled Web!'" 140. Subsequent references are given in the text.

14. Bulosan had an intellectual relationship with Carey McWilliams, who wrote the foreword to *America Is in the Heart,* and with Louis Adamic, and he had a correspondence with William Saroyan and Richard Wright. However, these American literary personages do not figure prominently in his texts.

15. Campomanes and Gernes, "Two Letters from America," 17.

16. Ibid., 22.

6. Reconstituting American Predicates

1. Frantz Fanon, "On National Culture," in *The Wretched of the Earth* (New York: Grove Press, 1963), 227, 236.

2. Benedict Anderson, *Imagined Communities: Reflections on the Origin and Spread of Nationalism* (New York: Verso Books, 1999), 30.

3. I would like to acknowledge Nikhil Singh for this formulation that guides comparative cultural analysis.

4. John Dominis Holt, *Waimea Summer* (Honolulu: Topgallant Publishing Co., 1976), 1. Subsequent references are given in the text.

5. Stephen H. Sumida, *And the View from the Shore* (Seattle: University of Washington Press, 1991), 152.

6. Susan Najita, "History, Trauma, and the Discursive Construction of 'Race' in John Dominis Holt's *Waimea Summer,*" *Cultural Critique* 47 (winter 2001): 169.

7. Ibid.

8. Ibid., 180–81.

9. See J. Kehaulani Kauanui, *Precarious Positions: Native Hawaiians and US Federal Recognition,*" *The Contemporary Pacific* 17: 1 (2005): 1–27; idem, "'A Blood Mixture Which Experience Has Shown Furnishes the Very Highest Grade of Citizen-Material': Selective Assimilation in a Polynesian Case of Naturalization to US Citizenship," *American Studies* 45:3 (fall 2004): 5–29.

10. Jessica Hagedorn, *Dogeaters* (New York: Pantheon Books, 1990), 3–9. Subsequent references are given in the text.

11. In television variety shows broadcast in Manila, the GI baby character, usually of phenotypically African American descent, with the unknown father, is a mainstay in comedy skits.

12. I thank Anita Sokolsky for this reading of the Narcissus myth. I also wish to thank Shilpa Raval for our discussion of Echo in the myth.

13. Claude Lévi-Strauss, *The Savage Mind* (Chicago: University of Chicago Press, 1966 [1962]), 17.

14. Fenella Cannell, "The Power of Appearances," in *Discrepant Histories*, ed. Vicente Rafael (Durham, N.C.: Duke University Press, 1995), 225. See also Martin Manalansan, *Global Divas: Filipino Gay Men in Diaspora* (Durham, N.C.: Duke University Press, 2003). Manalansan explores the role drama and beauty/*byuti* plays in the lives of Filipino gay men in New York in negotiating their Filipino and American identities.

15. According to Garth Alexander, a journalist covering Manila during the 1970s and 1980s, one of these Filipino beauty queens turned revolutionary is Nelia Sancho: "there were other beauty queens who helped the Communists," Alexander explained, "but she was the only one who joined the party" (private communication).

16. The same question could be asked of the tethering of Puerto Rico to the United States as an Associated Free State/"Estado Libre Asociado," evoking autonomy and dependency at the same time.

17. Rachel Lee, *The Americas of Asian American Literature: Gendered Fictions of Nation and Transnation* (Princeton, N.J.: Princeton University Press, 1999), 79.

18. Paul de Man, " The Rhetoric of Temporality," in *Blindness and Insight: Essays in Contemporary Criticism* (Minneapolis: University of Minnesota Press, 1983), 209.

Coda

1. See Oscar Campomanes, "Filipinos in the United States and Their Literature of Exile," in *Discrepant Histories: Translocal Essays in Filipino Histories*, ed. Vicente Rafael (Philadelphia: Temple University Press, 1995), 159–92.

2. Homi Bhabha, "Day by Day . . . with Frantz Fanon," in *The Fact of Blackness*, ed. Alan Reed (Seattle: Bay Press, 1996), 191.

3. Like Bush, "GMA," as the Philippine press refers to Arroyo, is herself the offspring of a former president.

4. Amy Kaplan, "Confusing Occupation with Liberation," *Los Angeles Times*, October 24, 2003, B19.

Index